the About.com. guide to
ONLINE
RESEARCH

Navigate the Web—from RSS and the Invisible Web
to Multimedia and the Blogosphere

Wendy Boswell
The About.com Guide to Web Search

Aadamsmedia
Avon, Massachusetts

About **About.com**

About.com is a powerful network of more than 600 Guides—smart, passionate, accomplished people who are experts in their fields. About.com Guides live and work in more than twenty countries and celebrate their interests in thousands of topics. They have written books, appeared on national television programs, and won many awards in their fields. Guides are selected for their ability to provide the most interesting information for users and for their passion for their subject and the Web. The selection process is rigorous—only 2 percent of those who apply actually become Guides. The following are the most important criteria by which they are chosen:

- High level of knowledge and passion for their topic
- Appropriate credentials
- Keen understanding of the Web experience
- Commitment to creating informative, inspiring features

Each month more than 48 million people visit About.com. Whether you need home-repair and decorating ideas, recipes, movie trailers, or car-buying tips, About.com Guides offer practical advice and solutions for everyday life. If you're looking for how-to advice on refinishing your deck, for instance, About.com shows you the tools you need to get the job done. No matter where you are on About.com or how you got there, you'll always find exactly what you're looking for!

About Your Guide

 Wendy Boswell has been on the World Wide Web for over a decade and has significant real-life experience in Web search strategies and Web search hacks and tricks, and knows where to find the "really good stuff"—from interactive tutorials to the latest on cutting-edge technology to the just plain wild and weird. Wendy's relevant Web experience includes coordinating a successful eBay business, overseeing a non-profit community Web site, doing technical writing for a CAD company, and writing a beginner's guide to search-engine optimization for Register.com. She also is the Weekend Editor for Lifehacker, and writes quite a few blogs for b5 Media, one of the largest blog networks on the Web today. Wendy has taken many in-depth classes and seminars on successful Web site design and optimization strategies. She makes her living and spends her fun time on the Web, and keeps up with the latest developments in Web search strategies and search-engine optimization.

Acknowledgements

This book is dedicated to my husband, Dean, who makes every day of my life worth living. Here's to many more years together from your M.O.W.

I also couldn't have done this book without the constant hugs and loving interruptions from my three children: James, Henry, and Emma. You three are the light of Daddy's and my lives—and yes, for the 467th time, we ARE going to Disneyland next year, okay? Thanks also to my mother and mother-in-law for their sweet encouragement, to my sister-in-law for always making me laugh and feel loved, and to all my family and friends who helped me keep on going to the end of this project.

ABOUT.COM

CEO & President
Scott Meyer

COO
Andrew Pancer

SVP Content
Michael Daecher

Director, About Operations
Chris Murphy

Marketing Communications Manager
Lisa Langsdorf

ADAMS MEDIA

Editorial

Innovation Director
Paula Munier

Editorial Director
Laura M. Daly

Executive Editor
Brielle K. Matson

Development Editor
Katrina Schroeder

Marketing

Director of Marketing
Karen Cooper

Assistant Art Director
Frank Rivera

Production

Director of Manufacturing
Susan Beale

Production Project Manager
Michelle Roy Kelly

Senior Book Designer
Colleen Cunningham

Published by Adams Media, an F+W Publications Company
57 Littlefield Street
Avon, MA 02322
www.adamsmedia.com

ISBN-10: 1-59869-503-7
ISBN-13: 978-1-59869-503-8

Printed in China.

J I H G F E D C B A

Library of Congress Cataloging-in-Publication Data
is available from the publisher.

This publication is designed to provide accurate and authoritative information with regard to the subject matter covered. It is sold with the understanding that the publisher is not engaged in rendering legal, accounting, or other professional advice. If legal advice or other expert assistance is required, the services of a competent professional person should be sought.
  —From a *Declaration of Principles* jointly adopted by a Committee of the American Bar Association and a Committee of Publishers and Associations

Many of the designations used by manufacturers and sellers to distinguish their product are claimed as trademarks. Where those designations appear in this book and Adams Media was aware of a trademark claim, the designations have been printed with initial capital letters.

This book is available at quantity discounts for bulk purchases. For information, please call 1-800-289-0963.

How to Use This Book

Each About.com book is written by an About.com Guide—a specialist with expert knowledge of his or her subject. Although the book can stand on its own as a helpful resource, it may also be coupled with its corresponding About.com site for further tips, tools, and advice. Each book not only refers you back to About.com but also directs you to other useful Internet locations and print resources.

All About.com books include a special section at the end of each chapter called Get Linked. There you'll find a few links back to the About.com site for even more useful information on the topics discussed in that chapter. Depending on the topic, you will find links to such resources as photos, sheet music, quizzes, recipes, or product reviews.

About.com books also include four types of sidebars:

- **Ask Your Guide:** Detailed information in a question-and-answer format
- **Tools You Need:** Advice about researching, purchasing, and using a variety of tools for your projects
- **Elsewhere on the Web:** References to other useful Internet locations
- **What's Hot:** All you need to know about the hottest trends and tips out there

Each About.com book takes you on a personal tour of a certain topic, gives you reliable advice, and leaves you with the knowledge you need to achieve your goals.

CONTENTS

CONTENTS . . . *continued*

Introduction from Your Guide

There's just no getting around it: the World Wide Web is here to stay. From TV commercials that advertise company Web sites to billboards with an official "dot com" address inviting you to click further for more information, evidence of the Web's influence is everywhere we look.

However, the Web is much more than ads and information. To be sure, the Web is primarily made up of masses of images and data, but it's evolving and changing all the time into something that's more personally meaningful and more a part of our daily lives. Anyone with an Internet connection can use the Web not only to find information but also to connect with people all over the world, watch video of news events happening in real time, or research century-old archives—and that's just the tip of the iceberg.

The Web has also become part of our common social lexicon. When we want to find something on the Web, we "Google" it. We want to record our thoughts, so we "blog." We want to become more mobile, so we use Web 2.0 technology that releases us from our cubicles and gets us anywhere we want to be. The Web is no longer a static medium—it's become a dynamic platform from which people all over the globe are launching themselves into a whole new way of living.

The Web can be somewhat overwhelming for the uninitiated. Where do you go to find information? How do you find information? How do you know if what you are looking at is actually credible? These are common dilemmas for both the inexperienced and experienced Web searcher, but there is good news: you can learn how to navigate the World Wide Web successfully, efficiently, and with confidence, no matter where you are on the knowledge spectrum. It just takes time, perseverance, and patience, and a little bit of know-how.

So many people miss out on much that the Web has to offer because they don't go past their comfort zone—that is, what they can find on the surface. I invite you to come with me past that Web search comfort zone into the vast wonderland that is the Web. There's so much good stuff to explore that it would be a shame to limit yourself to what you are used to. Anyone, from elementary-school age to elderly, can learn how to search the Web and mine its incredibly rich resources.

By the time you reach the end of this book, I promise you will have the skills to find what you need on the Web with a minimum of fuss and frustration. The Web's resources are not just for those folks with a solid grasp of technology—they are meant for anyone who has the tools in their Web search toolbox to locate them. And that's what this book is all about: giving you the tools and knowledge you need to find what you're looking for on the World Wide Web.

Using the information that you'll read about in this book and my About.com Web Search site, you'll be able to confidently search the Web for anything you might need to find. My goal is for you to walk away with the skills that you need to unearth a video . . . search for a podcast . . . locate relevant blogs . . . evaluate sites for credibility . . . and use Web-based tools to simplify and organize your life. This might sound like a tall order, but if you take one small chunk of information at a time, you'll be a savvy Web searcher before you know it.

Chapter 1

An Introduction to the World Wide Web

How Do You Define the Web?

More people than ever before are using the World Wide Web for a variety of reasons: to shop; to pay bills; to connect with other people via e-mail, online communities, etc.; to track the news; to work; to play.

However, most people aren't really sure what the Web actually *is*. They use it, but if they had to come up with a definition, they might be stuck. (My first inclination would be to look the definition up on the Web!)

We know what we use the Web for. It's where we Google something, score our bargains on eBay, pay bills via secure servers, connect with like-minded individuals on MySpace, and a whole lot more. It's definitely a useful addition to our lives; in fact, many people even use the Web to make a living nowadays. The Web is incredibly integrated into our lives, yet there are so many other things that it offers us. For instance, did you know that, among many other things, you could use the Web to:

- watch African lions visit a watering hole in real time?
- collaborate with people all over the world for a business project?
- find freeware that's just as good as (or better than!) stuff you would pay for?
- listen to personalized radio stations?
- download free movies, free music, and free books?

At this point in my ongoing exploration of the Web, even though I have discovered a pretty good chunk of what the Web has to offer, I can say with absolute certainty that I've barely scratched the surface. I must warn you: once you realize all that the Web has got going on (and how much fun it is to explore!), you'll find it utterly addicting and amazingly full of resources. For instance, you can use the Web to research a thesis paper on Shakespeare's plays, listen to streaming speeches from historical people of renown, or do a detailed search on little-known health issues. The possibilities are endless. Let me put it this way: it's a good thing that I do this for a living, otherwise I don't know how I would get around to "working."

Let's figure out exactly what the Web is. We know what we use it for, but do we know what the Web really is? Where did it come from, and where is it headed? In order to become a truly well-rounded Web citizen, it's imperative to step back and see what the Web is actually made of, to see the forest instead of the trees.

WHAT'S HOT

▶ Are you a "Web head"? Do you go online to do . . . well, pretty much everything? Perhaps you're the only person in your circle of friends who actually knows what a Boolean search is, or maybe you are a whiz with at least ten different search engines and subject directories. Well, it's time to put that knowledge to the test and take the "Are you a Web Head?" quiz found at http://about.com/ websearch/webhead.

One of the best ways to get a picture of the Web is to take a look at its beginnings. The Web looks a *lot* different than it did when it was just a wee twinkle in the eye of **Tim Berners-Lee**, that's for sure, and it's fascinating to see how far we've come from those beginning days. I'm pretty sure that the good folks who started all of this in motion never *dreamed* that the World Wide Web would look the way it does today.

To delve into the origins of the Web, we have to look at the backbone on which the Web was created: the Internet. Let's go back in time to around 1957, when the first attempts of possible connectivity through computer networks were just beginning to get off the ground in the United States and Europe.

A Brief History of the Internet

It would be easy to zoom right to a quick definition of the Web; however, if you want to figure out how the Web fits together, you've got to start by looking at its foundation: the Internet. Without the Internet, there would be no Web, so it's important to look at how the Internet got started, how it flourished, and what it looks like today.

The simplest definition of the Internet is this: the Internet is a communications network made up of many internal networks, which are themselves made up of many computer systems, just like the ones in your house and mine. The Internet is basically the underlying foundation on which the Web is built; the bus carrying the passengers, if you will.

The Internet is the superstructure of the Web. It is the underlying backbone on which the information of the Web is processed, merged, shared, etc. We do not find information on the Internet, we find it using the Internet.

ELSEWHERE ON THE WEB

▶ For a look at the origins of the Web, visit the personal bio page of Sir Tim Berners-Lee at www.w3.org/People/Berners-Lee/ShortHistory.html. Sir Tim is credited with the idea of using hypertext links to connect information together on what is now known as the World Wide Web. Best quote? "The dream behind the Web is of a common information space in which we communicate by sharing information."

Did Al Gore invent the Internet?

▶ In a word, no, Mr. Gore did not invent the Internet. Here are his exact words: "During my service in the United States Congress, I took the initiative in creating the Internet." Taken out of context, it certainly does appear that he's taking credit for inventing something that he really didn't; however, it's just awkward phrasing that when coupled with the rest of his statement (mostly focused on economic growth) actually does make sense.

How did the Internet get started? The Internet initially got its start as an idea to connect networks in the late 1950s in the United States Department of Defense. To explore this newfangled idea, an interagency was formed with the acronym of **ARPA** (also known as ARPANET): Advanced Research Projects Agency. Originally, the Internet was made up of a paltry three main terminals (communication stations, if you will) that traded research information back and forth.

The only problem was that there wasn't a universal "language" that the terminals were able to use in order to trade information efficiently—each communications network had its own unique protocols, which made for slow going, connectivity-wise. The main issue was this: how do you make it possible for many small networks to communicate as one large network? The answer: **Internet protocols** that enable users from any physical distance to send and share information.

The problem of universal network connectivity was solved with the invention of **packet switching**; basically, this consists of shunting information from node to node until it gets to its proper destination. Once this seemingly insurmountable problem was taken care of, the Internet grew from those measly three main terminals at an astonishing rate.

Suffice to say that this growth didn't stop or even slow down for a moment. But with this phenomenal growth came a unique dilemma: how in the world was all this information going to be accessed in a user-friendly way? That's where the Web comes in.

The Web got started in the late 1980s. A CERN (Conseil Européen pour la Recherche Nucléaire, known as European Organization for Nuclear Research) scientist named Tim Berners-Lee came up with the idea of hypertext, information that was "linked" to another set of information. His idea was more for convenience than anything else; he just wanted the researchers at CERN to be able to communicate more easily via a single informational network, instead of many smaller networks that were not linked with one another in any sort of universal way. This hypertext technology included **hyperlinks**, which enabled users to peruse information from any linked network merely by clicking a link.

One of the main reasons that the Web grew as fast as it did was the freely distributed technology behind it. Tim Berners-Lee managed to persuade CERN to provide the Web technology and program code for free so that anyone could use it, improve it, tweak it—you name it. It's interesting to speculate on how things would be different had Berners-Lee and CERN decided *not* to be so magnanimous!

Obviously, this concept took off in a big way. From CERN's hallowed research halls, the idea of hyperlinked information went first to other institutions in Europe, then to Stanford University—and then Web servers began popping up all over the place. According to the BBC's write-up of Web history, "Fifteen Years of the Web," (http://news.bbc.co.uk/2/hi/technology/5243862.stm) the growth of the Web in 1993 was at a staggering 341,634 percent as compared to the previous year.

Here's the original announcement of the technology that changed the world from Tim Berners-Lee to the alt.hypertext **newsgroup** he chose to debut it:

"The WorldWideWeb (WWW) project aims to allow links to be made to any information anywhere. [. . .] The WWW project was started to allow high energy physicists to share data, news, and documentation. We are very interested in spreading the web to other areas, and having gateway servers for other data. Collaborators welcome!" —August 2, 1991.

Here's a quick summary of the key Web and Internet history points:

TOOLS YOU NEED

▶ You can refer to my short and sweet "History of the Web" timeline over at http://about.com/websearch/historyofweb for reference; it's a summarization of a few of the most interesting events that have shaped Web history in the past two decades. Highlights include the debut of Yahoo, the entry of the White House onto the World Wide Web, and the inevitable burst of the dot-com bubble.

What was the very first Web site?

▶ The very first Web site (alas, it's long been gone and no screenshots are available) was at http://info.cern.ch/hypertext/WWW/ThePro ject.html. From the CERN page for the creation of the Web (http://info.cern.ch/): "Visitors could learn more about hypertext, technical details for creating their own webpage, and even an explanation on how to search the Web for information." It's amazing to realize how far we've come, from one Web site to literally millions.

- **1950s:** ARPA (Advanced Research Projects Agency), a small agency within the U.S. Department of Defense, is formed. One of their key projects is communication between networks.
- **1960s:** Network communication gets a huge boost with the invention of packet-switching technology, a way to break down large amounts of data into manageable, transferable packages.
- **1970s:** More nodes join various networks in Europe and North America. Packet-switching protocols get even more refined, and the Internet is on its way to becoming a global communications network.
- **1980s:** Sophisticated Internet technology protocols, namely Transmission Control Protocol/Internet Protocol (TCP/IP), are developed, enabling networks to communicate more effectively. The number of nodes (also known as hosts) on the Internet hovers around the 10,000 mark.
- **1990s:** CERN researcher Tim Berners-Lee comes up with the idea of hypertext, a way to link different documents on different networks via point-and-click links. Berners-Lee and CERN freely release the coding technology behind the idea of hypertext, and the Web grows at an astonishing rate.

How the Web and the Internet Fit Together

As I said earlier, the Internet is not part of the Web, but the Web is part of the Internet. The Internet is a network. The Web is an information-sharing **subnetwork** that lives on the Internet and uses the superstructure of the Internet as well as special protocols in order to make this information available to users.

The Internet is a superstructure on which the Web is built. However, here's something that might really blow your mind: the Web is the largest subnetwork of the Internet, but it's not the only one. There are many subnetworks that work together as one giant entity, each with different purposes.

Every subnetwork is created from an underlying foundation known as a protocol. We don't ever see much of what is going on behind the scenes with these subnetworks, but the protocols serve very important purposes: basically, they make things work right. A few of the most important subnetwork protocols include:

- Hypertext Transfer Protocol (HTTP)
- Secure Hypertext Transfer Protocol (S-HTTP, HTTPS) or HTTP over Secure Socket Layer (HTTP-SSL)
- For e-mail: Simple Mail Transfer Protocol (SMTP), Post Office Protocol (POP), Mail Application Program Interface (MAPI)
- File Transfer Protocol (FTP)
- Internet Relay Chat (IRC)
- Instant Messaging (IM)
- Gopherspace (GOPHER)
- Telnet (TELNET)
- For discussion groups: Network News Transfer Protocol (NNTP)
- Peer-to-Peer Networking (P2P)
- Transmission Control Protocol/Internet Protocol (TCP/IP), which binds all of the above protocols together.

Each of those protocols consists of its own subnetwork with a specific purpose. Have you ever looked at a Web address?

ELSEWHERE ON THE WEB

▶ The World Wide Web Consortium, also known as W3C, put together a wonderful timeline for their tenth anniversary at www.w3 .org/2005/01/timelines/time line-2500x998.png. This timeline has loads of interesting information about the early days of the Web, including such information as the period of time from pre-Internet days to the present day and the growth of Web servers worldwide. It's a good way to see how far we've come from such humble beginnings.

The HTTP is for Web pages. What about when you log into a secure banking page? The HTTPS guarantees your security. Do you use Outlook? Chances are you've had to configure your SMTP/POP settings for e-mailing correctly. Each subnetwork has its own preprogrammed purpose that makes it a useful part of the whole.

Now, I know my head kind of exploded when I was first handed this information, but don't worry: all you need to really take away from this is the fact that the Web is a series of subnetworks and protocols that work together on top of the Internet superstructure in order to provide a well-rounded online experience.

HTML: The Language of the Web

Without Tim Berners-Lee's invention of the hypertext markup language, or **HTML** for short, the Web as we know it would not exist. What is HTML? It's text that is linked to other text via hyperlinks, and it's the defining feature for the entire World Wide Web. Without hypertext, without HTML, you wouldn't be able to jump easily from one Web page to the other—and the growth of the Web would never have occurred at such a staggering rate without it.

What does HTML look like? That's a very good question. Here's a quick peek at what almost every existing Web page looks like under the hood, so to speak:

```
<html>
<head>
<title>My Web Page</title>
</head>
<body> Text on the page. </body>
</html>
```

Yep, that's about it. What you're looking at here are HTML **tags**, simple words and symbols that, once put together, form a Web page. Now, I know that if you've never seen HTML coding

▶ We all know that the Internet has grown at a fantastic rate, and with it the Web's network of linked information. But are there any rules governing this mass influx of resources? Are there any governing bodies that have a say in how the Internet is run? Or is it just a giant free-for-all? The answer lies somewhere in between. Read my article titled "Internet Regulations: Rules for the Internet" to better understand your search results, here: http://about.com/websearch/internetregulations.

before, it can look a bit mystical. But let me assure you: it's simple to learn, and once you've got the basics down, you can understand how Web pages really tick—and your Web searches will be better because of it.

Anyone can write HTML. You may not have known this, but if you have a simple word processing program (Microsoft Word, Notepad, etc.), you can write HTML. There are many WYSIWYG (what you see is what you get) HTML editors out there that make the process of writing Web pages even simpler; Dreamweaver and Homesite are among the most notable. In addition, there are quite a few online HTML editors that you can use to write a quickie Web page:

- Google Page Creator: www.pages.google.com
- RealTime HTML Editor: http://htmledit.squarefree.com/
- Lissa's HTML Editor: www.lissaexplains.com/htmlarea/html editor.shtml

You might be asking yourself: why should I care about HTML? Most people won't ever dip their toes into the HTML pool, and that's okay. However, if you're serious about learning what the Web is all about, you'll need to have at least a working knowledge of what HTML is; after all, it *is* the language of the Web.

Web Pages, URLs, Domains, Oh My!

So we know what the Web is, we know what the Internet is, and we even have a pretty good idea of what HTML is—hey, we're doing pretty good so far! Now let's take a quick look at Web pages and links, also known as URLs, and figure out how these things work together to create a seamless Web experience.

URL stands for Uniform Resource Locator. Basically, a URL is an address for information on the Web. Every chunk of content on the Web has its own specific URL in order to be found more easily.

Here's a good way to get a grasp on how URLs work: think of an old movie where a character picked up the phone and asked the operator to give him (for example) "Delta 1-2-3." This was in the days when very few people actually had telephones, and so simple phone numbers like this made sense. Fast forward to the present day, when millions of people have phones, and this arrangement is no longer feasible—thus the complicated organizational phone number system that is in place today.

It's the same with URLs. Currently there are around *50 billion* Web pages on the World Wide Web—and every single one has its own specific URL in order to differentiate it from every other Web page (and make it easier for you to find it!).

Let's see how a URL works. In order to really get a grasp on how a Uniform Resource Locator works to differentiate each Web page, we're going to take one apart and examine it, piece by piece. Here's what a basic URL looks like: http://www.websearch.about .com/od/bestwebsites/a/siteoftheday.htm. A few things you'll notice right off the bat are:

- **There are no spaces in the URL.** This makes it easier for Web servers to serve up individual Web pages without interruption.
- **There are a lot of forward slashes.** This is just to separate the different parts of the URL, similar to the way a file path separates directory, subdirectories, and document name with backslashes.

▸ Anyone who's looking to learn how to code HTML from the ground up should definitely check out W3C's W3Schools at www.w3 schools.com. There are all kinds of fun HTML tutorials here—text, frames, links, and much more. It's a great way to really get your feet wet with HTML, but not get overwhelmed with a lot of bells and whistles.

- **The URL starts with "http."** Almost every URL you will come across will start with the prefix "http," which is an acronym for Hypertext Transfer Protocol.

Okay, so let's get under the hood of this particular URL and figure out what makes it tick, shall we? I'll take it chunk by chunk:

- **http://:** I know when I see the http at the front of a URL that this particular file is hosted somewhere on the Web. A Web server that gets an HTTP request (for instance, from you typing in a URL) will recognize this as an HTTP protocol, and will send the appropriate HTML page that this URL corresponds to. Lost yet? Well, you can also think of the HTTP as the area code in a phone number; you're just starting the dial-through process.
- **www:** The next part of the URL is "www," which stands for World Wide Web. **Note:** Not all URLs will have the www, but that doesn't mean that they're not on the Web. Some URLs will have a different subnetwork protocol at the beginning; this just tells you which subnetwork that particular URL is originating from.
- **websearch.about.com:** This is the part of the URL that tells you the domain name, what you might recognize as the actual name, or title, of a site. This site's name is About Web Search, and the domain name reflects that. The **.com** part is a suffix that indicates which **top-level domain** this particular URL belongs to. A top-level domain, or TLD for short, tells you whether the site is a business, educational, organizational, or governmental address, as well as what its country of origin is (we'll get to more about that in just a bit).

WHAT'S HOT

▶ Sometimes URLs can get really long. Really, really long; in fact, if you've ever tried to copy and paste a URL that you wanted to share and e-mail it to a friend, you might have found that the URL "broke," and it became difficult for your friend to see what you were so excited about. Enter TinyURL, a site that shortens those long URLs into shorter, more manageable segments. Visit http://tinyurl.com to learn more.

- **/od/bestwebsites/a/:** This part of the URL tells the Web server exactly where to go to retrieve the files. It's a directory road map that drills down into file folders. In our phone number analogy, this would be the local area prefix after the area code.
- **siteoftheday.htm:** This is the specific address of the Web page inside the folders indicated by the forward slashes in the /od/bestwebsites/a/ part of the URL. "Siteoftheday" is the file name of the page you would be looking at if you were viewing this URL on the Web. The **.htm** suffix (which could also be .html) indicates that this is indeed an HTML file. To round out our phone number analogy: this would be the last four-digit segment of a phone number.

Yes, it's a lot to take in—but remember the phone number analogy to keep it as simple as possible. A URL is just an organizational tool to help you find Web pages more easily. Without URLs, it would be daunting, to say the least, to attempt to retrieve specific information from the vast amount of it on the Web, let alone organize what's there into any kind of manageable whole. Plus, once you know the anatomy of a URL, you'll find that you can do a lot of pretty advanced Web searching (we'll get to that in later chapters).

Let's examine some top-level domains. I noted in our URL breakdown that you can tell a lot about a URL from the TLD, or top-level domain (such as .com). There are many different types of TLDs, but we're just going to look at five: country of origin, governmental, organization, educational, and commercial.

- **Country of origin TLD:** A country code top-level domain is a top-level domain used and reserved for a country or a dependent territory. For instance, Germany's TLD code is .de, Spain's TLD code is .es, Brazil's TLD code is .br, and so on.

- **Governmental TLD:** Specifically in the United States, the domains that belong to government entities end in the suffix .gov. These domains, obtained through the General Services Administration of the federal government, can belong to federal, state, or local entities. Within the U.S. government's vast array of Web properties, there's also the .mil domain or .fed or .us. Most of the American military Web sites, for example, use the .mil suffix.

- **Organization TLD:** The organization TLD, or .org, started as a characterization for those sites that weren't easily fitted into any other category, such as nonprofits. The charitable organization World Vision, for instance, has a domain name registered at http://worldvision.org, indicating its noncommercial status.

- **Educational TLD:** Virtually every accredited higher-level educational institution in the United States is registered under an .edu domain—for example, www.stanford.edu. Most other educational facilities in the world have opted not to use the .edu domain; instead, they use a combination of their institution's title and their specific country codes.

- **Commercial TLD:** The commercial top-level domain, or .com, is the most common of all the TLD designations. Originally, the .com TLD was intended to signify business Web sites; however, anyone can register a .com domain no matter what they intend to use the domain for.

There is a reason why we need all these TLDs. To put it mildly, there are a lot of people on the Web, and these people have registered a lot of Web sites. There had to be some kind of organizational structure put in place from the beginning; otherwise, the

ASK YOUR GUIDE

Is the entire URL necessary in order to get to a Web page?

▶ Not any more. In fact, you can usually leave out the http://www part of a URL and just type in the directory and file part. For instance, say you wanted to navigate to CNN's Web site. Just type in "cnn.com" and you're all set. In fact, some Web sites are so well-known that you can navigate to them simply by typing the name in your browser, such as "wikipedia."

Web would be one big, goopy, unorganized mess. That's why it's so important to understand the basic structure: URLs, domains, top-level domains, etc.—it's so you can get around more easily. With the billions of Web sites there are on the Web, I'm thankful that this system is in place; it sure makes searching the Web much easier.

Web Stats: Just How Many People Are on the Web?

To say that Web use has grown (and is growing) at an astonishing rate would be an understatement. According to ClickZ Stats (www .clickz.com/showPage.html?page=stats/web_worldwide), an organization that tracks online statistics in all sorts of sectors, the estimated worldwide Internet-using population came to around 1.08 billion in 2005. The projection for 2010? At least 1.8 billion, and I think that number is conservative.

Nielsen/Net Ratings, a company that specializes in Internet statistical research, has come up with these intriguing numbers for people using the Web:

- The average person visits around 1,400 Web pages per month.
- The average person visits around 60 different domains per month.
- The average time spent on the Web: nearly 29 hours a month.

In the United States alone, as of March 2007, 70 percent of the population was on the Internet in some fashion. Oceania/Australia follow with 53.5 percent of the population online, and in third place is Europe, with nearly 40 percent of the population online. The number of new users increases exponentially each year according to www.internetworldstats.com/stats.htm. Since the birth of the Web in 1991, this yearly growth has become almost ordinary, and all signs point to this escalation continuing at an extremely rapid pace.

That's how increasingly important the Web has become, and there's no sign of this trend slowing down, that's for sure. As this growth continues, it's more important than ever to educate ourselves about the wide and wonderful world of the Web and to broaden our horizons as more technology becomes accessible to the general public.

Get Linked

Want more information on what you've just read? Check out these resources at my About.com Web Search site to dig deeper.

HOW THE WORLD WIDE WEB HAS CHANGED SOCIETY

The Web has become a major part of many people's lives. We use it for communication, work, school, entertainment, and more. Read more about the history of the Web and its impact on our society.

http://about.com/websearch/websociety

TCP/IP—THE LANGUAGE OF THE INTERNET

What is the language of the Internet? Computers have a common "language" that they use to talk to each other on the Net, which is called Transmission Control Protocol/Internet Protocol, or TCP/IP. Find out more here.

http://about.com/websearch/languageofinternet

HTTPS: WHAT DOES THIS MEAN?

If you've ever seen an "https" in the URL address of a Web site, you might have wondered what it stands for. Hint: If you're shopping online, you'll definitely want the HTTPS protocol in your site URL.

http://about.com/websearch/https

Chapter 2

The Basic Web Search Toolbox

Getting the Most out of Browsers

To take advantage of all that the Web has to offer, you'll need to use a Web browser. A Web browser, simply put, is a software program that allows you to access, view, and interact with all the information out there on the World Wide Web. Without a browser, it would still be possible to use the Web and find what you're looking for; however, a HUGE part of the rich Web search experience that we enjoy today would be lost.

There are a lot of browsers available out there, which is nice—you have plenty of choices from which to pick a program you'll be spending a lot of time with. The browser you choose has a big impact on what kind of Web search experience you ultimately will have, so obviously your choice is important. The top browsers on the market today are:

- Microsoft Internet Explorer (**www.microsoft.com/windows/ie/default.mspx**)
- Firefox (**www.mozilla.com/en-US/firefox/**)
- Opera (**www.opera.com/**)

And there is a whole host of other choices. However, the browser field is pretty well divided between **Internet Explorer**, one of the first browsers on the Web browser scene, and **Firefox**, a relative newcomer to the browser arena.

No browser is better than the others. Which one you use really depends on your personal preferences. Many people start out with Internet Explorer, or IE for short, because it was one of the first full-bodied Web browsers on the market and is automatically bundled with every Windows operating system as part of the full meal deal. In fact, that's a big reason why Internet Explorer took off as big as it did!

However, most people couldn't care less which browser they use, as long as they can get to where they're going on the Web. I was like that for a long time—I only used Internet Explorer because, well, it was just there. It got me where I needed to go with a minimum of fuss and that was all I needed, right? Actually, I couldn't have been more wrong—your choice of browser makes a *huge* difference in how good or bad your Web search experience is. That's why, a couple of years ago, I started researching other browsers than Internet Explorer, most notably Mozilla Firefox.

When I first started looking at Firefox, I had been a die-hard Internet Explorer user for many years; however, I'd noticed that certain annoyances such as constant pop-ups, slow load times, and lack of useful browser extensions were really starting to become more of a problem. Firefox solved all these problems for me—in

ELSEWHERE ON THE WEB

▶ For an extremely detailed look at the history of the Web browser—and I mean extremely detailed (you'll really know your stuff when you're done reading it!)—I invite you to read Wikipedia's entry on Web browsers at http://en.wikipedia.org/wiki/Web_browser. It's an interesting look at the early life and times of Web browsers, the 1990s browser wars, and what's going on in the Web browser scene today.

fact, Firefox is rapidly becoming known as the "searcher's browser." Why? There are quite a few reasons, but here are my own personal favorite Firefox features:

- **Tabbed browsing.** Once you go tabbed browsing, you'll never go back to the old days of "open new window." It's just that useful.
- **Advanced security options.** Once I started using Firefox, I never saw another pop-up. Not one. That's kind of a big deal, since pop-up ads tend to slow down your computer system and put a cramp in your Web surfing.
- **Useful add-ons.** More useful extensions, toolbars, and add-ons have been programmed for Firefox than for any other browser. For example, you can search multiple search engines and research sites simply by installing the Firefox search engine add-on (you can find this at https://addons .mozilla.org/search-engines.php).

Ultimately, it's up to you which browser you choose, but speaking as someone who spends a lot of time on the Web, I couldn't recommend Firefox more highly. You can download it for free at www.mozilla.com/en-US/firefox/. If you're used to using another browser, do what I did and give Firefox a try for one month: I can almost guarantee that you won't be switching back.

Every Web browser has the same basic features. Since you're going to be using your Web browser quite a bit with this book, it's a good idea to familiarize yourself with the basic parts so you can follow along. Here's a basic browser anatomy lesson—the bare bones of what a browser looks like (you might want to pull up your chosen browser right now so you can see what I'm talking about):

ASK YOUR GUIDE

Do Web browsers include security options to keep me safe on the Web?

▶ Yes—and in my opinion, Firefox is one of the most security-conscious browsers on the market today. For instance, Firefox will prevent intrusive pop-ups from ever appearing within your browser window (I've had Firefox for years now and haven't seen one pop-up yet—how's that for security!) once you set proper security settings . . . which you can learn how to do here: http://about.com/websearch/ firefoxsecurity.

▶ Many people have made the switch from Internet Explorer, still the dominant Web browser with the lion's share of users, to Firefox. However, if you're wondering what all the fuss is about, read this excellent Forbes article titled "Internet Explorer vs. Firefox," found at www.forbes.com/tech nology/2004/10/04/cx_pp_ 1004mondaymatchup.html. It's a good look at how the browsers are different, which one has what features, and might give you some idea of which browser you'd like to choose for your Web search needs.

- **Menu bar:** Includes headings such as File, Edit, and View that when clicked will open drop-down menus. Notice that you can close everything on a browser except the menu bar—it's always there, as it is in all Windows applications.
- **Status bar:** This is the bar at the bottom of your browser window. The status bar displays all sorts of information, depending on what you're doing at the time, but mostly it's for showing load speed and the URL of whatever address your mouse is hovering over. The status bar also can display privacy or security information, depending on what browser you're using.
- **Address bar:** This is the box at the top of your browser window that displays the entire URL, or Web site address. For instance, if you decide to surf over to About Web Search, your address bar would display this URL: http://websearch .about.com/About_Web_Search.htm. You can type a URL directly into the address bar of your browser.
- **Title bar:** The title bar is at the very top of your browser window. You'll see the title of the Web page there; for example, again, if you navigated to About Web Search, you'd see the title displayed as "About Web Search - Learn How To Search The Web."
- **Toolbar icons:** The browser toolbar and the icons found on the toolbar are at the top of your browser window right underneath the title bar. This is where you'll see the Back button, the Home button, the Refresh button, etc.
- **Display window:** The display window is just a fancy term for your browser workspace; it's the frame through which you see a Web site.
- **Scroll bars:** If you've ever been to a Web site where you had to "scroll down" to read something, then you've used the scroll bars. They're just navigational/directional aids.

Now, there is a lot more to a browser than this—security features, **toolbar** options, password recovery procedures, etc.—and we'll get into some of those things. However, this basic one-size-fits-all description should get you around your browser just fine; after all, we're more interested in what we can do with our browser than what's under the hood, right?

Try out toolbars and add-ons. Your mileage may vary, but over the past few years I've experimented with a lot of browser toolbars, add-ons, buttons, etc., and I've figured out which ones do the job that I need them to do.

The Google Toolbar (http://toolbar.google.com) comes in both Internet Explorer and Firefox flavors, and is a great way to search Google without actually navigating to Google itself. In addition, the Toolbar will warn you automatically if you come across Web pages that are unsafe (e.g., have malicious applications running that could be harmful to your computer), check your spelling, automatically fill in words for you as you type, and delight you with many more features. I've had the Google Toolbar installed on my computer with no problems from the day they first debuted it—it's a great help with Web searches.

There are many search engine add-ons for Firefox. Go to Firefox and you'll notice that in the upper right-hand corner they've provided you with a search box containing a few popular search engines (Google, **Amazon.com**, etc.) that you can instantly access from this box. You can add many, many more search engines and Web sites to this search box, making it one of the most useful tools in your Web search arsenal. To add search engines to your Firefox toolbar, just head on over to https://addons.mozilla.org/en=USfirefox/browse/type:4 and click the sites and search engines that you want.

Now, whenever you want to search, for example, eBay, you can type what you are looking for directly into the search bar and

TOOLS YOU NEED

▶ If you want to feel like a kid in a candy store, you'll want to visit these add-on links: First, the official site for Microsoft Internet Explorer add-ons is found at www.ieaddons.com. Here's where you'll find security extensions, time-saving applications, and all kinds of entertainment goodies for Internet Explorer. Second, the official add-ons site for Firefox is found at https://addons.mozilla.org/. A wide variety of add-ons is available here, from Web development to in-browser Web chats.

▶ One fun thing you can do with your Google Toolbar is pop some buttons onto it— check it out at the Google Toolbar Buttons Gallery (http://toolbar.google.com/ buttons/gallery). You can add buttons for your favorite Web search activities from shopping to checking up on Wall Street, or you can even create your own. The most popular buttons currently are Weather, Dictionary, Mood Ring, Google Earth, and Google Blog Search.

select the eBay icon from your search engine toolbar, instead of typing the eBay URL into your Web browser's address bar and *then* finding what you're looking for. It's an excellent shortcut that I use constantly.

CustomizeGoogle (https://addons.mozilla.org/firefox/743/) is a Firefox extension that enhances Google search results by adding extra information (like links to Yahoo, Ask.com, MSN, etc.) and removing unwanted information (like ads and **spam**). What I like best about this extension is that it simply gives me more search options to play with.

There are many other toolbars and add-ons out there for your browser; however, I find that the mantra "less is more" definitely does apply here. You don't want a lot of extra features on your browser that don't do much of anything except look pretty—you want just the absolute best software applications out there that deliver an incredible Web search experience. In my opinion, you can't go wrong with the three that I've detailed here, but if you want to explore even more browser toolbars and add-ons, I invite you to visit my article "Search Toolbars" (http://about.com/web search/searchtoolbars) to try out a few more.

How to Set Your Home Page

The next Web search job is setting your **home page**. Remember playing kick the can when you were little, and whoever made it to home base first was the winner? Well, just as in kick the can, you need a home base while searching the Web—and I'm going to show you how to get one.

You'll notice that at the top of your browser there is an icon that looks like a house—this is your home page icon. You can set your home page to anything your heart desires, but just make sure that it's a page you don't mind seeing every time your browser starts up for the first time, or every time you click the home icon.

Here's how you set your home page in Internet Explorer:

1. Click Tools, then Internet Options.
2. At the top of the General tab of the pop-up window will be a section titled Home Page.
3. The Web address where you currently are will show up in the Address box.
4. If you want to set the current page to be your start page, click the Use Current button. If you'd like to set it to a different page, type that address into the Address box.

Ta da! All set. If you want to change it later, just go through the above steps again for the new page.

And here's how it's done for Firefox:

1. Click Tools, then Options.
2. Click the General tab.
3. At the top of the General window, you'll see a section titled Home Page and a box labeled Location. If you're already at the page you'd like to set as your home page, then all you need to do is click Use Current Page. If you'd like to set it to a different page, type that address into the Location box.

You're all set. If you want to change it, just go through the above steps again for the new page.

There are a few search services out there that offer what is known as a portal page for searchers; this is where you can cluster all your Web goodies onto one page, such as your e-mail, weather, movie times, latest news, **bookmarks**, etc. I've had my home page set on My Yahoo (http://my.yahoo.com) for as long as I can remember; it's a convenient way to access all I need in one handy location. If you'd like to use My Yahoo for your home page, head on

ASK YOUR GUIDE

What if I want to add a Web site to my Firefox search toolbar that isn't listed at the Mozilla site?

▶ It's relatively easy to add your own sites to this search toolbar. Start by picking the search engine or specific site that you want to add to your toolbar. If you'd like to build your own specialized Firefox extension for your favorite site, read this article titled "Make your own Firefox search plug-in," here: www.lifehacker.com/software/firefox/make-your-own-firefox-site-search-plugin-202923.php. It's easy to do, I promise.

over to the My Yahoo home page to get started; it's pretty self-explanatory once you start the process.

Bookmarks and Keyboard Shortcuts

You probably already know that the Web is a pretty big place, and there are scads of Web sites out there that are pretty amazing. What happens if you'd like to save a site to come back and visit later? Do you have to write it down on a Post-It and hope you can find it? Thankfully, that is definitely not the case—you can use your bookmarks instead. In addition, keyboard shortcuts will save you an amazing amount of time once you start spending time on the Web—you'll be surprised at how streamlined your searches will become once you master the basics.

Bookmarks are saved shortcuts to your favorite sites. All browsers have **bookmark managers** built into them, and there are also standalone Web-based bookmark services that you can use not only to store your own bookmarks, but also to share them with others (we'll get more into those services in Chapter 7, "Using the Social Web in Searches").

Here's how you make a bookmark in Internet Explorer (note: these shortcuts are specific to PCs and not to Macs):

1. Find a site you'd like to come back to.
2. Click the Favorites icon in your browser toolbar, or click the word "Favorites" in the menu bar above it.
3. After you click the Favorites icon, a left-side screen window will pop up; if you clicked "Favorites" on the menu bar, you'll get a drop-down menu. Select "Add . . ." or "Add to Favorites" and click OK. You can rename the page at this point if it's got a long or particularly unhelpful title.

TOOLS YOU NEED

▶ Setting your home page is a major step toward customizing your Web search experience, and one of the most popular components on these home pages for many people is Web-based e-mail, available through portal sites such as Yahoo, Google, AOL, MSN, and more. These e-mail services are all completely free! You can compare free e-mail services here: http://about.com/email/freeemail.

You've just created a Favorite!

There's also a quick keyboard shortcut that you can use to make a favorite in Internet Explorer: simply press the CTRL key (or the CMD key on a Mac) and then press D. Voilà! Instantly added to your favorites.

Here's how you can create bookmarks in Firefox:

1. Select Bookmarks in your browser's menu bar, and click Bookmark This Page.
2. At this point, you'll be asked where you would like to save the new bookmark. This is your opportunity to create a new folder, or, if you already have organized your bookmarks into manageable folders, you can select the appropriate folder from the list.
3. Select the folder you want and click OK. If you want this favorite to go straight to the Firefox toolbar rather than be stored in your bookmarks manager, click Bookmarks in the menu bar and then click Manage Bookmarks, and either make a new bookmark using New Bookmark or drag an existing bookmark to that folder.

That's it—you've just created a new favorite in Firefox. There's also the quite handy CTRL+D keyboard shortcut for creating a bookmark, as well as the CTRL+Shift+D keyboard shortcut that will let you bookmark multiple tabs at once.

Get in the habit of organizing your bookmarks into folders. Believe me—you don't want a mess of 3,421 favorites that are not organized into any kind of system . . . speaking completely hypothetically, of course. Every time you make a new favorite, whether it's in Internet Explorer or Firefox, be sure to either plop that site into an appropriately named folder, or start a new folder—

WHAT'S HOT

▶ Google has made available a Google Personalized Homepage product (available at www.google.com/ig). You can arrange this page any way you want by checking off the boxes of the modules you'd like to add; once you're signed in, you can drag and drop titles of these modules to arrange the page to your liking. In addition, you can add more stuff to your Google home page by clicking the link appropriately named "Add Stuff."

***How do I organize
my Internet Explorer
favorites?***

▶ There's a lot you can do
with your favorites, and
I've written up a step-by-
step tutorial complete with
screenshots titled "Microsoft
Internet Explorer Favorites
Tutorial" (you can find it at
http://about.com/websearch/
explorerfavorites). I'll show
you how to create, organize,
delete, and print a list of your
favorites.

it's much easier to do it as you go along than all at once. Plus, as
you become more and more Web-savvy, you're going to want your
Web search finds to be in a manageable "database" of sorts so you
can use them to build other Web searches, projects, queries, etc.

Basic keyboard shortcuts are crucial time savers. I've used
basic keyboard shortcuts to streamline my Web search experience
for as long as I can remember. Here are the ones that I use most
frequently (the first is for Windows, the second for a Mac):

- **CTRL + A or CMD + A:** Highlights all the text on a page or
  in a text box.
- **CTRL + C or CMD + C:** Copies the highlighted text.
- **CTRL + V or CMD + V:** Pastes the text that you just copied
  from a Web site to anywhere else.
- **CTRL + P or CMD + P:** This tells your computer to print
  the Web page.
- **CTRL + D or CMD + D:** Saves a bookmark in both Internet
  Explorer and Firefox.

That's about as fancy as I get with keyboard shortcuts; however, if you really want to go mouseless and use the keyboard for
virtually all of your Web search adventures, you'll want to check
out the Mozilla Keyboard Shortcuts page at **www.mozilla.org/
support/firefox/keyboard**. This printable chart shows keyboard
shortcuts for Firefox, Internet Explorer, and **Opera**.

Media Players

One of the best parts about the Web is the amazing variety of
media content that you can find there. However, in order to
play most of this content, you're going to need a **media player**
of some type.

Windows machines will already have Windows Media Player automatically baked in, and it's a great media player for most content (if you don't already have it, you can download the latest version at www.microsoft.com/windows/windowsmedia or for Mac users, here: www.microsoft.com/windows/windowsmedia/player/mac/default.aspx). In addition to Windows Media Player, I also use Apple iTunes, which comes with every Mac computer, to play streaming radio stations or watch movie trailers (if you don't have it, download it for your Mac or PC at www.apple.com/itunes/). I find that the combination works out pretty well.

A Good Web Search Strategy

I suggest that you commit time to learning Web search strategy. This might seem like an odd tool to add to our Web search toolbox, but in my experience as the About.com guide to Web searching, I've found that time commitment is one of the most important, yet most often neglected, elements in developing a successful Web search strategy.

In order to become a savvy Web searcher, it's important to realize that you're going to have to spend time figuring it all out. It doesn't come naturally—you don't just wake up one morning suddenly able to parse Boolean search strings or find the average rainfall in Bolivia (complete with audio!). If you want to learn how to search the Web, it's imperative that you devote time to learning how to do it—and realize that, even with this commitment, there is always something new to be learned. The more I learn, the more I realize I have to learn.

In addition, it's very important to realize that some Web searches can't be successfully accomplished quickly. Sure, there's the relatively simple ones that can be whipped up in a fraction of a second, but then you come up against search problems that require more effort, more creativity, more . . . you guessed it . . .

TOOLS YOU NEED

▶ I found a Firefox add-on that will help me tackle my bookmarks, the Bookmark Tags Firefox Extension (http://dripfeed.myweb.uga.edu/bookmarktags/): Instead of deciding on the one, appropriate folder to place a bookmark in, you assign it any number of "tags," or categories, and let Bookmark Tags organize your bookmarks for you. I've had this up and running for a few days now and it's been a big help—try it yourself and see what you think.

time. Some of my most frequent reader e-mails concern this very theme, and while I'm all about making searches more efficient, it's crucial to recognize that the Web is not a magic genie that pops out answers instantly.

Be willing to try new things. It's easy to get bogged down into a predictable routine when searching the Web; in fact, I fall prey to that quite often myself! We find what works for us, and we stick with that, never trying anything new or venturing out of our safe little Web search boundaries. This is a sad situation to be in, folks—there are just too many Web search goodies out there to ignore. Throughout the course of this book, I'm going to introduce you to some things that you've probably never seen before. While these technologies might have some unusual vocabulary, be difficult to figure out (at least at first), or be outside your comfort zone, I encourage you to try everything at least once. Don't be afraid to stretch your Web search boundaries—you might be surprised at what you find!

Persevere when answers aren't immediately available. One of the worst mistakes you can make in your Web search experience is to expect instant success. If you're an experienced searcher, you know that while the search process has come a long way, it still takes a bit of effort to find exactly what you are looking for, especially if what you are looking for is highly specialized.

The best thing to do when searching the Web is to be patient and keep at it. The more you learn about how to refine your Web searches, the faster and more enjoyable the process will become. In fact, you might start enjoying the hunt more than the actual results—or maybe that's just me as a search geek talking. Bottom line is this: don't give up easily. If at first your Web search does not succeed, try it again a different way.

Get Linked

Here are some additional resources on my About.com Web Search site that should help you find even more great information about searching the Web.

TOP TEN WEB SEARCH TRICKS

There are Web search techniques that I use every day in order to find what I'm looking for. I've put together a list of a few of my favorite tricks.

http://about.com/websearch/toptentricks

FREE E-MAIL CLASS—LEARN HOW TO SEARCH THE WEB WITH WEB SEARCH 101

Web Search 101 is a free class made up of thirteen weekly lessons that will come to you in your e-mail inbox; every week, I'll show you how to do something different on the Web. It's a great introduction, and will get you well on your way to becoming a more experienced (and less frustrated!) Web surfer.

http://about.com/websearch/websearch101

DEVELOPING A SEARCH PLAN

Even if you're just doing a casual Web search, it can be a good idea to identify exactly what it is you are looking for from the beginning, and if possible, narrow down your target to make it easier to find.

http://about.com/websearch/searchplan

Chapter 3

Using Search Engines

Information Overload on the Web

There are literally billions of Web pages, and that number increases every day. How do you find something? Sure, you could probably just type in your favorite URL, but what if you want to go beyond those boundaries? How do you explore the vast deposits of information out there on the World Wide Web that are literally free for the taking?

All these fantastic resources were making their way onto the Web, but with little chance of being found unless you knew the exact address—and probably very few of us memorize the URLs of all the Web sites that we've ever visited so we could come back again. There had to be some way to organize this information so that people could access it more easily.

Enter search engines and Web directories. Thankfully, this dilemma has been addressed by some very smart folks who recognized that as the Web got bigger and bigger there had to be some

How many Web pages are there on the Web?

▶ The number is astronomical, and continues to grow. Depending on which source you ask, there are anywhere from 4 billion to 100 billion pages. One of the better sites to get this kind of information from is WorldWideWebSize. com (http://world widewebsize.com/); every day, they update various graphs that show relevant Web growth information. Currently, the Web is clocking at about 15 billion pages . . . give or take a few million.

way to organize the glut of information. There needed to be some structure, some boundaries, some way to find relevant resources without taking too much time: in other words, we needed the organizational structure of a search engine.

What Is a Search Engine?

If you've been on the Web for more than five minutes, you've probably used a search engine to find something—a map, a recipe, a phone number, the news, etc. A search engine at its most basic can be compared to a library card catalog arrangement—you think of a topic, and then you can pull up information on the topic based on an underlying structural system that organizes information according to strict subject guidelines. And since the card catalog (i.e., search engine) is organized in a categorical/hierarchical fashion, you are usually able to retrieve relevant information in a timely manner.

Search engines provide a quick and easy way to find what you're looking for from the vast resources of the Web. Sure, you can still search the Web without a search engine, but you can miss out on a lot of good information that way. In addition, search engines retrieve results in a very short amount of time; this timeliness especially comes into play if you're writing a report, about to head out the door, need a quick answer, etc. Obviously, the benefits of using a search engine are many.

A lot goes into a search engine's information retrieval. While search engines do make searching the Web much easier, there's some pretty convoluted stuff going on underneath their deceptively simple and streamlined surfaces. Search engines are extremely complicated software programs that use complex math algorithms, data retrieval solutions, and other somewhat scary math-type things in order to find what you've asked them to look for.

Search engines consist of three basic components: spiders, indexes, and ranking and relevancy programs.

Spiders—not the creepy crawly kind—are just software programs that follow, or "crawl," links on the Web, grabbing content from sites and adding it to their particular search engine indexes.

Everything that these spiders find out on the Web goes into the search engine's index, or database. This is like the card-catalog-at-a-library analogy that I've already mentioned: all the books have corresponding cards in the card catalog that tell you exactly where to find them in the library based on subject, author, title, etc. It's very similar with search engine indexes.

If you had to pick one component of search engines that was the most useful, ranking and relevancy programming would probably be it. Every search engine ranks information according to a variety of factors: relevancy, incoming links, content on the page, etc. Without this final piece of the puzzle, search engines would be serving up one big mess of information with little or no organizational structure, and obviously this wouldn't be much help.

Let's get under the hood and see how search engines work. Honestly, there are brainy people who have gone to school for a very long time who still don't understand how these complicated programs work, so we're not going to get the full picture in one small chapter. However, at their most basic (and I'm talking bare-bones basic here!), search engines generally work like this: you type in a query, the search engine's programming uses your query to find relevant material within its index, your results are displayed.

There's much more to the inner workings of search engines—relevancy algorithms, query processing, result rankings, etc.—but that's the short version. Search engines really are fascinating when you start delving into their component parts, and it's especially

TOOLS YOU NEED

▶ It's quite interesting to try different search engines, especially extremely targeted "niche" search engines (did you know that there's a search engine dedicated completely to finding new cocktail recipes?). I try to test out a new search engine at least once a week—it's amazing how different the search results can be from engine to engine. You can visit my table of search engines at http://about.com/websearch/searchenginetable.

interesting how search engines just keep evolving and changing to fit the needs of an ever more demanding Web search population. In fact, we could be here together for a very long time digging into the mechanical workings of your average search engine. However, you're reading this book not to find out how search engines work, but to find out how you can make them work for you. Right? Right.

Basic Search Engine Commands

So search engines find all the good stuff, round it up, and then present it, right? Not exactly. It's kind of like the whole "needle in a haystack" scenario: there's absolutely no lack of information coming at you, but finding relevant information is a whole other story.

While search engines have done most of the heavy lifting for us, it still can be somewhat difficult to find exactly what you're looking for using a search engine, especially if you're looking for something that's just a bit obscure or relatively complicated. However, there are quite a few tricks you can use to tame your favorite search engine into humble submission. It's just a matter of knowing the right buttons to push, and the right questions to ask.

There are a few one-size-fits-all commands that work on pretty much any search engine. These are the absolute basic tools you'll need to make your search engine queries more effective and cut down on the Web search frustration factor. Plus, these basic commands have the added benefit of helping to cut through the chaff and get right to the needle in the haystack, to mix a couple of metaphors.

The main search trick is to use quotation marks. Why? Because without the use of these simple punctuation marks, the search engine will look for your query words both as a whole

ASK YOUR GUIDE

When you type in a query to a search engine, are you actually searching the Web?

▶ Well, kind of. You're actually searching the search engine's index, or the pages that the search engine's spiders (software programs that go out and explore the Web via links) have crawled and have been included in the database.

phrase and separately, making for a pretty unorganized page of search results.

For example, say you're searching for the topic of "warthog habits." Using quotes around these words will tell the search engines that you would like this query designated as a whole concept, in the exact order that you typed it in, rather than as two individual topics, warthogs and habits.

Another great Web search trick is to use targeted phrases. This one might seem obvious, but the more focused and targeted you can make your Web search queries from the very beginning, the better.

For example, if you want to find the best pizza in San Francisco, it would do you no good to just type the word "pizza" into a search engine and expect it to come back with anything remotely useful for you (although you might get some good pizza recipes that way); however, this is starting to change with personalized search engines that are able to grab your geographical location based on your computer's ISP. Regardless, it's a good idea to be as specific as possible—after all, you're not always going to be at your home computer. Search engines cannot read your mind—not yet, anyway. So it behooves you when using a search engine to try to be as targeted as possible. If you're searching for pizza in San Francisco, then by all means type in "pizza San Francisco."

In addition, don't be afraid to type in a question or longer phrase; for example, say you want to find the best Crock-Pot chicken recipe on the Web. You might find some pretty good results by simply typing in "what is the best chicken crock pot recipe?" Don't be intimidated or nervous—tell that search engine exactly what you are looking for and you'll most likely be surprised at what you can turn up.

ELSEWHERE ON THE WEB

▶ If you're looking for some of the best up-to-date search engine news on the Web, you'll want to pay a visit to SearchEngineWatch.com, a site that is updated every time a search engine so much as twitches. SearchEngine-Watch is pretty much the authority when it comes to anything to do with search engines. You'll find the latest developments, commentary, and news here; they've also got archived news back to 2001 as well as detailed search engine tutorials and comparison charts.

Use basic math symbols to refine your searches. Similar to Boolean searches which use the words "and" and "not," the basic math symbols plus (+) and minus (-) can be a tremendous help in focusing or widening your Web search efforts.

First, let's look at using the plus symbol. The + sign before a word tells the search engine that you really, really want it to locate *all* the words you've entered in your search query, not just some of them. For example, suppose you're looking for information on both Shakespeare and Hamlet. Note: There should be no spaces (unless otherwise indicated) between the operator and the query. Here's what your query would look like:

```
+Shakespeare +Hamlet
```

You've just instructed the search engine to come back with *only* pages that contain both of these words in your search results. Here's another one:

```
+Shakespeare +Hamlet +Ophelia
```

This query tells the search engine that you are looking for pages that have all three of these words on them.

Now, you might be asking yourself how this is different from just using quotation marks around Web searches. Actually, it's quite different. Using quotes effectively tells the search engine that you want the words within the quotes found in that exact order, and in that exact proximity; in other words, you'd like the search engine to find what you're looking for exactly the way you wrote it.

Sounds simple, right? Well, again, search engines can't read your mind—they need exact instructions in order to carry out your commands. When you use the + symbol in front of a series

TOOLS YOU NEED

▶ If you're doing a big research project and need to keep track of the sites that you come across in your Web search travels, I recommend Google Notebook (www.google.com/notebook). Google Notebook makes Web research of all kinds easier and more efficient by enabling you to clip and gather information even while you're browsing the Web. Google Notebook "lives" in your Web browser, so all your notes are in one convenient place.

of words, you're telling the search engine that you don't mind if these words are nowhere near each other on the page; you just want them all on the same page *some*where. Make sense? Okay, then let's move on to the next basic math search engine helper: the minus symbol.

To keep going with the basic math search technique, the - symbol is useful when you're looking for one subject that might be commonly associated with a second subject and you'd like to exclude that second subject from your search results. Clear as mud, right? Well, let's take a look at an example:

```
Superman -Krypton
```

In this search query, the search engine is being instructed to look for pages that mention Superman, but not his home planet of Krypton. Let's keep going with this subtraction thing:

```
Apple -iPod -iTunes
```

You've just told the search engine that you would like pages returned that mention Apple, but you would like all instances of both iPod and iTunes removed from the search engine results. This is going to return narrowed results. Let's do one more:

```
Darth Vader -anakin -skywalker -padme -kenobi
```

This particular search query is telling the search engine that you would like it to come back with all pages that mention Darth Vader, but you would like it to specifically exclude pages that mention the words Anakin, Skywalker, Padme, and Kenobi.

Obviously, the subtraction symbol comes in pretty handy when you want to refine a Web search. But wait—it gets even better!

ASK YOUR GUIDE

Are these "basic math" searches the same as Boolean searches?

▶ Not exactly. Boolean logic is the term used to describe certain logical operations that are used to combine search terms in many search engine databases and directories on the Net. The basic math commands I've given you are related to the Boolean search commands of AND, OR, and NOT; you can get a lot more involved with Boolean searching, however.

Let's talk about the combo platter—the basic math Web search combo platter, that is.

Add quotation marks for a better focus. Wait until you see what you can do with some simple combinations of quotation marks and basic math! Here's an example using one of our previous searches.

Instead of this:

> Darth Vader -anakin -skywalker -padme -kenobi

Try this:

> "Darth Vader" -"anakin skywalker" -"padme skywalker" -"obi wan kenobi"

Instead of inserting the subtraction symbol every two seconds, you can type entire phrases, put them in quotation marks, and plop the minus symbol in front for a much more refined and successful search.

Try a wildcard search. A wildcard search will still work in Google, Yahoo, Ask, and AOL Search. Unfortunately, many other search engines no longer support the wildcard syntax.

A wildcard search works like this: you type in a phrase—e.g., Chinese food—and add an asterisk (*) to indicate to the search engine that you would like it to fill in the blank, so to speak. Let me give you an example:

> Quilting * classes

ELSEWHERE ON THE WEB

▶ If you're not comfortable typing in these simple math commands to narrow your searches, never fear—most search engines will do this for you in their Advanced Search options. Try it at Google Advanced Search (www.google.com/help/refine search.html); the folks at Google do a tremendous job of walking you right through what you want to do.

This query will come back with the search engine substituting other words for that asterisk; for example, I just did a quick search in Google with this exact phrase and came back with quilting and sewing classes, quilting and patchwork classes, etc. Here's another example:

```
How to * better
```

This search query came back with a ton of interesting material: how to get better fuel economy, how to build a better password, how to communicate better, etc. The wildcard is not the absolute best way to narrow down your searches, but it's certainly a good way to retrieve material that you might not have seen otherwise.

There is plenty more in the way of search commands and syntax, but I've found that these basics, while simple, can narrow down your search engine results surprisingly well. I'll go into further detail on more search commands in later chapters.

The Most Effective Engine for Your Search

As the guide to Web searching for About.com, I have the opportunity to play around with a lot of search engines. And there are a lot. New search engines (and improvements to the old ones) seem to be popping out faster than I can write them up every day! Which brings me to this commonly asked question from my Web Search readers: Which search engine should I use?

There's not really a right or wrong answer for this one. Every person is different, and every person's search needs are different. And there are just so many fun search services to play around with that it seems pretty restrictive to limit yourself to just one.

TOOLS YOU NEED

▶ For a good comprehensive look at which search engines support which search commands, I invite you to visit UC Berkeley's "Recommended Search Engines: Tables of Features" at www.lib.berkeley.edu/TeachingLib/Guides/Internet/Search Engines.html.

There are so many search engines out there that you might be tempted to limit yourself to just one. Or perhaps you are enticed to go the other way and use a new search engine for every single search you attempt. My recommendation is to strive for a happy medium between these two extremes. Here is a list of the five top search engines to include in your daily Web search routine:

WHAT'S HOT

▶ Can't decide whether to use Yahoo or Google? Try GahooYoogle (www.gahoo yoogle.com/), a fun search site that searches both Google and Yahoo at the same time. It's interesting to search for the same term on both sites and see how different the search results are.

- **Google.com:** With its ease of use, mammoth index, and consistent result relevancy, Google receives the majority of most people's search engine queries throughout the day. You can use Google not only to find answers but also to search domains, search within URLs, and do other useful and interesting things (more on all that in Chapter 4).
- **Yahoo.com:** Yahoo is not only a search engine; they have peripheral properties such as Yahoo Education, Yahoo Answers, Yahoo TV, etc. Use Yahoo as a backup search when you're not satisfied with Google's answers, or if you want a different perspective on a general search.
- **Ask.com:** Formerly known as Ask Jeeves (remember the butler?), Ask has definitely come a long way. Originally Ask marketed itself as one of the few natural language search engines—i.e., you could type in a question and Ask would answer it for you. Ask is especially known for their Image Search—their results are unique and relevant.
- **Technorati.com:** Technorati is a blog search engine, meaning that it only searches the blogosphere (the term for all the blogs on the Web). Technorati is a tremendous resource if you're looking for what other people have to say on any particular subject; in addition, Technorati updates its listings frequently, so it's kind of like the water cooler of the Web. We'll talk more about the blogosphere in Chapter 12.

- **YouTube.com:** YouTube is one of the best-known video search services on the Web today; in 2006, it became part of Google's ever-expanding empire. YouTube is the place to go to find free video content of all kinds, from the Larry King interview you missed last night to short documentaries about any subject.

It's pretty interesting what you can find with the same search on different search engines. As you can see, these search engines are all quite diverse but they all have the same common purpose: they find content on the Web for you.

A Quick Tour of Search Engines

As I already mentioned, there are a lot of search engines on the Web, with more popping up every day. Here are just some of the search engines available for your searching needs.

First, let's look at some all-purpose search engines. For your everyday average search, you can't go wrong with the big three:

- **Google:** It's the number one most popular search engine on the Web for three reasons: It's easy to use, it returns extremely relevant results, and it's got a massive index.
- **Yahoo:** This is also a good choice for general searches. I find myself using their News search quite often.
- **Ask:** I can highly recommend Ask as a good all-purpose search engine. The Ask team is constantly innovating and improving their search service.

Now, let's look at some answer search engines. Answer, or fact-finding, search engines are a relatively new concept, but in my opinion, this is where many search engines are heading. The ones I think work the best are:

- **Brainboost.com:** Brainboost is great for finding quick answers for basic facts.
- **Factbites.com:** Got a research question you need a short and sweet answer to? Factbites is a good resource.
- **Answers.com:** I use Answers.com to give more background to preliminary research; they do a great job of pulling in sources from all over the Web.

These are great for when you just need a quick answer—for instance, "Why is the sky blue?" or "When was the battle of Gettysburg?"

Visual search engines are another great resource. These comparatively new search engines present their results in a more visual format—e.g., screenshots, or **tag clouds**, or Flash-based interfaces. The ones I find the most relevant are:

- **Kartoo.com:** This is a search engine that presents its results in an interactive map format; this makes it easier for you to pull in results you might not have originally included in your query.
- **Quintura.com:** This search engine allows searches within a tag cloud, a collection of terms usually related to each other in some way either by context or links. I find that Quintura's setup helps me add information to basic concepts.

There are academic search engines, too. These search engines have a more research-oriented index of listings. Among the best ones are:

- **FindArticles.com:** This is a search engine dedicated to finding articles from leading academic, industry, and general interest publications; perfect for finding credible resources. You have to pay to access many of the articles you find here; however, you can limit your search to only the free stuff.
- **Scirus.com:** This science search engine is dedicated to searching science-specific content.
- **Dictionary.com:** This is much more than just a dictionary search engine—it includes tabs for a thesaurus, an encyclopedia, and a multiple-reference search.

As you can see, there are search engines out there dedicated to specific purposes, from helping you find the best scientific periodical for your research to enabling you to visually connect concepts that you might not have connected before.

Let's find some images with image search engines. Most general search engines have the capacity to search for images. The one that I use most frequently is Google Images (http://images.google.com/), but I've also written up a long list of both image-specific search engines and image search sites here: http://about.com/websearch/imagesearch.

One of my favorite image search engines is Ditto (www.ditto.com), an image search engine that enables users to search for images. Ditto recently announced that they have 500 million pictures in their image search (and counting). Basically, Ditto is a way to find images quickly and effectively—they've also been around for a pretty long time in Internet years (I remember using them back when they started in 1999).

Another good image search engine is Picsearch (www.picsearch.com), a search engine dedicated solely to finding images on the

Web. Finding images on the Web with Picsearch is simple—just navigate to the Picsearch home page and type in a query.

I need to caution you that just because an image is on the Web does not mean that it's available for your use on a Web site or blog. Please read the fine print before using images from any of these image search engines or image search sites. Different photos and sites have different usage licenses, some of which might restrict your use of their image, and you can get yourself in trouble if you don't obey the rules.

Get Linked

Here are some more resources on my About.com Web Search site that will help you learn even more about search engines.

CRIME AND LAW ENFORCEMENT SEARCH ENGINES

Find crime statistics, crime scene investigation information, police information, and more with these Crime and Law Enforcement Search Engines.

http://about.com/websearch/crimesearch

WHAT IS A SEARCH ENGINE?

Exactly what is a search engine? Basically, a search engine is a software program that searches for sites based on the words that you designate as search terms. I've also written up the difference between search engines and search directories here.

http://about.com/websearch/whatissearchengine

WHICH SEARCH ENGINE SHOULD I USE?

Pick the best search engines for your searching needs with Search Engines 101, a great way to explore more of your search topic, try a new search engine, and search more of the Web.

http://about.com/websearch/bestsearchengines

Chapter 4

Google Tips and Tricks

A Quick Introduction to Google

Google (www.google.com) is without a doubt the most popular search engine on the Web. Google is a crawler-based engine, meaning that it employs software programs designed to "crawl" the information on the Net and add it to Google's searchable database. Google has a great reputation for relevant and thorough search results, and is a good general, all-purpose first place to start when searching the Web.

How did Google get its start? From small beginnings in a Stanford University dorm room, the search engine originally known as BackRub in 1996 has certainly come a long way. Stanford University students Sergey Brin and Larry Page, the creative geniuses behind the Google juggernaut, came up with the idea of a search engine in 1996 that garnered its results from the analysis of **backlinks**, links that were pointing at any given Web site. The more backlinks a Web site had, the more popular it was deemed to be, and the more relevant to keyword queries. This is also where the idea of **PageRank** originally got its start.

How Google Works

Google works by using PageRank. Very simply put, PageRank is Google's way of measuring how important (or how relevant) a Web page is. PageRank, which is largely based upon the number and quality of backlinks a Web page has, is an important factor in how well a particular Web page ranks within the Google search results.

PageRank affects Google searches in several ways. By no means is PageRank the only factor in determining what comes back in Google's search results when you send them a query, but it does help with the quality and relevancy of results that you receive. A Web site with a PageRank of 7, for example, is most likely more reliable information-wise than a Web site with a PageRank of 2. Again, this is not always the case, but PageRank can be a somewhat reliable gauge to factor in the quality of a site.

In addition, PageRank plays a big part in making your Google searches actually worthwhile. It's a categorization tool, just one of the many factors that Google uses to determine relevancy when retrieving your results.

How does Google work to get my results? No one really knows (other than Google, and they're a bit close-mouthed with this info!) exactly how Google ranks its results. That's pretty much considered proprietary information, and since the search engine field is a very competitive one, this information is definitely kept private. However, Google's search engine does have some basic parts that work together to serve up millions and millions of search results all around the world every day (remember the basic parts of a search engine from Chapter 3?):

ELSEWHERE ON THE WEB

▶ Google spoofed themselves with a joke explanation of PageRank, er, I mean PigeonRank (www.google.com/technology/pigeonrank.html). Basically, Google took something that many people on the Web get very obsessed about and made a joke of it, telling the world that instead of complicated algorithms underneath search results, there were actually crack teams of highly trained pigeons. It's worth a look if you need a laugh.

- **GoogleBot:** This is the name of the Google spider that crawls hyperlinks from Web page to Web page, and then adds these pages to the Google index.
- **Google Index:** This is the database where the GoogleBot's finds are stored.
- **Google Processors, Interface, Servers, etc.:** This is where the queries coming in from Google users are processed, analyzed, and collated into relevant results.

That's an extremely simplified explanation; for a much more detailed resource, visit "How does Google collect and rank results?" at the Google Librarian Center, www.google.com/librariancenter/articles/0512_01.html.

Okay! Now that we know basically how Google works internally to bring us all those lovely search results, let's see how we can really rev up the Google search engine to make it work for us at maximum speed.

The Basic Ten Google Search Tips

I have to admit it: I'm a Googleholic. I love their streamlined services, the way that my search results are (almost) always completely relevant and fast, and how massively huge Google's index is—this all makes for a pretty powerful search combo.

However, most people barely get below the surface of this incredibly complex search engine. There's so much that Google is able to do, but very few Web searchers really take advantage of it. No more! Here are the top ten Google search tips that I use on a regular basis. There are many more, but these are the ones that I use throughout the day as I'm working.

Google phrase search: We've already covered phrase searching in Chapter 3, but it's worth repeating. If you want Google to return your search as a complete phrase, in the exact order

What's with all those Google home page drawings?

▶ You might have noticed that Google dresses up their logo on special days: Christmas, Halloween, Van Gogh's birthday, Martin Luther King Jr. Day all have their own specific logos. All of them are carefully collected for viewing at Google Holiday Logos (www.google.com/holiday logos.html). And just as a bit of trivia, the artist who draws them all is named Dennis Hwang—he's been serving up specialized Google logos since 2001.

and proximity that you typed it in, you'll need to surround it with quotes—e.g., "three blind mice." Otherwise, Google will just locate these words both separately and together.

Google negative search: This is the minus sign business we've already talked about, used to exclude terms from your search results. You can tack on as many exclusions, each preceded by a minus sign, as you want; I've experimented with up to twelve for a really complicated search string.

Google forced search: Google automatically excludes common words like "where," "how," "and," etc. because it tends to slow down your search. However, if you're looking for something that actually needs those words included, you can "force" Google to include them by using our old friend the plus sign—e.g., Spiderman +3—or you could use quotation marks—e.g., "Spiderman 3."

Google site search: This is one of my most frequent Google searches. You can use Google to actually search within a site for content. For example, say you want to look inside of About Web Search for everything on "free movie downloads." Here's how you would frame your search at Google:

```
site:websearch.about.com "free movie downloads"
```

Voilà! You would type the "site:" command, plus the URL of the Web site, plus the phrase (notice the quotations?). This is an extremely useful search command, since many sites' search functions are not that great at pulling up what you're looking for.

Google number range search: This is one of those "wow, I can do *that*?" kind of Google searches. Here's how it works: simply add two numbers, separated by two periods, *with no spaces*, into the search box along with your search terms. You can use this number range search to set ranges for everything from dates (Babe

Ruth 1920..1930) to weights (1000..10000 kg Jeep). But be sure to specify a unit of measurement or some other indicator of what the number range represents, otherwise Google will not be able to process your query correctly. Here's one that you could try:

```
nintendo wii $100..$300
```

You're asking Google to find all the Nintendo Wiis within the price range of $100 to $300. You can ask for pretty much any kind of numerical data; the trick is in putting the two periods in between the two numbers.

Google define: Ever come across a word on the Web that you don't know? Instead of reaching for that bulky dictionary, just type "define" (you can also use "definition") and then the word you want to look up and Google will come back with a host of definitions. I use this one all the time not only for definitions (mostly tech-related), but also because it's a great way to find detailed articles that can explain not only the word you're looking for but the context in which it most commonly occurs. For instance, searching for the buzz phrase "Web 2.0" using the Google syntax of "define web 2.0" returns some really interesting and practical info.

Google calculator: Anything that helps with math gets a vote in my book. In addition to using Google to solve simple math problems, you can use it to convert measurements. Here are a few examples of this—simply type these right into the Google search box:

```
Half a quart in tablespoons
```

ELSEWHERE ON THE WEB

▶ One of the best places on the Web to learn more about how to search with Google is Nancy Blachman's site, Google Guide (www .googleguide.com). The site is designed as an interactive tutorial, with levels for both the beginning and intermediate user. I always come away from this site with useful Google tips that I can't wait to try out.

```
5 miles to kilometers
```

```
sqrt(8912)
```

TOOLS YOU NEED

▶ You can combine many of these simple Google search commands into one powerfully focused search string. Here's an example: intitle:1040 form site:irs.gov. You've just asked Google to search the IRS site for a form 1040. There are a lot of combinations that you can try; don't be afraid to pair up various Google search commands to see what you can come up with.

And so on. Google can also do much more complex problems and conversions; you can find out how to build your queries so Google knows what to do with them at the official Google Calculator help page, www.google.com/help/calculator.html.

Google PhoneBook: Google has a gigantic phone book directory, as well they should—their index is one of the largest, if not *the* largest, on the Web. Here's how you can use Google's PhoneBook to find a phone number or address (United States only at the time of this writing):

- first name (or first initial), last name, city (state is optional)
- first name (or first initial), last name, state
- first name (or first initial), last name, area code
- first name (or first initial), last name, zip code
- phone number, including area code
- last name, city, state
- last name, zip code

Don't want your information in the Google PhoneBook? You'll want to visit this page: Google PhoneBook Name Removal (www.google.com/help/pbremoval.html).

Google spell checker: For some strange reason, I have never been able to spell certain words without a spell checker—and since we don't always work within a medium that offers an automatic spell check on the Web (blogs, message boards, etc.), it's nice to have a built-in Google spell checker. Here's how it works: you just type the word you're struggling with into Google's search box, and Google will very politely come back with this phrase: "Did you mean . . . (correct spelling)?" This is probably one of the most useful Google inventions ever.

Advanced Google Search Tips

Now that we've got some of the more basic Google commands under our belts, it's time to move on to even more fun with Google in the form of a few more advanced commands you can use to find what you're looking for with Google.

Google Book Search: Google has many "sections," or peripheral search properties, and one of my favorites has to be Google Book Search (**http://books.google.com**). You can search the full text of books here for quotes or information, or just to browse; it's like your own personal library of information. In order to search for books with Google, all you need to do is type in the book's title: "book jane eyre." Your search results will come back with direct links to that book in the Google Books index.

Google cache: The Google cache command will help you find the cached copy—the way the Web page looked when Google's spiders last indexed it—of any Web page. This especially comes in handy if you're looking for a Web site that is no longer there (for whatever reason), or if the Web site you're looking for is down due to an unusually high volume of traffic. Here's an example of how you would use the cache command:

You've just asked Google to return the cached copy of the About Web Search page with the words "web search" (remember the quotation marks? That means you'll see the words in exactly that order on the page) highlighted. Actually, almost every site you come across using Google will have the option of accessing the

ELSEWHERE ON THE WEB

▶ Google Book Search is working with several major libraries to include their collections and make them more accessible to the public at large. The Library Project has some basic goals: they want to make it easier for people to find relevant books on the Web and off the Web, but at the same time they are endeavoring to respect the lawful authors' and publishers' copyrights. You can find more information at the Google Book Search Library Project: http://books.google .com/googleprint/library.html.

cached version right there in the search result. Clicking "cached" will bring you immediately to the last copy Google made of that particular page.

Google links: Want to find out who's linking to any page? Just try the Google link command:

```
link:websearch.about.com
```

Notice that there are no spaces between the colon and the URL; it won't work right if you put a space there. The link command will return all the Web pages that have links to the Web site that you specify. This comes in handy, especially if you have your own site and want to see who is linking to you.

Google related: Want to see other sites that might be similar to the one that you're looking at? Try this:

```
related:nike.com
```

Again, no space between the colon and the URL. The related command will return every site that is similar in content to the specified site. You can also access this function simply by clicking the Similar Pages option in almost every returned search result.

Google info: The info query is kind of like the Google Swiss army knife—it returns all of the above information and a few other useful tidbits in one handy chunk:

```
info:websearch.about.com
```

Note that, again, there's no space between the colon and the URL. This is what you get with the info command: a one-stop-shopping search syntax that comes back with the Web site's description, Google's cache for that site, sites that link to that site, Web pages that are linked *from* that site, and pages that contain that particular Web site's URL.

Google stocks: For anyone who wants to get virtually real-time reporting on their favorite stocks, Google's got you covered with the stocks command. Here's how it works:

```
stocks:goog
```

One drawback is that you have to type in the exact ticker symbol in order for this to work (you can't just type in the company name). Since most of us probably don't know ticker symbols off the top of our head for every company we might like to research, this is definitely something that Google needs to make more user-friendly.

Google complete title search: The title of a Web page can be seen in the strip at the very top of your browser; for instance, if you navigate to **www.google.com**, you can see that the title for the Google home page is quite appropriately Google. If you want to restrict your searches only to page titles, here's what it looks like:

```
allintitle: summer camp
```

You've just instructed Google to come back with pages that have either the words "summer" or "camp" in the title area; for an even more targeted search, you could put quotation marks around this phrase.

WHAT'S HOT

▶ Want the latest information on stocks, bonds, and the markets? You'll want to visit Google Finance (http://finance.google.com/finance), a Google peripheral service that collates market summaries, the most recent financial news, top movers, and updated stock quotes. It's a great place to catch up on your money news.

▶ I love watching movie trailers (sometimes more than I enjoy watching the movie itself!), so when I found a whole Google subsite completely dedicated to movie trailers . . . well, let's just say that I became a little distracted. Check it out for yourself at Google Video New Movie Previews (http:// video.google.com/movietrailers.html). Both current and upcoming movie trailers can be viewed here, and the picture quality is pretty amazing.

Google title and page search: The allintitle command tells Google to search only page titles. However, you can use the intitle command to search both page titles and the Web page itself:

```
intitle:horses saddle
```

This command string tells Google to return pages that have the word "horses" in the page title and the word "saddle" either in the title or anywhere on the Web page itself.

Google complete URL search: Not all URLs are created equal, and I've found that you can discover some pretty interesting Web pages by using Google to look for words within the URL itself. The allinurl command will do this for you:

allinurl: cascade mountains

This query will return only those pages that have both the words "cascade" and "mountains" in the URL.

Google URL and page search: If you would like to search both URLs and Web pages, you can use the inurl command:

```
inurl:government passports
```

This command instructs Google to come back with URLs that have the word "government" in the URLs, and the word "passports" anywhere on the page.

Google file search: One of my favorite Google search features has to be the ability to search for specific file types. At the time of this writing, you can search for thirteen different types of file formats:

- Adobe Portable Document Format (pdf)
- Adobe PostScript (ps)
- Lotus 1-2-3 (wk1, wk2, wk3, wk4, wk5, wki, wks, wku)
- Lotus WordPro (lwp)

- MacWrite (mw)
- Microsoft Excel (xls)
- Microsoft PowerPoint (ppt)
- Microsoft Word (doc)
- Microsoft Works (wks, wps, wdb)
- Microsoft Write (wri)
- Rich Text Format (rtf)
- Shockwave Flash (swf)
- Text (ans, txt)

Being able to search for specific file types is a *huge* shortcut. For instance, say you wanted to find all the Word documents about astronomy in Google's sizable index. Here's how you would do it:

```
astronomy filetype:doc
```

Every result will be a Microsoft Word document, with the word "astronomy" somewhere either in the title of the document or on the page itself.

Google movie search: Google is constantly improving and adding to their search features, and one of the more recent additions is the ability to search for movies. If you want to find reviews and showtimes for movies playing in your area, type "movies" or "showtimes" or the name of a currently playing movie into the Google search box.

Google also has a specific movie: operator that will help you hunt down that movie that you can't quite remember the name of, research an actor, explore plot twists, and more. For example, you get reviews, direct links, and much more with this command.

```
movie: you will be assimilated
```

Google music search: Find all sorts of good information about artists, songs, albums, and the best places to buy the music you are looking for. If you enter the name of an artist into the Google search box, you'll see user reviews, song titles, stores to purchase the music, and other useful information related to that artist at the very top of your search results page.

At the time of this writing, only artists who are popular in the United States are included in this particular search syntax. Google is always adding to and updating their various search services, so if you're not in the United States and really would like this kind of instant info on your favorite artists, just sit tight—chances are it will be coming your way very soon.

Google search by number: One of the absolutely coolest Google search features has to be the ability to search for package tracking numbers so you can see just how fast that Star Trek phaser is going to make it to your house for your husband's birthday (hypothetically speaking, of course). Every time you order something online, you are given a tracking number that the company (and now, you) uses to keep track of where and when that package will be traveling. You do not need to include quotation marks; all you need to do is copy the number into the Google search bar and Google will automatically know from which service it comes. Here's a quick rundown of all the number strings that Google recognizes (these are just example numbers):

- UPS tracking numbers example search: 1Z9999W99999999999
- FedEx tracking numbers example search: 999999999999
- USPS tracking numbers example search: 9999 9999 9999 9999 9999 99
- Vehicle ID (VIN) numbers example search: AAAAA999A9AA99999

WHAT'S HOT

▶ You can use Google to keep track of any topic you're interested in and deliver appropriate content right to your e-mail inbox with Google Alerts, a service that notifies you as news on your chosen subject happens. Google Alerts are simple to set up, and they're a great way to save time when you're particularly interested in a story (but don't want to keep coming back and searching for it). Find out how to set up your own Google Alerts here: http://about.com/web search/googlealerts.

- UPC codes example search: 073333531084
- Telephone area codes example search: 650
- Patent numbers example search: patent 5123123 (remember to put the word "patent" before your patent number)
- FAA airplane registration numbers example search: N199UA (an airplane's FAA registration number is typically printed on its tail)
- FCC equipment IDs example search: fcc B4Z-34009-PIR (remember to put the word "fcc" before the equipment ID)

And you don't need to put the package company's ID before the tracking number ID, by the way—Google automatically figures it out. Pretty neat, huh?

Google maps: Find maps of any U.S. address quickly just by entering the address in the Google search box. If you want to plan out a whole road trip, you can by navigating over to Google Maps (http://maps.google.com). Here's where you can print out driving directions, get local points of interest, or find businesses in your area.

Obviously, you can do a lot with Google—and believe it or not, I've covered only a fraction of it here. I could write an entire book just about Google, there's that much to it! Now that you've got just a few of the best Google search tips under your belt, let's explore even more of what Google has to offer us in the way of what I like to call peripheral search sites—Google subsites that are completely dedicated to finding targeted objectives for you.

The Best Google Peripheral Search Services

By now, we're all pretty familiar with Google's incredibly useful search engine. It's even become a verb ("Let me just Google this").

ASK YOUR GUIDE

What are some of the best undiscovered Google services out there?

▶ Google has many, many subsites in addition to the ones that I've listed in this chapter. Among some of the more notable are Google Catalogs (http://catalogs .google.com), Google Earth (http://earth.google.com), Google Scholar (http:// scholar.google.com), Picasa (http://picasa.google.com), and Google Docs and Spreadsheets (http://docs.google .com). Go ahead and give these services a look—I think you'll be surprised at how much you can actually accomplish with Google.

▶ The folks at Google Maps have generously opened up the core programming within this application (this is called an Application Programming Interface, or API), and many talented programmers have used this API to create Google Map "mashups." Google Maps Mania (http:// googlemapsmania.blogspot .com) is a wonderful site that keeps track of the many Google Maps mashups out there—you can find anything here from the top beaches with wireless access, to the nearest Starbucks coffee shop.

But did you know that Google is not just a general Web search engine? Yep, there are many more aspects of Google searching for us to explore. For instance, Google has created many subsites that are targeted on finding just one specific topic area for you, and these topic-specific sites can give you some great search results. Let's go off the beaten path for a second and see what else we can do with Google. Here are my picks for the top Google peripheral services.

Google Blog Search: Google has a pretty good blog search engine, found at http://blogsearch.google.com/. (Don't know what a blog is? We'll talk about blogs in Chapter 12, but meanwhile here's a quick definition: blogs are online journals created by people in all different walks of life. Here's my blog: http://about.com/websearch/ blog.)

In order to use Google's Blog Search, just type in a topic you're interested in reading about—for instance, George Bush. You'll get back results from what is called the **blogosphere**, the name given to all the blogs (millions of them) on the Web, in order of last published and/or relevance to your query. I find that this is a super way to find blogs that I wouldn't have necessarily found on my own and add them to my subscription list (you can find out more about this in Chapter 5, "Searching the Web with RSS").

Google Special Searches: Google has set up special search engines just for certain topics in addition to the ones that we've covered. They are:

- **Google University Search** (www.google.com/options/univer sities.html): Search pretty much any higher-level institution in the United States with Google University Search. A great way to find admission info, alumni updates, etc.
- **Google U.S. Government Search** (www.google.com/ig/ usgov): Formerly Google Uncle Sam. You can search any

government site from here, from local to federal, as well as keep up on government-related news.

- **Google Linux Search** (www.google.com/linux): Any Linux fans out there? Use Google's Linux-specific search to scour the Web for anything related to Linux, an open-source operating system.
- **Google Mac Search** (www.google.com/mac): Here you can search Mac and Apple sites, as well as download free Google applications developed specifically for Mac users.
- **Google Microsoft Search** (www.google.com/microsoft.html): Search Microsoft-related sites using Google Microsoft Search. This is a great way to find out the latest Bill Gates news, as well as keep on top of the most recent Microsoft developments.

Google Image Search: Absolutely one of the best places on the Web to go to find quality images is Google Image Search (http://images.google.com). If you have trouble finding what you're looking for here, you will want to try out Google Advanced Image Search (http://images.google.com/advanced_image_search?hl=en). Note: Just because you find an image using Google's Image Search does *not* mean that it's free for your use. If you do end up using an image on a Web site or blog, be careful to track down the original owner of the image, and give credit where credit is due by including a link back. It's considered very bad Web manners not to do so.

Google News: With over 4,500 news sources updated almost in real time throughout the day, you can't find a much better source of news than Google News (http://news.google.com). Google News is divided into categories from World to Health, and is constantly scouring the Web for new stories to add.

TOOLS YOU NEED

▶ The use of images on the Web can be tricky. Many people don't realize that images are not actually just free for the taking—correct procedures need to be followed in order to stay within copyright law. However, there are many sites that offer completely royalty-free and copyright-free images for public use. One of the best is Stock Xchng (http://www.sxc.hu/), the site that I use the most for free stock images.

As you can see from this chapter, Google has a lot to offer . . . and this is barely the tip of the iceberg! Be sure to try out some of the Google search tips that I've given you, or visit one of Google's peripheral search services—you'll be glad you did. However (there's always a "however"), even with all of Google's extraordinary capabilities, savvy searchers know that they should never limit themselves to only one search engine tool in their Web search toolbox. Google is a fantastic search engine, but it's not the only search engine on the Web. Keep reading on for additional useful Web search utilities, search engines, and tips that will help you discover more of the Web.

Get Linked

Here are some resources on my About.com Web Search site that will help you learn more about Google.

GOOGLE SEARCH ENGINE BASICS

In the last few years, Google has attained the ranking of number one search engine on the Web, and has consistently stayed there. Find out the basics of this powerful search engine.

http://about.com/websearch/googlebasics

GOOGLE FREE REVERSE PHONE NUMBER LOOKUP

You can do a free reverse phone number lookup with Google—it's fast and pretty simple.

http://about.com/websearch/googlephone

Chapter 5

Searching the Web with RSS

What Is RSS?

You're browsing your favorite Web site, and all of a sudden, you come across a little orange button that says "XML" (whatever that is), or a text link that invites you to "subscribe to this **feed**" (huh?), or an icon labeled with "Sub with Bloglines," "Sub with FeedReader," etc. When you click these links, you're brought to a somewhat intimidating page full of confusing text and programming—have you entered the Web Twilight Zone? Nope, you've just discovered an RSS feed.

RSS is an acronym for Really Simple Syndication, Rich Site Summary, or Ready for Some Stories (depending on who you ask). Here's a short and simple definition of RSS: RSS is a simple XML (programming language similar to HTML) tool that was originally created to help people syndicate and share updated content from their Web sites. It's a streamlined way for you to get the content

Why do I see programming language when I click an RSS subscribe button?

▶ When you click to subscribe to an RSS feed, you'll usually see a mishmash of computer language that will seem to make no sense. That page is meant for software that is programmed to read RSS feed data and make it more user-friendly through feed readers and e-mail. Once you've signed up for a feed reader, you can use it's subscribe button to go straight to a more understandable interface.

that you want all in one place—a **feed reader**—without visiting Web sites hoping for updated information. In other words, RSS brings the Web to you, instead of you going to the Web.

Basically, RSS is an avenue by which anyone on the Web can publish content and make it more accessible to the people who want it. There are different kinds of RSS, different versions, different definitions—but guess what? None of that is really important in the grand scheme of things. RSS can get pretty complicated when you start digging into coding, etc., but we don't need to worry about that: all we need to concern ourselves with is how we can make RSS work in Web searching.

RSS is a huge timesaver. This is why so many people consider it an extremely important part of their Web search toolbox.

Say you have roughly 100 sites that you like to visit on a weekly or even daily basis. You navigate to a particular site, hoping that it's got something new for you since the last time you visited, but nope—you'll just have to visit again. And again. And again, until the moment that particular site decides to put up something new. Talk about frustrating and time-consuming!

But that's where the beauty of RSS comes through—you don't have to visit your favorite site every five minutes in hopes that it will update; instead, you can sit back and let your new best friend RSS do the work for you. Using RSS, you can subscribe via something called a feed to any Web site that is syndicated, meaning that it has an RSS feed (most sites have RSS feeds nowadays—it's almost a necessary part of being on the Web). Once you subscribe, instead of visiting your favorite sites to get the latest content (and being disappointed when there's nothing new), you can sit back and let the content come to you. It will be collated nicely in what's called a feed reader (we'll get to those in a minute), which is basically a list of your subscribed feeds. See what a time saver that is? I don't know how I ever got along without RSS; it allows me to read literally hundreds of sites' content every day within minutes, rather than hours.

Okay, so what's a feed reader? A feed reader is a very simple tool that allows you to group all of your RSS feeds in one place, much like a newspaper gathers stories from all sorts of different locations and contributors. It's a way for you to read all the content from your feeds in one streamlined interface. Read below for more on feed readers.

Subscribing to RSS Feeds

The best analogy I can think of to explain this is simple: look around your home and count how many magazines or newspapers you are subscribed to. How did you happen to be subscribed to these publications? You informed the various companies that you wanted them to keep you in the loop, so to speak, and from that point on, instead of you having to go to the store to pick up the latest copy of (insert publication here), the content comes to you instead.

RSS feeds are similar in nature. You find a site that you would like to subscribe to, and you tell that site—via one of various easy-to-implement methods—that you would like to stay updated, through RSS, with all their content as it is published. There are three different methods by which you can subscribe to a Web site's RSS feed:

- **An orange feed icon** is pretty much becoming the standard for feed subscription. If you happen across this symbol on the Web site that you wish to subscribe to, click it and you'll be subscribed to that particular site's RSS feed; it will then start showing up in your feed reader of choice.
- **"Subscribe to this feed."** Plenty of sites nowadays will give you a variety of options in order to get you subscribed via

TOOLS YOU NEED

▶ Is there a specific news topic or point of interest that you'd really like to keep track of as it happens? You can track developments in almost any content category via this nifty tool that turns any Google News search into an RSS feed—try it at www.justinpfister.com/gnewsfeed.php. The process is simple: just type in what you want to keep track of and specify format, region, and language, and you're off and running.

RSS to their site. You'll either see it written out ("Subscribe to this site," for example) or you'll see a list of feeder chiclet icons all smooshed together for easy access. Clicking any of these links will enable you to be subscribed to that feed's content.

- **Subscribe via a feed reader button.** Most feed readers have made it possible for you to do a "one-click" subscribe: you find a site you're interested in, you notice that your chosen feed reader has an icon displayed, and you click that icon. The process differs from reader to reader, but overall, the process is the same and pretty simple—you just click and you're subscribed.

What Is a Feed Reader?

You know what an RSS feed is, you know how to subscribe to one, but what do you do with these feeds once you're subscribed? Where do they all go? That's where feed readers come in.

Feed readers are at their most basic an aggregator of content. They combine all the feeds that you've subscribed to in one easy-to-access master list. Feed readers come in different shapes and sizes, but they all do essentially the same thing: organize your RSS feeds in a convenient, easily readable format.

Think of a feed reader as a newspaper with hundreds of different items—stories, ads, etc.—from all over the world. When you open up that newspaper, you don't have to read each item on a new and separate page; if you did, that newspaper would have to be hundreds of pages thick. Instead, each item you're interested in appears in a list with all the other items you're interested in, allowing you to get all your news in one convenient place. In essence, you're creating your very own newspaper, containing only the content that you are interested in.

WHAT'S HOT

▶ Stumped on where to find feeds on a particular subject? You might want to try out the FeedFinder (http://feedfinder.feedster.com/), a search tool that scours RSS feeds according to the keywords that you specify. For instance, want to find some RSS feeds on knitting? Just enter in the word "knitting" and you'll have more interesting Web sites—accompanied by their respective RSS feeds—than you'll know what to do with.

All feed readers make it possible for you to quickly scan headlines and/or full stories at a glance, from a variety of different providers, all in one place. A variety of feed readers is available to you for free on the Web; they fall into five distinct categories, designed for different ways of reading feeds: Web-based feed readers, desktop feed readers, browser built-in feed readers, e-mail-based feed readers, and mobile feed readers.

Web-based feed readers: If you want to read all your feeds from within your browser, you want a Web-based feed reader (these are the most convenient and easy to set up). Examples of Web-based feed readers are Bloglines (www.bloglines.com), Google Reader (www.google.com/reader), Kinja (www.kinja.com), My Yahoo (http://my.yahoo.com), and NewsGator (www.newsgator.com/home.aspx).

Desktop feed readers: If you want to read all your feeds separate from your browser and to have the reader actually installed on your system, you want a desktop feed reader. These usually come with more powerful features than the Web-based feed readers, but are definitely for the more technologically advanced crowd. Examples of desktop feed readers are BlogBridge (www.blogbridge.com), RSS Bandit (www.rssbandit.org), AmphetaDesk (www.disobey.com/amphetadesk), and FeedDemon for Windows (www.newsgator.com/NGOLProduct.aspx?ProdId=FeedDemon).

Browser built-in feed readers: There are some browsers out there on the market that come with baked-in feed readers; there are also loads of extensions and plug-ins that provide this functionality for you. Three of the easiest to use browser built-in feed readers would be Firefox's Live Bookmarks (www.mozilla.com/en-US/firefox/livebookmarks.html), Opera (www.opera.com/), and Internet Explorer 7 (www.microsoft.com/windows/products/winfamily/ie/default.mspx).

ASK YOUR GUIDE

Which feed reader do you use?

▶ I've tried quite a few feed readers and the one that I like the most is Bloglines (www.bloglines.com). It's easy to set up, simple to organize, and updates my content quickly. If you want to see the sites that I've subscribed to, feel free to browse my public Bloglines folders at www.bloglines.com/public/abwebsearchguide. You might come across a site in my subscriptions that you will want to subscribe to yourself via RSS.

E-mail-based feed readers: If you would like all of your feeds delivered to you via e-mail, you're going to want an e-mail-based feed reader like Mozilla Thunderbird www.mozilla.com/en-US/thunderbird/), Newsgator Inbox (www.newsgator.com/NGOLProduct.aspx?ProdID=NewsGator+Inbox), or Google Alerts (www.google.com/alerts). You can adjust the frequency of e-mails with each one of these readers.

Mobile feed readers: More and more, people are getting their Web search content while they're out and about, through a variety of mobile devices. If you are one of these people, you might want to check out one of these feed readers/access services made especially for mobile devices: Yahoo Mobile (http://mobile.yahoo.com/), Google Mobile (www.google.com/mobile/), AOL Mobile (http://mobile1.aol.com/portal/mobile-feed-reader), and WINKSite (http://winksite.com/site/).

I know this is a lot of new information to digest, so here's a summary of the two basic steps you'll need to take in order to get started with RSS: First, you need a feed reader—there are plenty to choose from, listed above. The easiest one to use is the Web-based Bloglines. Second, you need some feeds. Most Web sites these days come with a handy RSS feed; all you need to do is copy and paste the Web site's address into your feed reader.

How to Set Up Specific Web Searches Using RSS

Now that you know the basics of how RSS and feed readers work, I want to show you how you can use the power and convenience of RSS to make your Web searches more streamlined.

The most popular use of RSS is simply to track stories as they happen—most commonly, breaking news, popular events, etc. For instance, say you wanted to know about the Chicago Cubs every time a story hit the presses. Instead of taking the time to labori-

ELSEWHERE ON THE WEB

▶ If you're interested in daily news about RSS and the feed reader field, take a look at A Feed Is Born at www.afeedisborn.com/. This interesting (and frequently updated) blog has news about RSS, Web feeds, and how to manage information overload. Since the RSS field is relatively new and always innovating, this is a good place to keep on top of what's going on.

ously scan various search engines, blogs, message boards, etc., you can set up an RSS feed with specific, customized boundaries.

Here's how: First, search for the Chicago Cubs in your favorite search engine. I'm going to pick Google, since I know they provide RSS feeds for all their news searches. (Not all search engines do this, but most are catching up. At the time of this writing, Yahoo, MSN, and Ask all provide RSS for news searches.) You're not going to want to subscribe to the general Web search results; you're looking for up-to-the-minute news, right? So you'll need to click the News tab.

Once you're in the News section, you have several ways to subscribe to this very broad search term. To the immediate left of your news search results about the Chicago Cubs, you'll see some RSS text subscribe options (you might remember that previously in this chapter, we discussed the various ways you can subscribe via RSS—this is one of them). You can click the RSS or Atom button to go straight to the RSS code page; once you're there, you'll want to copy that link and paste it into your feed reader. Additionally, you can set this particular search up as a Google Alert, meaning that once a day (you can set your frequency, anything from once a week to once an hour to as it's available) you'll receive e-mail alerts notifying you that there is new news.

Also, there's always the feed reader button option. Most feed readers (Bloglines included) have buttons available for you to add to your browser toolbar. This makes it exceedingly simple when you come across a site you'd like to subscribe to via RSS; all you need to do is click the button, choose the folder you want that feed to be organized into, and away you go. The Bloglines button can be found at www.bloglines.com/help/easysub.

Refine your searches with RSS. That first Cubs search was a pretty vague one. You're going to get a lot of search results in your

▶ All of us could use some help getting more organized; thankfully, there are plenty of sites dedicated to this very thing. RememberTheMilk (www.rememberthemilk .com/) is one of the best "getting to done" Web sites out there, offering you many different ways to access your lists of pretty much anything—including RSS. Just sign up, and then once you have a list all written up, you can put your RememberThe-Milk username in this URL and subscribe to it: www .rememberthemilk.com/rss/ yourusername/. Easy and convenient.

RSS feed . . . maybe too many (especially during baseball season!). You can definitely refine this search to reflect only the specific Chicago Cubs news that you want updates on, and here's how.

First, instead of just typing in the words "Chicago" and "Cubs," you're going to want to put that phrase in quotes: "Chicago Cubs." That will narrow down your results by at least half right off the, um, bat.

Secondly, say you want information only on Chicago Cubs baseball statistics. That's a pretty narrow search parameter, and if you want to set this up (again, through Google), all you would need to do is type: "Chicago cubs" statistics. Yep, this is just Web search basics again, only this time we're using the basics right along with RSS. Again, the process is the same once you go to subscribe to this news feed of your customized Google search query.

It doesn't take much to set up a relatively customized news feed for yourself on pretty much any topic. Once you have it all set up, you'll start getting updates almost in real time, without having to scour the Web.

Other Ways to Use RSS

I'm constantly amazed by the ways people twist this incredibly useful technology to serve a variety of purposes. The most common uses for RSS feeds are to keep up with news, a favorite site, a favorite blog, customized searches such as the Chicago Cubs example, etc., but there are plenty of other uses for RSS as well. Here are just a few of the ways you can use RSS to do your Web searching for you:

Monitor message boards. I've been on a few Yahoo Groups message boards for almost ten years now, and I receive all my board updates through the magic of RSS within my feed reader.

Sports scores. Want to monitor your favorite team? See ESPN's list of specific sport feeds at http://sports.espn.go.com/espn/ news/story?page=rssinfo. You can also use Yahoo's My Yahoo page (found at http://my.yahoo.com/); just go to your Bookmarks section and click Add; you'll be prompted to enter the URL address of the site where you usually monitor your team's scores. Once you do that, these scores will show up on your My Yahoo page. Yahoo also offers an entire page of syndicated sports feeds; you can find these at http://sports.yahoo.com/nfl/rss.

Weather reports. Get weather reports delivered to you, not only for local weather conditions, but also for impending severe weather situations. Try NOAA's feeds for watches, warnings, and advisories at www.weather.gov/alerts. There are also RSS feeds from the Weather Channel at www.weather.com/weather/rss/subscription?from=footer, Yahoo Weather at http://weather.yahoo.com/ (type in your zip code or country and you'll be taken to the specific page for your area; you can subscribe by adding this page to My Yahoo or your feed reader), and Weather Underground at www.weatherunderground.com, where you can get weather reports for many cities all over the world.

Shopping at Amazon.com. I'm a little bit addicted to Amazon.com, and who can blame me—there are incredible deals at this huge online shopping site, on everything from books to groceries. You can track price changes on your favorite items at Amazon.com with RSStalker (www.rsstalker.com/), a nifty RSS feed utility that takes the URL of any specific product or category at Amazon.com that you'd like to track and generates a feed for it. Using RSStalker, you receive price updates almost in real time; this could potentially save you a lot of money.

EBay listings. EBay has quite a few RSS feeds that you can take advantage of, from system announcements to message boards to (last but not least) actual store and auction listings. You can also "mix" specific RSS feeds for eBay using RSSAuction (www.rssauction.com/), where you can create customized eBay searches to be delivered either by RSS or by e-mail.

ASK YOUR GUIDE

What do I do if I come across a site that doesn't have an RSS feed?

▶ That's where RSS feed scrapers come in. The term "scraping" in the context of RSS basically means you're creating an RSS feed for a site that doesn't actually provide one for you. Sites such as FeedYes (www.feedyes.com) and PonyFish (www.ponyfish.com) can be used to create RSS feeds for sites that do not offer them.

Craigslist. Craigslist (www.craigslist.org) is one of the most popular sites on the Web. It's basically a local classified ads section with worldwide locations, with anything from personals to real estate. You can subscribe to specific searches on Craigslist in nearly every ad category simply by clicking the RSS button at the bottom of the page, or dropping the URL into your feed reader. Note: Some searches (such as "furniture") are updated very frequently, so be cautious when subscribing since some feed readers will only keep items fresh for you up to a certain number (Bloglines goes up to 200 and then stops).

Blogs. Almost every blog (online journal) on the planet has an RSS feed. If you find a blog you like, you'll most likely be able to subscribe to it via the variety of methods we've talked about in this chapter. Not sure where to find a good blog? Try Technorati (http://technorati.com/), a blog search engine where you can simply type in a subject that you're interested in and get a whole host of blogs that reference that topic.

Flickr. Flickr (www.flickr.com) is a digital photo-sharing Web site where you can upload your photos for the community at large and view other people's photos. Flickr has a number of RSS feeds available at www.flickr.com/services/feeds/. If you want to subscribe to a specific photostream or Flickr user, you can use PonyFish (www.ponyfish.com/), a free RSS tool that allows you to create your very own RSS feed. All you do is drag and drop the URL and ta da! You're subscribed.

Social sites, such as Listible, Furl, Spurl, del.icio.us. You can find some pretty wonderful sites on the Web all by yourself, but you can also see what other people are looking at and bookmarking via a variety of social bookmarking communities where these lists are made publicly accessible. At all of these sites, each topic and every unique user has a separate RSS feed you can subscribe to.

iTunes and other music subscription sites. Love music? Stay on top of the latest and greatest with RSS feeds. Apple has an entire page of music-related RSS feeds at www.apple.com/rss/; you should also check out Yahoo Music feeds (http://music.yahoo.com/rss/), Sony Music feeds (www.sonymusic.com/rss/), VH1 Music feeds (www.vh1.com/rss/), and Rolling Stone music feeds (www.rollingstone.com/rssxml/music_news.xml—just copy and paste this URL into your feed reader of choice).

YouTube. YouTube (www.youtube.com) is one of the largest video sites on the Web. You can both upload and watch pretty much any kind of video here. If you'd like to stay on top of the latest videos from a particular artist or user or topic, visit this page: www.youtube.com/rssls.

Specific keywords and categories within Web sites. Say you want to be alerted when a site posts updates, but you're only interested in certain topics. Many larger sites have specific RSS feeds for each category they post in. For instance, if you love Lifehacker (www.lifehacker.com) but only want to get updates on Windows Media, you can subscribe to http://tags.lifehacker.com/software/windows-media/?format=rssfeed.

Calendars of events. You can create a calendar of events and share it with others via RSS (or subscribe to public calendars) either with Upcoming.org (http://upcoming.org/), an online social events calendar, or with RSSCalendar (www.rsscalendar.com/rss/), a site where you can create your own public or private calendar and then people who are interested can subscribe via RSS.

Job search engines. You can track your job market via RSS from pretty much any job search engine out there. Indeed (www.indeed.com), Monster (www.monster.com), and Dice (www.dice.com) all have RSS feeds enabled. Just create a search—say, for systems administrators in New Orleans—and then subscribe to that search. All new listings for that query will show up in your feed reader.

Track packages. You can track the whereabouts of your FedEx packages via RSS. Technology blogger Ben Hammersley came up with this shortcut: just tack your tracking number on the end of the URL www.benhammersley.com/tools/fedextrack.cgi?track=. Then copy and paste the entire URL into your feed reader—you'll get updates as the package moves. In addition, you can use the Web site SimpleTracking.com (www.simpletracking.com) to generate a custom RSS feed for your package or shipment.

Find travel deals. Many online travel sites are offering RSS feeds so you can stay on top of the latest travel deals. At the time of this writing, feeds are offered by Travelocity (http://travel.travelocity.com/feeds/Subscription.do), Expedia (www.expedia.com/daily/outposts/rss/expedia_rss.asp?CCheck=1&&), Orbitz (www.orbitz.com/App/ViewRSSHelpPage), Sidestep (www.sidestep.com/deals-rss_travel_feed), and Kayak (www.kayak.com/labs/rss/).

Watch the stock market. Anyone who is into stocks knows that in many deals, time is of the essence. Track your favorite stocks and financial news via the Yahoo Ticker (http://edit.ticker.yahoo.com/config/slv4_page?.p=ticker), CNN Money's RSS feed (http://money.cnn.com/services/rss/), or MarketWatch's personal finance news (http://feeds.marketwatch.com/marketwatch/pf/).

Vanity check. Okay. Show of hands—how many of us have typed our names into a search engine to see what comes up? Well, now you can indulge this even more via RSS. Simply type your name into Google, for example, and then copy and paste the URL of these search results into your favorite feed reader. You can also set up a Google Alert for your name so news will come via e-mail rather than via your feed reader.

Comics. I get a daily dose of Dilbert in my feed reader, and you can, too. Go to www.dilbert.com and just copy and paste the link into your feed reader. In addition, you'll definitely want to look at

Tapestry Comics (www.tapestrycomics.com), a huge directory of Web comic strips that have RSS feeds.

Software updates. Keep on top of the latest Windows updates by subscribing to RSS feeds for your software of choice. Version-Tracker (www.versiontracker.com) is an excellent place to get updates, as well as PCWorld's most popular downloads of the week (http://feeds.pcworld.com/pcworld/downloads/weekly). There's also CNET's weekly downloads feed (www.cnet.com/4520-6022 -5115100.html), Microsoft's RSS feeds for all sorts of interesting stuff (www.microsoft.com/windows/rss/default.mspx), and RSS information for all of Apple's products and services (www.apple.com/rss/).

Airport and travel conditions. See what the airport, parking garages, and general travel conditions are before you head out the door. You can do this very easily with FlightStats (www.flightstats .com/go/Downloads/addAirportDelaysRSSToWebSite.do). Many individual airports also have RSS feeds—Shanghai International (www.einnews.com/rss_services/china/newsfeed-shanghai-pudong -international-airport), London City Airport (www.londoncityair port.com/fids/rss/), and Marseille Provence Airport (www.mrsair port.com/eng/wap_pda.jsp).

Movie reviews and info. Anyone who is a big movie fan (as I am) will appreciate this. You can subscribe to many movie review sites and showtimes right in your feed reader. Try Movies.com (www .movies.go.com/rss), Yahoo Movies (http://movies.yahoo.com/rss), the New York Times movie reviews (www.nytimes.com/services/ xml/rss/), or Apple Movie Trailers (http://images.apple.com/trailers/ rss/newtrailers.rss), one of the best sites to find high-quality movie trailers as soon as they're made available.

TV listings. Just as with movie info, you can get all the television news and updates you can handle via RSS. Try KTYP (www.ktyp .com/rss/tv/), TvRSS (www.tvrss.net/), Yahoo TV (http://rss.news

TOOLS YOU NEED

▶ If you enjoy National Public Radio (NPR), you'll be glad to know that they offer quite a few different RSS feeds, including All Things Considered, Fresh Air, and Song of the Day. You can also subscribe to specific topic feeds (culture, politics, education, etc.) as well as member station feeds. Find them all at www.npr.org/rss/.

▶ Wouldn't it be nice to have an instant community of smart people available to answer pretty much any question you asked at any time? Well, you can—they're at Yahoo Answers (http://answers.yahoo.com). One of the best things about Yahoo Answers is that you don't have to keep checking back to see if there are any new answers or questions; you can subscribe to any topic simply by dropping the URL into your feed reader.

.yahoo.com/rss/tv), or Zap2It (www.zap2it.com/tv/), or find out which movies will be coming your way in high definition with HDNet (www.hd.net/movies_schedule_sevenday.html).

Government news. Pretty much any news agency or news source out there is going to have an RSS feed, and that applies to government sources as well. For instance, you could subscribe to the official NASA breaking news feed at www.nasa.gov/rss/breaking_news.rss, the radio addresses of the President of the United States (www.whitehouse.gov/rss/radioaddress.xml), the Department of Education news (www.ed.gov/rss/edgov.xml), instant earthquake information (http://earthquake.usgs.gov/eqcenter/recenteqsww/catalogs/eqs7day-M2.5.xml), White House press briefings (www.whitehouse.gov/rss/pbriefing.xml), or the Yahoo News feed for the U.S. Senate (http://rss.news.yahoo.com/rss/ussenate).

Recipes. I love to cook, but I have to have a recipe in order to make it work. This is where RSS feeds really started to get convenient for me! Try AllRecipes (http://allrecipes.com/help/aboutus/rss.aspx), Drinknation for mixed drink and cocktail recipes (www.drinknation.com/rss/), Betty Crocker's recipe of the day (www.bettycrocker.com/Meal-Ideas/Recipe-of-the-day), or, one of my favorite recipe sites, About.com's Southern Cooking (http://about.com/southernfood/rssfeed). Try not to drool on your keyboard.

Newspapers. Tired of paying that pricey newspaper subscription? More and more newspapers are making their papers completely free via RSS. A few sites have pulled many newspaper feeds all together in one place: try the UK National newspaper feeds (www.dave.org.uk/newsfeeds/), or The Media Drop (www.themediadrop.com/archives/001588.php) for a good listing of newspapers that offer RSS feeds. If you can't find the newspaper you're looking for, try a search with the full name of your paper plus the letters RSS; you'll most likely be able to find a feed this way.

I'm sure that once you start fooling around with all the fun ways you can use RSS, you'll wonder how you ever got along without it. Basically, you can use RSS to accomplish any Web search task that you do on a regular basis. Once you set it up, you won't have to worry about it; the results just come to you, quickly and conveniently.

Get Linked

You can go to my About.com Web Search site for resources to help you to do even more with RSS.

WHAT IS RSS?

What are RSS feeds? Perhaps you've seen text or image buttons on various Web sites inviting you to "Subscribe via RSS." Well, what does that mean exactly? What is RSS, what are RSS feeds, and how do you get them to work for you?

 http://about.com/websearch/whatisrss

FIFTY THINGS YOU CAN DO WITH RSS

RSS, a simple technology that makes content come to you, can be used literally hundreds of different ways to simplify your life. Here are just fifty different things you can do with RSS.

 http://about.com/websearch/fiftyrssthings

TEN THINGS YOU DIDN'T KNOW YOU COULD DO WITH RSS

What are RSS feeds and how can they help you? You'd be surprised. Keep reading for ten things you didn't know you could do with RSS feeds.

 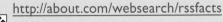 http://about.com/websearch/rssfacts

Chapter 6

The Niche Web

Instant News

The Web is a bonanza of resources, and that can be both a good thing and a bad thing. It's good because there's a seemingly never-ending supply of information, but it's bad because, well, because there's a seemingly never-ending supply of information!

It boils down to this: *How do I find the good stuff? Where do I go?* In this chapter, I'm going to unlock a virtual treasure trove of undiscovered information—I'm going to show you where I go for all the best sites in specific niche categories, from News to Shopping to Entertainment.

There are countless Web sites for news and information. We've already discussed using search engines for news in Chapter 3, and they are an excellent source. However, there are many sites out there that you can use to make yourself a more informed person. Here are my top Web sites, including a few

About.com

that you might not have heard of, for keeping on top of the news from around the world.

BBC (http://news.bbc.co.uk/): The BBC (British Broadcasting Company) is not only one of the best news sources in the world, but they also have quite an extensive site with resources such as free language courses (www.bbc.co.uk/languages/) and an extremely useful BBC Radio page (www.bbc.co.uk/radio/) where you can listen to live streaming broadcasts from the BBC.

Topix (www.topix.net): Topix is a gigantic news aggregator; at the time of this writing, they were funneling in news on more than 360,000 different topics from thousands of sources. One of the most useful features of Topix is the ability to subscribe via RSS to virtually any news topic, as well as stay on top of local news: just type in your zip code if you're in the United States, and you'll get a personalized page of news from an approximate 100-mile radius.

The Drudge Report (www.drudgereport.com): The Drudge Report is a mammoth compilation of stories from hundreds of different sources. It's also become famous (or infamous, depending on how you want to look at it) for breaking news ahead of most of the mainstream news and media outlets.

CNN (www.cnn.com): News coverage just wouldn't be complete without CNN, and although many of us do get CNN on our television sets, it's my opinion that the Web site is even better. You can find free streaming video here of any news story, in-depth coverage, and supplementary links to help you dig even deeper.

Time (www.time.com/time): Yep, *Time* magazine has its own site, and it's a good one. You can read many stories here from the current issue of *Time*, and you can also view photo galleries, read the Quote of the Day, and read the most popular stories as determined by page views (the number of times a story has been actually pulled up by readers).

ELSEWHERE ON THE WEB

▶ Sure, it's great to keep up with the daily news, but if you're in the mood for something a bit . . . weirder, try News of the Weird (www.newsoftheweird.com), The Onion (www.theonion.com/content), or the Fortean Times (www.forteantimes.com). All of these sites feature extraordinary happenings, satiric commentary, or just plain "what were they thinking?!?" kind of news, perfect for anyone looking for a bit of the lighter side.

The New York Times (www.nytimes.com): The Gray Lady is up on the Web, and after a series of revampings, the site is better than ever.

OhMyNews (http://english.ohmynews.com): OhMyNews, originally started in Korea, is one of the best citizen journalism news sources on the Web today. Readers are the reporters, which makes this news site one of a kind.

Techmeme (www.techmeme.com): Techmeme is for anyone who wants to keep up with the latest technology news, almost in real time. It's the first place I visit when I want to see what the technology geeks are all talking about; anything from the newest Nintendo Wii controller to rumors of satellite radio companies merging can be found here.

NPR (www.npr.org): NPR (National Public Radio) is not necessarily well-known for their Web site, and that's a shame, because their site is just as good as their stellar lineup of programs. Listen online live, or visit archived NPR programs here.

MSNBC (www.msnbc.msn.com): In the last few years, MSNBC has quietly revamped their news site to become one of the best informational reporting properties on the Web. They consistently are ahead of most of their competitors in putting up timely news items, and do a superb job of giving background information.

Those are the Web sites that I tend to check on a daily basis to get all the news I need; however, there are many more sites that you might be interested in. Additional sites for news and information include:

Slate (www.slate.org): Online magazine of news and commentary on culture and politics.

PBS (www.pbs.org): Features companion Web sites for nearly 250 PBS programs and specials, as well as seven different online news shows. An excellent resource for in-depth coverage.

TOOLS YOU NEED

▶ Need your news in a video format? You'll want to check out Blinkx.tv (www.blinkxtv.com), an amazing wall of video content. You can search through dozens of media sources, from ABC News to the BBC, and you can turn up a lot of interesting video here that you won't find anywhere else. Two caveats: not all of these videos are appropriate for younger viewers, and the site is best viewed with a high-speed Internet connection.

▶ That depends on whether your local news station has a Web site. If you know the call letters of your favorite TV station, try typing them into a search engine—for instance, FOX 12. If your TV station is on the Web, you should be able to find it this way. There are more ways to watch your local news online that I'll go into in Chapter 11.

The Wall Street Journal (http://online.wsj.com/public/us): Anyone who is looking for the most up to date and in-depth financial news would do well to check out the *Wall Street Journal* online.

USA Today (www.usatoday.com): *USA Today* does a fantastic job of presenting somewhat complex news stories clearly and concisely. A great place to get a quick news rundown for the day.

Salon (www.salon.com): This online magazine reports on news, politics, culture, and life.

The Best Lifestyle and Entertainment Sites

I'd be lying to you if I told you I only used the Web for research. Au contraire! There's so much good stuff out there that it's a bit difficult to pry myself away from the computer sometimes. Here are just a few of the best lifestyle and entertainment sites that I visit at least daily.

The Complete Review (www.complete-review.com/main/main.html): At the time of this writing, there were over 1,800 book reviews in this site's database. It's one of the first places you should go on the Web to get the latest in book reviews.

MoOM (www.coudal.com/moom.php): I'm a sucker for museums, so the Museum of Online Museums is high on my list of must-visit sites. Any museum in the world that has a Web site is represented here; in addition, you can visit selected special exhibitions as featured on the site. An amazing resource.

Orisinal (www.ferryhalim.com/orisinal): Orisinal is a games site . . . but not just any old games site. Orisinal is a collection of some of the most beautifully designed Flash games on the planet, plus (and all you parents out there will appreciate this one) the music that goes along with the games is actually quite beautiful—lots of acoustic piano, for example.

ZeFrank (www.zefrank.com): It's hard to really explain what ZeFrank is; mostly, you just need to experience it. Learn how to dance from instructional videos (trust me), watch semi-daily video-casts, or play with a whole plethora of interactive toys.

BoingBoing (www.boingboing.net): BoingBoing is an eclectic, frequently updated site full of offbeat finds that the Web community (and the four contributors to the site) discover on the Web.

The Food Network (www.foodnetwork.com/): I love to cook, so the Food Network is one of my frequently visited sites. Download recipes, watch shows, or participate in the forums.

The Internet Movie Database (www.imdb.com/): The IMDb is the largest movie information Web site in existence. You can find information not only on pretty much *any* movie or TV show here, but you can also research actors, read scripts in their entirety, and watch movie clips and trailers.

YouTube (www.youtube.com/): Millions of videos all in one place – that's YouTube. I like to visit YouTube for clips from the Family Guy cartoon I missed, or maybe my favorite '80s hair band music video. There's also a ton of homemade content here that ranges from simply stupid to utterly brilliant.

Yahoo Music (http://music.yahoo.com/): All your music needs are covered here, from breaking news to videos to streaming music you can download for a nominal fee.

Poetry Daily (www.poems.com/): This one is pretty much what it sounds like—you can sign up for a new poem in your e-mail inbox every single day. A great way to experience poetry of all kinds, in small doses.

The Web is a great place for shopping. Don't worry—I definitely won't leave out the shopping. I've been a huge fan of shopping on the Web pretty much since it started; in fact, I do the

ELSEWHERE ON THE WEB

▶ If you're looking for older news, you can use Google News Archives (http://news.google.com/archivesearch). This wonderful resource searches more than 200 years' worth of news for you, providing an easy and absolutely fascinating way to explore historical archives. It's a great place to go if you are doing any kind of historical research. Google News Archives even can create a timeline of events for you.

majority of my Christmas shopping and back-to-school shopping on the Web. Some of the best shopping sites include:

Amazon.com (www.amazon.com): You just cannot go wrong with Amazon.com. They've got everything from books to clothing here, and it's usually at a much better price than what you could find it for in the "real" stores.

eBay (www.ebay.com): eBay is the original auction site; they started out with just a couple of Pez dispensers and now have millions of items up for sale at any given time. EBay is great for collectors, but you can also find some pretty amazing deals on things you actually *need*; I was able to buy all three of my kids' complete back-to-school wardrobes here for a shockingly low price.

Etsy (www.etsy.com): Now here's where we go off the beaten path a bit. Etsy is an online crafts marketplace, where people all over the world with any kind of artistic bent can sell their handiwork to you. I've found some astonishingly good pieces of art here (along with really *bad* stuff, but thankfully there's much less of that!).

Zafu (www.zafu.com/): This is for the girls, especially if you're as tired as I am of not finding jeans that actually fit. Zafu takes your exact measurements, style, preferences, etc. and then matches you to the stores that stock jeans for your unique body type.

Epinions (www.epinions.com): Technically, Epinions is not a shopping site; but it's definitely one of the most useful sites on the Web for shoppers. Epinions is a community consumer review site: anyone can register to submit a review on what they've purchased, good or bad. It's a good place to check before you buy, especially before you make a major purchase.

Helpful Finance and Career Web Sites

Finance information and help for job seekers is available for free on the Web. You can get the latest stock quotes, research financial

TOOLS YOU NEED

▶ In addition to shopping sites, there are hundreds of comparison shopping search engines, where along with a dizzying array of consumer choices you also can pick the best prices from a variety of sources. Some of the best comparison shopping search engines include Yahoo Shopping (http://shopping.yahoo.com/), PriceGrabber (www.pricegrabber.com/), and ShopZilla (www.shopzilla.com/).

news, find a job, network with other job seekers, and more. Below are what I consider the best career and finance Web sites.

The Web has some excellent finance sites. This is just a taste of the helpful financial tools that you can find on the web.

Yahoo Finance (http://finance.yahoo.com/): Yahoo Finance nicely categorizes essential financial information, from stocks to breaking news, in one place. In addition, you can do some pretty serious background research here.

Google Finance (http://finance.google.com/finance): Google Finance is relatively new at the time of this writing, but it's already made quite a mark. The best use for Google Finance is for up-to-the-minute breaking financial updates.

CNN Money (http://money.cnn.com/): I really appreciate CNN Money, not only because they provide good financial coverage, but also because they offer a lot of interesting finance-related articles, such as "The Bizarre Lives of the Filthy Rich" or "Will Housing Bring Down the Economy?" Definitely worth a bookmark.

IRS.gov (www.irs.gov/): Surprisingly enough, for such an unpleasant subject, the IRS has done an exemplary job of putting their site together. You can download any IRS form here, as well as get advice from tax professionals.

There are great job Web sites out there. You can find a job and network with other job seekers, all available for free on the Web. In addition, many job sites give you the ability to subscribe to searches via RSS. Here are my picks for the best job Web sites:

Monster.com (www.monster.com/): Most people would consider Monster.com to be the biggest, most comprehensive job search engine on the Web today. You can search hundreds of thousands of jobs in just about any category you can think of,

ASK YOUR GUIDE

Can you really find a job using the Web?

▶ I think that the Web must be part of any successful job hunter's toolbox—but it's definitely not something you should focus your entire job search on. The best site I've come across for finding a job and staying on top of job search trends has to be Alison Doyle's About.com Job Searching site (http://jobsearch.about.com/). She does some fantastic work there; it's frequently updated with new research, articles, and much more.

network with other job seekers, and read in-depth career articles from a rotating panel of experts.

Dice (www.dice.com/): Dice is one of the best job search engines out there specifically targeted toward careers in the technology sector.

Yahoo Hot Jobs (http://hotjobs.yahoo.com/): Yahoo Hot Jobs is one of the biggest job search engines on the Web; I've always appreciated how many jobs in my local area it can turn up.

Indeed.com (www.indeed.com/): Indeed is probably my favorite job search engine, mostly because it seems to turn up interesting job positions that don't necessarily find their way into the more mainstream engines. Indeed gives you the ability to subscribe to any job search via RSS.

SimplyHired (www.simplyhired.com/): SimplyHired is another job search engine that seems to turn up the jobs less traveled. Try their page of Special Searches (www.simplyhired.com/specialsearches.php) in order to really narrow your job search.

Craigslist (www.craigslist.org/): Honestly, what *isn't* Craigslist good for? Seriously. Not only can you use Craigslist to repopulate your living room, buy a new house, or sell your truck, but you can also find some incredibly good job postings here from all over the spectrum.

Useful Travel Sites on the Web

This past Christmas vacation, I planned an entire Disneyland trip for five people completely online, from airfare to tickets to coupons for area attractions. There are great travel sites out there that not only can find you the best deal from thousands of sources, but can also make planning your next vacation incredibly convenient and time-saving. Here are my picks for the best travel sites on the Web:

Iexplore (www.iexplore.com/): This is where you're going to find some serious adventure travel ideas, anything from privately guided Tahitian tours to a Mount Everest adventure to a ten-day Switzerland excursion. Make sure you check out the Travel Discounts and Specials page (www.iexplore.com/specials/specials.jhtml).

National Park Service (www.nps.gov/): The National Park Service has done some revamping of their site, making it possible for you to get information on almost any park in the United States and to make camping reservations directly from the site itself—an extremely convenient feature.

Theme Park Insider (www.themeparkinsider.com): Like theme parks? If you want to get the most out of your visit (and save some serious coin), you'll want to visit Theme Park Insider, a great site for roller coaster aficionados.

Expedia (www.expedia.com): Expedia is a comparison travel search engine: you tell it what you're looking for, and it goes out and grabs hundreds of possible solutions for you, organized by price, quality, etc. This is an especially good place to find last-minute deals—I was able to shave $700 (!) off a combined flight, hotel, and car rental package.

Fodor's (www.fodors.com): If you want your travel plans to go a bit off the beaten path, you'll want to check out Fodor's. Great travel articles here.

Travelocity (www.travelocity.com): Travelocity is similar to Expedia; it's a comparison travel search engine. You can find some pretty amazing deals here.

SeatGuru (www.seatguru.com): SeatGuru is a site that helps you figure out where you're sitting on the plane. Sounds simple, doesn't it? Well, SeatGuru is one of the most useful travel sites on the Web because (as you probably know) not all airplanes are built alike . . . and it's certainly convenient to know ahead of time where you're sitting.

Priceline (www.priceline.com/): Priceline is a good place to grab last-minute travel deals as well as plan vacations or trips ahead

ASK YOUR GUIDE

How do you know if you're getting a good travel deal online?

▶ I personally never rely on just one source, whether that's on the Web or in real life with a travel agent. Instead, I'll usually pick at least three travel search engines and/or specialty sites (depending on where I'm going), and come up with a mini-spreadsheet of various price points. If I don't feel like I've reached a good deal at this point, I'll usually call a local agent. So far, this method has worked very well.

▶ If you're looking for information about a specific disease or disorder, one of the
best places I've found to get
accurate, easy-to-understand
information is Healthline.
com (www.healthline.com/).
Healthline's database includes
over 200 health-related
"channels" (specific health
topics ranging from Acne
to Sleep Disorders), peer-
reviewed articles, and much
more.

of time. Not only does Priceline offer the standard airfare/car/hotel
packages, they also give you the opportunity to compare cruise
packages—a nice touch.

Site59.com (www.site59.com/): Site59 is perfect for last-
minute getaways, especially if you're looking for something on the
weekend. You can book deals as late as three hours before your
departure time!

Byways.org (www.byways.org/): I've long been a fan of the
road trip, having crossed the United States three times already, so
Byways really caught my eye as one of the travel sites I need to
keep track of. You can plan a fascinating road trip here; take advantage of the inside knowledge of both the Byways staff and travelers
in the forums.

MouseSavers (www.mousesavers.com/): Planning on going to
a Disney resort anytime soon? You won't want to miss Mouse-
Savers, the best Disney vacation money-saving site on the Web.
Here's where you go to find all the "insider" deals, such as deeply
discounted hotel rooms, car rentals, and park tickets. I also check
MouseSavers for special in-park events that might be happening
when we arrive (we are confirmed Disneyholics in our family!).

Trustworthy Health and Medicine Sites on the Web

Whether you're trying to find a good alternative remedy for an
earache or researching more about a relative's cancer scare, the
Web is definitely a great place to do it. However, that being said,
medical information that you find on the Web should never substitute for a doctor's care or advice. The following sites are for
informational purposes only.

WholeHealthMD (www.wholehealthmd.com): One of the
best Web sites for finding more information about alternative
medicine and methods.

Trauma Pages (www.trauma-pages.com/): Many of us have gone through traumatic events in our lives, and Trauma Pages aims to help you make sense of them with an outstanding set of resources and articles.

FoodFit (www.foodfit.com/): Want to learn how to eat more nutritiously? You'll want to check out FoodFit, one of the best Web sites around for teaching yourself the value of good nutrition and exercise.

Weight Watchers (www.weightwatchers.com): Weight Watchers is one of the longest-running diet programs out there for good reason: it actually *works*. Many people are able to lose weight successfully with the WW online program; you can journal, interact with other dieters, and get recipe support—all online.

3 Fat Chicks on a Diet (www.3fatchicks.com): Well, with a name like that, how could you not love the site? It's pretty much what it sounds like: three women on a quest to lose weight, the healthy way. Lots of good articles and support can be found here.

National Institutes of Health (www.nih.gov): The NIH is a gargantuan site, loaded with health and medical information. This is one of the best places to find out what's going on in the world of medical research.

WebMD (www.webmd.com): I love WebMD, mostly because they present somewhat complicated health-related information in an easy to understand manner. They also offer interactive surveys and quizzes to help you figure out what might be going on in your body.

HealthFinder (www.healthfinder.gov): Another great health-related Web site from the U.S. government that includes information from over 1,500 health organizations.

WHAT'S HOT

▶ If you're interested in staying on top of the latest health and medical research, you can't do much better than Science Daily ([www.science daily.com](www.sciencedaily.com)), an aggregator of a variety of health, medicine, and science topics. There's also Science.gov ([www.sci ence.gov](www.science.gov)), Yahoo's special Science News section (http://news.yahoo.com/i/753), and Science News Online ([www .sciencenews.org](www.sciencenews.org)), the companion site to the *Science News* journal.

*What about kids and
safety on the Web?*

▶ I've had to lay down some
guidelines for my kids on the
Web, such as setting clear
boundaries about which sites
are appropriate, monitoring
time on the Web, and mak-
ing sure that there's some
accountability between the
parents and the kids. I've
written an article (http://
about.com/websearch/kid
safety) that talks about this
very thing; I also give practical suggestions as to how
you can monitor your child's
Web surfing.

The National Institute of Mental Health (www.nimh
.nih.gov): A great place to start your research into mental health
issues.

The Diet Detective (www.nutricise.com): Good site for
learning more about health, nutrition, and exercise; it also has
motivational articles.

Fun and Safe Sites for Kids on the Web

As the mom of three wonderful kids, I've seen more than my share
of both good and horribly bad Web sites for kids. Over the years,
there have been a few kids' sites that have consistently shown
themselves to be of good quality. Here are my picks for the best
kids' Web sites out there.

Sports Illustrated for Kids (www.sikids.com): This site provides a great way for kids to learn about their favorite sports.

BBC History for Kids (www.bbc.co.uk/history/forkids/index
.shtml): There is so much good stuff here, including interactive
timelines, games, and lots of great information. Perfect for kids
interested in history or who need to learn about a specific time
period for a school project.

Yahoo Kids (http://kids.yahoo.com/): Formerly known as
Yahooligans, Yahoo's network of sites especially aimed toward kids
is one of the best. You can find games, coloring activities, just-for-
kids movie trailers, even homework help.

PBS Kids (www.pbskids.org): This is the first place my six-
year-old wants to visit on the Web. Every show that you can watch
on PBS is represented here with videos, activities, coloring pages,
and more.

Seussville (www.seussville.com/main.php): Dr. Seuss's home
on the Web! Read stories (or have them read to you), play fun
Seuss activities, or print out Dr. Seuss coloring pages.

Animal Planet (www.animal.discovery.com): Got an animal lover in your family? My kids love Animal Planet; they can watch fascinating animal videos here or get behind the scenes of their favorite Animal Planet/Discovery Channel shows.

Bill Nye The Science Guy (www.billnye.com): I've been a fan of Bill Nye since his earliest days, so I was so thrilled to see that he had a Web site. You can play games here, as well as learn more about any of the science topics that Bill has featured in his shows.

Jan Brett's Activities Pages (www.janbrett.com/activities_pages.htm): Jan Brett is a celebrated children's book author and illustrator, and her site is a treasure trove of coloring pages, flash cards, free books, and printables of all kinds.

The Magic School Bus (http://www.scholastic.com/magicschoolbus/): Get on board with Miss Frizzle and the gang at the Magic School Bus site. Plenty of fun activities here, including games, guided tours, and streaming videos.

Neopets (www.neopets.com): Are your kids longing for a pet, but for whatever reason just can't have one? Well, you might want to check out Neopets, the largest virtual pet site on the Web. All the fun of a pet without the mess!

Orisinal (www.ferryhalim.com/orisinal): I already mentioned Orisinal in my best fun sites section, but I have to include it in the Kids section as well—it's that good. If your kids are itching to play games on the Web, and you're concerned about finding appropriate games for them, you'll be relieved to find Orisinal: it's absolutely kid-safe (plus, there are no annoying graphics or loud music!).

StoryNory (www.storynory.com): Do your kids love having stories read to them? Well, of course they do! StoryNory is a wonderful site full of free, downloadable, iPod-ready stories for your kids. I've downloaded quite a few of these for my kids to listen to as they are going to sleep.

ELSEWHERE ON THE WEB

▶ Want another great kids' site? Try Ask.com's Ask For Kids (www.askforkids.com). You'll find a dictionary, a thesaurus, an almanac, science articles, astronomy research, math help—you name it, it's probably here. In addition, they have a whole section dedicated completely to news just for kids, homework help, and (of course) games.

While I've given you quite a few sites in this chapter to check out, this is only a tiny sample of what the Web has to offer. Find a new site that you'd love to share? Come on over to the About Web Search forums (http://about.com/websearch/forums) and tell us all about it.

TOOLS YOU NEED

▶ One of the best ways to find well-done kids' sites is by checking your child's school district Web site. Most school districts have a reviewed list of kid-friendly sites somewhere within their pages. In addition, you can find great kids' sites simply by reading my article titled "The Best Kids' Sites on the Web" (http://about.com/websearch/bestkidsites); many of my own kids' favorites made the cut here.

Get Linked

Here are a few more resources on my About.com Web Search site that will help you find the best Web sites out there.

BEST WEB SITE OF THE DAY

From crazy to community, social to reference, search helps to cutting-edge, you'll find it here at the About Web Search Site of the Day, updated daily.

http://about.com/websearch/siteoftheday

TOP TEN TIME WASTERS ON THE WEB

Got some extra time, or just feel like putting something off? Don't say I didn't warn you, but these sites are addictive! Here are the top ten time wasters on the Web.

http://about.com/websearch/timewasters

MOST POPULAR WEB SITES

Here's my mega-list of the best Web sites in a wide variety of categories, from e-cards to MySpace video codes.

http://about.com/websearch/popularsites

Chapter 7

Using the Social Web in Searches

The Social Web as a Web Search Tool

I've got a little secret: I don't find all these wonderful Web sites on my own. In fact, I rely on thousands and thousands of other searchers—people just like you and me—who are eager to find useful (and, admittedly, not so useful) sites and share them with others. How did I find these people? How did I tap into their network(s), so to speak, and start taking advantage of their collective mass wisdom? Why, through the vast **social Web**, of course.

What is the social Web? Basically, the social Web is very simple: it is an ever-growing distribution of people all over the world who find great Web sites and, instead of keeping these sites to themselves, share them with the Web at large.

The Web originally connected content to content. For example, say you're a physicist and you just wrote your most brilliant

About.com

*How did the social Web
get started?*

▶ The idea of the social
Web—a network of people
sharing content over the
medium of the Internet—
was introduced officially in
1998 by Peter Hoschka. You
can read the paper in which
he discussed the concept,
"From Basic Groupware to
the Social Web," at http://
portal.acm.org/citation.cfm
?id=290576.

paper ever. How do you get more of your academic community to read it? You can publish it in a journal, sure, but that reaches a very limited audience. So you decide to publish it to the Web, where anyone can read it and then share it with others. The Web is a platform to share content like nothing else in history, and the social Web is just building upon that original premise.

The social Web works by sharing bookmarks. Basically, you find something you like and share it with other people in a variety of social bookmarking or social networking communities, using tags to help categorize what it is that you're bookmarking. Let's go through what each of these terms mean.

Social Bookmarking and Social Networking

Social bookmarking is the practice of saving and categorizing a particular site and sharing it with others via social bookmarking communities. Users can share their own personal Web bookmarks, but they also have the wonderful option of discovering other people's bookmarks and adding them to their own collection. More sites can be discovered, more treasures unearthed, if you work together as a whole instead of by yourself.

Social networking is related to social bookmarking: you can make as many bookmarks on the Web as you want, then once you start sharing these bookmarks with other people, interacting with them, starting conversations through a variety of methodologies, you are networking. You are part of the social networking community the instant you share a bookmark with someone else. There are a number of ways that you can make yourself part of the social Web community at large; it's a wonderful way to connect to other people with like interests all over the world.

Tags are essential in the social Web lexicon. Tags are basically keywords or phrases that you can use to categorize something, to make it easier for other people to find it later.

For instance: Say you found a wonderful site all about the Civil War, and you want to add it to your arsenal of personal bookmarks. If you really liked how this particular site treated Abraham Lincoln, you might add a note in your titling of the bookmark: "Civil War—Abe Lincoln article." Guess what? You've just given that Web site a tag. Tags are at the core of what makes social bookmarking communities run smoothly. Without this simple yet effective self-organization, social bookmarking communities would have burnt out a long time ago.

That's the social Web in a nutshell: the Web connects content; the social Web connects content and people through the novel use of tagging. It's a simple concept that has taken off in a very powerful way.

Think of it. Instead of just one lone scout hunting for Web treasures, you have an enormous army of Web searchers busily finding and cataloguing some of the most cutting-edge, useful, and just plain wild Web sites out there—and as part of the social bookmarking community, you get to take advantage of all these wonderful finds. I don't know how I got along before social bookmarking—it not only saves me time by doing so much of my legwork, so to speak, but it also gives me advance notice of what new trends are emerging and what kinds of things other searchers are looking for. Social bookmarking sites have changed the Web landscape over the last few years, making it easier than ever before to find and share good information.

One other benefit of social bookmarking sites is that they allow you to make your Web bookmarks portable. You can access your favorite sites from anywhere—from home, work, a coffee shop, you name it.

TOOLS YOU NEED

▶ Tags are quickly taking off as one of the best ways to organize a site, both for visitors and the site owner. I've rounded up a few Web sites that use tags to organize their content here: http:// about.com/websearch/tags. I use tags myself to organize my content in the blogs that I write or contribute to; it's a simple way to make everything more accessible. For instance, Flickr (www.flickr .com) helps you find photos more easily with specific tags for each image.

Are there any composite social bookmarking sites?

▶ My Web search life got a whole lot easier in one fell swoop with the onset of Popurls (http://popurls .com), an innovative site that tracks at least twenty-five (more are added all the time) social bookmarking, social networking, and community content sites across the Web. Now, instead of going from site to site, I can just check Popurls for what's hot.

What Makes a Social Bookmarking Site Worthwhile

Plenty of social bookmarking sites have popped up in the last year or so to take advantage of what is becoming one of the hottest trends on the Web. I've pared down this overcrowded field and picked the best of the best, based on five criteria:

1. **No spam** (or a minimum of spammy entries). I'm pretty sure that most people don't appreciate wading through useless content on the Web, and while social bookmarking sites for the most part do a pretty good job of policing themselves, the odd spam entry does make its way through. The best social bookmarking sites have a zero-tolerance policy on submissions that meet the spam requirements, and do a great job of weeding them out.

2. **Lots of users.** The whole point of social bookmarking is to piggyback on the searches of other people who have gone before you. A social bookmarking site with only a few users pretty much defeats the purpose. I tend to look for communities that are thriving with many users; yes, I've probably missed out on a few good ones with this particular criterion, but so far it's served me well. The more, the merrier!

3. **Easy to use.** This is probably the number one feature that I look for in social bookmarking sites: is it easy to use? How fast can I get going with this? If I have to read a twenty-page user's manual to get up to speed on some fantastic new service, chances are I probably won't use it. If it's easy to use and easy to understand, I'll come back (and recommend it to other people). Social bookmarking is not meant to be difficult; its original purpose was to make it easier for everyday searchers like you and me to find and share the good stuff.

4. **RSS feeds.** I won't use a social bookmarking site if it doesn't come ready-made with RSS feeds for tags. Why? Because for me, that is one of the most basic components of *any* site, not just social bookmarking communities. I need to have an RSS feed capacity so I don't have to keep coming back and checking to see if there's something new. In addition to RSS feeds, I like to have the option of bringing in or carrying out bookmarks from another social bookmarking service; more and more sites are making this option available as a matter of course and it's good to see.

5. **Quality content.** This is a no-brainer. If I am going to keep using a social bookmarking site, I need to have consistent quality. For me, that does not involve seeing a link to the latest cute-kitten-on-the-piano video over and over again. There will be some of that kind of thing, sure, but there will be more links to really good undiscovered Web sites. This particular criterion can only be assessed after using a social bookmarking site for a period of time.

The Best Social Bookmarking Sites on the Web

I've been using a variety of social bookmarking sites for some time now, so I know what works and what does not.

First on the social bookmarking scene was del.icio .us. Most of us couldn't figure out how to spell this, let alone use it, when it first came out! However, del.icio.us (http://del.icio.us/) soon proved its worth with its easy-to-use interface and large user base.

You can also use del.icio.us to see the interesting links that your friends and other people bookmark, and share links with them in return. You can do make this search even easier by searching with tags.

ELSEWHERE ON THE WEB

▶ How do you keep track of all the social bookmarking sites proliferating on the Web? Fortunately, there are a couple of sites completely dedicated to the social bookmarking phenomenon. I highly recommend Mashable (www.mashable.com), a site that obsessively tracks new Web technology, as well as Programmable Web (www .programmableweb.com), a site that stays on top of not only new Web technology, but small startups that have interesting potential.

What is the biggest benefit of using social bookmarking sites?

▶ For me, the biggest benefit is the opportunity to see what other Web searchers are finding in their travels on the Web. I love to tap into what the Web community is thinking, feeling, talking about—I feel connected to people I've never even met. Plus, I'm only one person, and while I find a lot of really cool stuff on the Web, it's wonderful to be able to plug into the greater Web search zeitgeist and take advantage of the wisdom of the crowd.

Tags, social bookmarking, social networking—it's all there with del.icio.us. But there's even more. You can also subscribe to various del.icio.us tags via RSS and get new additions as they come in, through your feed reader of choice. For instance, I am subscribed to the del.icio.us tag for **e-books** (http://del.icio.us/tag/ebook); this way, I get a head start on new e-books that frequently show up on del.icio.us.

Furl is another excellent social bookmarking site. I use LookSmart's Furl (www.furl.net) almost as often as I use del.icio.us. Furl could be considered one of the granddaddies of social bookmarking; it was on the scene way before some of these other, better known whippersnappers.

Furl is a bit different than other social bookmarking sites; for one thing, the bookmarks here tend to be on the more academic side, probably because Furl was mostly picked up by academia (librarians, professors, researchers, etc.) when it first emerged. You still see that influence in the bookmarks that Furl turns up, which to me is a big plus.

In addition, Furl differentiates itself by allowing users not only to clip and share their favorite sites on the Web, but to actually save physical copies of them. Basically, this means that you are able to create your own searchable database of your favorite sites.

And then there's Reddit. This is another of my favorite social bookmarking sites. Reddit (http://reddit.com/) works pretty much like Furl and del.icio.us: you register a username and password, and then start submitting and sharing your bookmarks. Reddit is similar to del.icio.us in that users are encouraged to vote on the links and stories that they feel are deserving of being in the top-dog spot.

There are many different "flavors" of Reddit called subreddits: these are channels of particular topics such as Science (http://sci

ence.reddit.com), Culture (http://freeculture.reddit.com), and Programming (http://programming.reddit.com). In addition to these channels, Reddit also owns Lipstick (http://lipstick.com), a subreddit that is a social bookmarking site specifically aimed toward gossip and entertainment news.

Yahoo's MyWeb is an up-and-comer. I use this site on a regular basis, too. MyWeb (http://myweb.yahoo.com/) is a relative newcomer to the social bookmarking scene, so it still has a lot of room for improvement, notably in consistent quality of submissions. However, the fact that Yahoo has such an inherently large user base makes MyWeb a surefire winner when it comes to quantity—there are goodies galore to grab.

In order to use MyWeb most effectively, you're going to want to check its tag clouds. A tag cloud is just a bunch of tags—keywords that help categorize information—in one convenient place. For instance, say you're looking for technology news on Yahoo's MyWeb; you can take a look at the tag cloud and click the Tech tag.

In addition, MyWeb is organized into three basic tabs across the top of your browser window: My Bookmarks, My Contacts, and Interesting Today. My Bookmarks is pretty much what it sounds like: your bookmarks, made either private or public. My Contacts is your personal MyWeb network; you can choose to invite other people whose bookmarks you find interesting and make them part of your network (del.icio.us has the same feature; it's just another way to connect with other Web searchers). Third, there's the Interesting Today tab, a collection of what people are bookmarking in real time. I've actually subscribed to this tab via RSS in my feed reader so I can keep myself constantly updated on what other MyWeb users are finding interesting out there on the World Wide Web.

ELSEWHERE ON THE WEB

▶ Most social bookmarking sites come with their own handy toolbars or buttons—this makes it easier for you to bookmark sites as you come across them without having to actually navigate to your favorite social site. For instance, del.icio.us has made buttons available (http://del.icio.us/help/buttons), **Furl has a customized Firefox browser extension** (https://addons.mozilla.org/firefox/1781/, **and Reddit has drag-and-drop** bookmarklets (http://reddit.com/bookmarklets).

Stumble upon some terrific Web sites! Social bookmarking site number five, and probably my favorite, is StumbleUpon (www.stumbleupon.com). StumbleUpon is different from the previous social bookmarking sites that I've talked about so far in several important ways.

First, the emphasis is definitely on sharing great sites with the greater StumbleUpon community. You can do this simply by installing the StumbleUpon toolbar, which you can find at www.stumble upon.com (I've got it installed on my machine and it's never given me any problems). As you come across great sites that you would like to bookmark and share, you hit the Thumbs Up button on the StumbleUpon toolbar, give the sites a few quick tags and categories to help other Stumblers more easily find what you're submitting, and then click Enter. That's the social bookmarking part of StumbleUpon.

However, the reason I'm so utterly enthusiastic about—and more than a little addicted to—StumbleUpon is this: I can wander from site to site within StumbleUpon's gigantic submitted database of Web sites. All I have to do is click the Stumble! button on my toolbar, and I am able to explore the Web as I've never been able to explore before. You have a couple of options here as well; you can choose to discover sites from any category or you can narrow it down to either predetermined topics or a topic of your own choosing. For instance, the other day I was interested in looking for Harry Potter sites, so I entered the term "harry potter" in the StumbleUpon search bar. Instantly, I had some of the best Harry Potter Web sites around available to me, along with quite a few that I had never seen before (and quite frankly, I'm not sure how easily I would've been able to find them on my own). You get the best of the Web without having to filter it.

That's the beauty of StumbleUpon, to my mind: you are able to take advantage of a vast network of dedicated Web searchers who are finding utterly brilliant sites and sharing them with you. I do have to warn you, though—StumbleUpon is an incredibly addicting way to search the Web. I found myself up till 1:30 AM one weekend, blearily clicking the Stumble! Button over and over again, because the quality of the sites are just so amazing; you just keep on coming across stuff that instantly merits a bookmark of your own. I highly recommend using StumbleUpon both as a social bookmarking community and as an absolutely vital Web search tool.

How to Use Social Web Communities to Enhance Your Search

We've gone over what a social bookmarking and social networking community actually is, and we've discussed my five favorite social bookmarking sites—but how do you actually use these communities to make your Web searches more efficient? In this section, we'll take a detailed look at each of the social bookmarking sites I've mentioned as being the best of the best, and I'll show you how I use them to make my Web searches more streamlined and just plain more interesting.

Del.icio.us is the best site for connecting with other people. You can use del.icio.us for many things; here are just a few of the uses that I've found for this user-friendly social bookmarking site.

To me, the most appealing feature of del.icio.us is the other users. Many very smart, very Web-search-savvy people use del.icio.us on a regular basis, and del.icio.us makes it simple to track what these people are doing—you can simply add them to your personal network. Once you've clicked the link to do this (it's usually right next to the username), you can follow along with what your chosen person is surfing. I also subscribe to various

ASK YOUR GUIDE

What's the most popular social content site?

▶ Popularity of these sites probably varies from day to day, but I think overall the winner would have to be Digg (www.digg.com). Digg is a social bookmarking and social networking site that is completely driven by its users. Diggers submit sites, and other Diggers vote them up or down depending on how good the content is. If the site is really good, your Digg might even make it to the front page, a coveted triumph for many in the Digg community.

del.icio.us users' searches via RSS; this makes it easy for me to get all their updates in one convenient place.

Another excellent use for del.icio.us is as an online list manager. Here's the thing: I find an endless supply of great sites, but since I do indeed have a life that includes activity outside the Web, I don't have all the time I need to read what is on all these sites. That's where del.icio.us saves the day for me. I've created a category under my username titled To Read Later where I can place all my findings that require more than just a cursory glance, and it will all be there waiting for me when I get around to it. Now, I could probably separate this particular category into even further subcategories—e.g., Articles, Fun Stuff, To E-mail—but so far my original categorization has served me quite well.

And since del.icio.us's interface is so simple and uncluttered, I'm able to see at a glance what is waiting for me. I can also subscribe to this particular tag via RSS and read the articles in my Bloglines feed; since I'm in Bloglines frequently during the day, I have found this to be a very workable option. Plus, since del.icio.us is not based on my computer, I can access these lists from any location. This came in very handy over Christmas holidays when I was visiting my mother-in-law and wanted to share a few sites with her.

Last but not least, you can use del.icio.us tags to really tweak your searches. You can do quite a few different things with these simple tags, including:

- **Monitor what's on the cutting edge with the del.icio.us/ popular tag:** I've subscribed to this particular tag via RSS so I'm always tracking what's new here.
- **Track any subject:** You can see a list of all the del.icio.us tags at the del.icio.us tag cloud (http://del.icio.us/tag/); new tags are added all the time. Just find the topic that you're interested in and click it. You'll be taken to the home page

for any new sites that are currently being tagged under that category; if you only want to view the most popular items in any one category, simply click the Popular link at the top of the page. For instance, here's the link for the most popular Apple items: http://del.icio.us/popular/apple.

Furl is an excellent mobile database. I use Furl primarily as an online, access-from-anywhere list/article database. However, unlike with del.icio.us, with Furl I can see a quick synopsis of the articles and sites that I Furl, rather than just a link with a brief sentence.

Here are a few Web search tasks that you can use Furl for:

Preserve old links. The beauty of Furl is that it actually saves copies of Web pages, rather than just the links; so if a link goes bad after a while (it happens), you can still access your content through Furl. This especially comes in handy if you're citing something in a research paper; if your professor wants to double-check your references and the link no longer works, you can simply direct him or her to your Furl.

You can search all of your saved bookmarks with Furl. Furl offers the convenient feature of full-text searching throughout all your saved Web sites; you can imagine how handy this is when you're looking for something specific.

Furl can be used as a collection point for pretty much anything you want to keep track of on the Web. Say you're in the market for a new couch. You could store listings from eBay, from Craigslist, from your local newspaper, etc. all in Furl and use it as a database for your couch hunt. Here's another one: you can store all the recipes you find on the Web in Furl, and create your very own mega-recipe Web—completely searchable, completely accessible even if for some reason the links are no longer valid six months down the line. I consider Furl not only a useful tool for bookmarking sites and

ELSEWHERE ON THE WEB

▶ One of the more interesting and innovative sites that's come out of the social content craze is Geni (www .geni.com/tree/start), a site where you and your family at large can work on your family genealogy in collaboration from all over the world. What a super way to create a lasting memory for generations to come!

articles, but also one of the best searchable treasure-troves of links on the Web.

Reddit is the easiest social bookmarking site to use. Although it is one of the newcomers in the social bookmarking sites that I've mentioned so far, Reddit's format makes it easier to navigate than the others mentioned.

- Reddit works as a democratic community, as well as a social bookmarking community. Reddit users vote for or against submitted stories, so the best links tend to rise to the top.
- Every time you use Reddit, the service gets to know you and your preferences better. What this means is that Reddit will start to show you Web sites that correspond to your personal criteria, making your Web searches more effective.
- Reddit tends to have a more interesting variety of submitted links, so if you're looking for some new blood for your Web searches, I would definitely recommend Reddit as a starting point.

Yahoo MyWeb is ideal because of the massive user base. If you have a Yahoo account (and millions of people do), you can start using Yahoo MyWeb almost instantly. MyWeb incorporates the features of del.icio.us and Furl in that it saves links in a searchable list format; like Furl, it also saves actual copies of the Web page for you.

Yahoo MyWeb offers many annotation features that help you keep track of your bookmarks more easily. You can add detailed, customized notes to your saved pages, use multiple tags to categorize, and even tag multiple pages all at once, which can save a lot of time.

TOOLS YOU NEED

▶ How about social bookmarking for one of our favorite pastimes—shopping! Wists is a great place to store images of goodies you come across on the Web, and it also lets you take advantage of what other savvy shoppers are coming up with. You can read more about Wists in my article "Wists—Share and Publish Your Shopping Lists" (http://about.com/websearch/wists), or access the site and start building your own Wist at www.wists.com.

Your MyWeb searches and bookmarks are integrated into your Yahoo search results; basically, you're helping Yahoo's search engine become more functional as you use their stable of services. As you personalize your searches, Yahoo "learns" from you and configures the searches it shows you to be more relevant to your needs. Since we're all interested in better and more relevant search engine results, this is definitely a great development. Because I'm a longtime Yahoo user, I like the fact that I can use Yahoo MyWeb right along with all the other Yahoo services that I'm using: Yahoo Mail, Yahoo search, etc. Since I'm already signed in, it's natural to just start bookmarking away.

StumbleUpon is one of the most creative ways to explore the Web. I use my StumbleUpon toolbar throughout the day to find new and interesting sites all over the spectrum. Because the StumbleUpon database is filled only with sites preapproved by yourself and other avid Stumblers, you know that you're going to find just the best results. There's a bare minimum of spam or useless links here, mostly because the StumbleUpon community does a stellar job of weeding them out.

The more you use StumbleUpon, the more it learns your preferences and starts to send sites your way that match what you like. It does this because one of the biggest StumbleUpon features is giving sites a thumbs up or down as you come across them; so, if you're not appreciative of the Menudo fan site you found, you can give it a thumbs down, telling StumbleUpon you don't want to see it again. Your preferences are saved and logged for future stumbles. There's also a StumbleUpon strictly for Web videos found at www.video.stumbleupon.com/ that functions pretty much the same way as the Web-search-specific StumbleUpon, except with videos. One thing to keep in mind with Stumble Video is that non-family-friendly videos do sometimes make it through, so be careful when

WHAT'S HOT

▶ Perhaps you're just not into these social content communities that I've pitched so far. Say you're looking for a hub created around American Idol, or the latest presidential race, or quilting. Then you should take a look at Ning (www.ning.com), a site that lets you easily create your very own social community on anything your little heart desires. Finally, a good place for my shoe obsession!

video-Stumbling with younger viewers (I found this out the hard way, unfortunately!).

And that's just the beginning! So, as you can see, the social Web is a pretty new development in the world of Web search, and it's innovating all the time with new features and benefits for the Web searcher. The social Web is all about connecting people in order to find what you need faster and more effectively.

The most compelling reason why I love the social Web has to be this: I am no longer searching alone, but with literally millions of other people who are scouring the Web for the best sites on a virtually limitless array of topics. Now that's the way to search the Web!

ELSEWHERE ON THE WEB

▶ Netscape has done some rearranging: they've gone from a portal site to a community site, where users can submit, vote on, and comment on stories, much like Digg, another popular social bookmarking/networking site. Read more about the new Netscape here: http://about.com/websearch/newnetscape.

Get Linked

Want more of the social Web? Here are some resources on my About. com Web Search site that will help you out.

SHARE2ME

Share2me is a free browser plug-in that allows you to share your favorite stuff on the Web with your friends across a variety of platforms with just one click.

http://about.com/websearch/share2me

HOW TO USE DEL.ICIO.US

Del.icio.us is a great social bookmarking tool that allows you to tag and share your favorite Web sites with fellow del.icio.us users all over the world. Find out more about del.icio.us and how to use it.

http://about.com/websearch/howtousedelicious

HOW TO USE DIGG

Digg is a user-driven Web site; all the content on Digg is submitted and moderated by Digg users. Learn more about this popular social community and how to use it.

http://about.com/websearch/howtousedigg

Chapter 8

Digging Deeper with the Invisible Web

What Is the Invisible Web?

The Web is a big place. In fact, many studies show that the visible Web—that which is actually indexed by search engines—is only ⅟₅₀₀th of the entire Web. That's a pretty amazing statistic!

So what does that mean exactly? Is there a secret part of the World Wide Web that's only accessible by some kind of secret password? No, of course not; actually, there's nothing really mysterious about it. First, there is the visible Web, the part of the Web that is generally accessible through search engines, search directories, etc. In other words, it's ready and waiting for you to find it.

Then there's the invisible Web, also known as the deep Web—the part of the Web that is *not* necessarily accessible through search engines or search directories for various reasons. The content may be password-protected, behind a firewall, in a format unfriendly to search engines, or simply not linked to anything else. The term "invisible Web" mainly refers to this vast repository of information that search engines and directories don't have direct access to. Unlike pages on the visible Web, information on the invisible Web is generally inaccessible to the software spiders and crawlers that create search engine indexes; this is slowly changing, but there is still a vast repository of information out there yet to be discovered and indexed by search engines.

Now, the term "invisible Web" is just a tad misleading. It certainly does not mean that there is a part of the Web that is invisible. The invisible Web just refers to information that is a bit more difficult to dig for than your average Web search query. For example, if you think of the Web as a mine to be explored, you know that there are diamonds down deep in the caverns, but you have to figure out how to get there. It's the same with the invisible Web; the information is there, the information is accessible—but you're going to have to dig deeper in order to get to it.

The Importance of the Invisible Web

Why is the invisible Web important? I can answer that in one word: quality. Most of the information on the invisible Web is very topic-focused, simply because most of this fantastic information is packaged in various databases concerning everything from archaeology to zoology. Because this information is so narrow—and for the most part, academically oriented—you're more likely to obtain higher than average quality search results in a shorter amount of time, which definitely comes in handy when you're trying to do a research paper on a deadline.

This is definitely not to suggest that the deep Web is somehow more important than the surface Web. The invisible Web tends to be more relevant to specific informational queries, while the surface, or visible, Web tends to have a virtual smorgasbord of content in answer to your query that might or might not be

ELSEWHERE ON THE WEB

▶ If you'd like to read an in-depth research paper on the deep Web, I highly recommend Michael Bergman's "The Deep Web: Surfacing Hidden Value" hosted at the University of Michigan's Web site (www.press.umich.edu/jep/07-01/bergman.html). The paper is full of interesting deep Web statistics, facts, and figures that will help you get a better picture of what the invisible Web is all about; plus, it really puts into perspective how big the Web actually is.

completely relevant. We're basically looking at two different pipelines of information that must be interpreted and extrapolated two vastly different ways.

A good searcher will not only use search engines efficiently but will also know how to dig deeper into the vast river of resources that is the invisible Web. A well-rounded approach to searching the Web includes a thorough understanding of both these search processes.

The invisible Web is also important because of its sheer size. Let me explain this point with a few statistics from a Bright Planet white paper on the deep Web (found at www.brightplanet .com/resources/details/deepweb.html):

- Public information on the deep Web is currently 400 to 550 times larger than the commonly defined World Wide Web.
- The deep Web contains 7,500 terabytes of information compared to nineteen terabytes of information in the surface Web.
- The deep Web contains nearly 550 billion individual documents compared to the one billion of the surface Web.
- More than 200,000 deep Web sites presently exist.
- Sixty of the largest deep Web sites collectively contain about 750 terabytes of information—sufficient by themselves to exceed the size of the surface Web forty times.
- On average, deep Web sites receive 50 percent greater monthly traffic than surface sites and are more highly linked to than surface sites; however, the typical (median) deep Web site is not well-known to the Internet-searching public.
- The deep Web is the largest growing category of new information on the Internet.

TOOLS YOU NEED

▶ The invisible Web has a gold mine of medical databases and specialized medical sites that just don't show up on a cursory search in the search engines; I've put them together here: http://about .com/websearch/invisible medicalsearch. My favorite resources on this list? The National Library of Medicine (www.nlm.nih.gov), Family-Doctor (http://familydoctor .org), and OmniMedical Search (www.omnimedical search.com). Please note: Online medical information should never substitute for the expertise of a real, live doctor. If you or someone you love needs medical attention, make sure you get it.

- Deep Web sites tend to be narrower, with deeper content, than conventional surface sites.
- Total quality content of the deep Web is 1,000 to 2,000 times greater than that of the surface Web.
- Deep Web content is highly relevant to every information need, market, and domain.
- More than half of the deep Web content resides in topic-specific databases.
- A full 95 percent of the deep Web is publicly accessible information—not subject to fees or subscriptions.

Now, you might be wondering why this content is not more accessible. To find out, we've got to go back to the origins of the Web that we covered in Chapter 1—basically, what makes the Web the Web.

The most relevant reason is this: hyperlinks. Remember, the Web is made up of links to content. Without these connections, this content would stand alone, defeating the original purpose of the Web, which was to encourage connectivity of all kinds—people, ideas, content, etc.

Dynamic links aren't always indexed. I'm going to skip the techno-jargon, but suffice to say that static links are more easily crawled than dynamic links by search engine spiders, the software that search engines use to discover and index links for their databases. Dynamic links—those commonly used in databases—are just harder to crawl, so these links are not always included.

Basically, searching the invisible Web is comparable to deep sea fishing. You don't really know what's going to come up in your net, and there's certainly going to be a huge number of things that you're going to miss out on. Why? The answer is simple: the Web

Why isn't the invisible Web better known?

▶ Most Web searchers content themselves with what they find on the first page of their search engine results—and that's perfectly okay. However, since the Web has grown at such a fantastic rate, it's no longer enough to merely scrape the surface. The vast volume of sites that are being published on the Web in database or other non-search-engine-friendly form invites us to dig deeper.

has grown at an incredible pace, and even the most technologically evolved search engines can't keep up with the glut of information that is out there.

You can't see what you're missing on the ocean floor, and neither can search engines: they scoop up a lot of information, to be sure, but they still miss a tremendous amount of it. Search engines can't find what they can't see, and that's why the invisible Web exists: It's content that is not immediately available in a cursory Web search.

Accessing the invisible Web could be likened to this scenario: You run to the grocery store for some ice cream, but before you can get to the Rocky Road you crave, you have to find the secret access point, hidden somewhere in the store, for the freezer section. Search engine spiders attempting to index invisible Web links are running up against the same problem, which is why this information is not readily accessible—unless you know how to find that access point/gateway, which is what we're about to learn how to do.

Invisible Web Gateways

We've learned so far that the invisible Web is vastly untapped because of its lack of accessibility. However, the invisible Web is hidden in plain sight. How do you learn to look for something that isn't really hiding? Why, you just change your methods of discovery.

We already know that most of the content on the invisible Web is contained within databases whose entry points are not directly accessible via your favorite search engine. Now, if we knew the URLs of the databases in which the content we wanted was to be found, we could type them into our browsers and be done with it, right? Well, in a sense. First of all, most of us don't know the URLs of these specialty databases off the top of our heads (I certainly don't, anyway), and secondly, unless we are laser-focused

ELSEWHERE ON THE WEB

▶ You can find a good, succinct discussion of dynamic links versus static links at Lori's Web Design Blog: "How Dynamic Web Pages Rank in Search Engines Compared to Static Web Pages" (www.loriswebs.com/dynamicstatic.html). Once you understand how dynamic and static links work, you get a feel for how the invisible Web started to actually become "invisible"—well, at least to search engines.

on what we are looking for, one database is probably not going to hold all the answers we need.

This is where invisible Web gateways come in. Basically, these are portals, hubs of information that very smart folks have put together to better categorize and organize the diverse resources on the deep Web. These gateways make it easier for searchers to find a wider breadth of information all in one place by topic. Instead of just one database about archaeology, for example, you'll be offered twenty different databases on archaeology, thereby giving you a much broader range of information to draw from. There are many invisible Web gateways currently on the Web, and listed below are the best of the best.

The amount of information offered on Gary Price's Invisible Web Resources (www.freepint.com/gary/direct.htm) is frankly overwhelming, so tread carefully. The best way to find what you're looking for here is to use the search tool offered at the top of the page; you can really narrow down the glut of resources. This site is an excellent place to start your invisible Web journey.

The University of Michigan has put together OAIster, (pronounced "oyster") and encourages you to "find the pearls" on the invisible Web. They have millions of records from more than 405 institutions as diverse as African Journals Online and the Library Network of Western Switzerland. Find it at www.oaister.org/.

The Library Spot (www.libraryspot.com) is a collection of databases, online libraries, references, and other good info from the invisible Web. Be sure to check out their "You Asked for It" section, where popular readers' questions are featured.

The U.S. government's official Web portal is USA.gov, an extremely deep (as in lots of content) site. You could spend hours here. It's interesting to note how much you can do online here as well, such as renew your driver's license, shop government auctions, and contact elected officials. Check it out at www.usa.gov.

The University of Idaho has put together an incredible repository of original sources at www.uidaho.edu/special-collections/iil.htm. This is a listing of over 5,000 different Web sites that offer treasure troves of original manuscripts, archives, excerpts from rare books, and other sources for anyone who's looking to do some research.

Need to access a scholarly journal? Most journals that you need can be found right online at the Directory of Open Access Journals (www.doaj.org): Over 2,500 journals in this directory; an excellent place to find scholarly journals of all kinds.

Infomine (http://infomine.ucr.edu), home of "scholarly Internet resource collections," is a gold mine of invisible Web resources. Infomine gives searchers a plethora of academic resources, from databases to bulletin boards to electronic journals and more.

Academic Info (www.academicinfo.us) is a subject directory of over 25,000 informational resources for students, as well as academic test preparation. It's a good collection of research-oriented resources.

The Librarians' Internet Index (http://lii.org) is probably my favorite deep-Web-oriented site—there is just *so much good stuff* here. I particularly enjoy the "New This Week" feature; you can subscribe via RSS or e-mail to receive about fifty new Web sites a week found by the LII staff.

BUBL Information Service (www.bubl.ac.uk/) is a gigantic database covering pretty much any academic subject area. And they're not kidding around, either—everything's here from philosophy to history, organized in a Dewey Decimal–like fashion.

Intute (www.intute.ac.uk) is a collaboration of seven different UK universities working together to find the best academic and

ELSEWHERE ON THE WEB

▶ Yahoo recently unveiled a service that would allow users to access more deep Web content, including services that were previously subscription-only access. You can check it out for yourself at Yahoo Search Subscriptions (http://search.yahoo.com/subscriptions). Note: Not all subscription content is available to non-subscribed users, but you do receive access to sites through this Yahoo service that were not necessarily available to you before in cursory Web searches.

research resources on both the visible and invisible Web. A fantastic source of all kinds of information.

NLM Gateway Search (http://gateway.nlm.nih.gov/gw/Cmd) is the U.S. National Medical Library's gateway to at least twenty different databases. You can jump from database to database, collecting what you need, and finding more content that you might not have discovered otherwise. This is literally the world's largest medical library/database; a vast wealth of information is available here. Currently, this is a page with a search box that lets you search the twenty-three listed databases simultaneously. You can also search them individually, with search refinements.

Invisible Web Search Engines

Amazing, isn't it, the amount of information so readily available once you're given the tools to access it? I hope you have a chance to poke through some of those invisible Web gateways that I've given you. But even though these hubs are pretty extensive, they don't even begin to cover the plethora of information available to you on the invisible Web. That's where invisible Web search engines come into the picture.

No single search engine can search the entire invisible Web. However, these invisible Web search engines are specifically targeted to only search through resources that are not readily available on the surface Web, and they have indexed hundreds of thousands of documents, sites, and otherwise inaccessible content.

CompletePlanet (www.completeplanet.com) is a deep Web search engine with fast service, relevant results, and an easy-to-use interface. CompletePlanet searches more than 70,000 searchable databases and specialty search engines, a pretty impressive number, and I found that my search results for a number of different queries

WHAT'S HOT

▶ Search through hundreds of thousands of U.S. patents at the official Patent Full-Text and Full-Page Image Database (www.uspto.gov/patft). Full-text patents from 1976 and forward are available, as well as full-page patent images all the way back to 1790. In order to get the most out of this database, try to have the official name of the patent item or idea that you're looking for readily available to make your search more efficient.

were right on target with credible, reliable results (most worthy of a good footnote or two). CompletePlanet is not just a great research tool for the casual Web surfer who's looking for some answers—for the student or researcher, it is absolutely invaluable.

Scirus (www.scirus.com/srsapp/) is a science search engine dedicated to searching only science-specific content, and all of it is research- and/or academically oriented. Currently, Scirus is searching over 250 million science-specific Web pages, filtering out those results that are not science-related in order for you, the user, to quickly pinpoint what you're looking for.

SurfWax (www.surfwax.com/) is an invisible Web search engine with some terrific features, including a peripheral database search for NCBI (National Center for Biotechnology Information). SurfWax gives you the option to grab results from multiple search engines at the same time, or you can sign up for free to get more SurfWax features; the Free level allows you to create three SearchSets, a customized set of your favorite sources that you find yourself using time and time again. In addition, SurfWax offers a WikiSearch (www.wikiwax.com/) that you can use to dynamically search Wikipedia, an online community encyclopedia; an RSS feed search (http://lookahead.surfwax.com/rss-index.html); and a fantastic news index with over 50,000 sources (http://news.surfwax.com/), separated by topic.

Turbo10 (www.turbo10.com) is a search engine that trawls the invisible Web for results. Turbo10 connects you to deeper, higher-quality information from niche-specific search engines, and enables the searcher to access databases from government entities, businesses, and universities. Basically, Turbo10 has cut out some of the middleman work you would have to do to get to these resources on your own.

IncyWincy (www.incywincy.com/) indexes millions of pages both on the visible and invisible Web. IncyWincy is definitely a

ELSEWHERE ON THE WEB

▶ Search through full texts of books and articles with Google Scholar (http://scholar.google.com/), a peripheral service of Google that gives you access to scholarly content. Not all content is fully searchable here; however, you will see links to journals, books, etc. that you can check out at your local library. This is a good place to start your research or check out a very small portion of the invisible Web.

good resource for anyone who's eager to dig deeper into the invisible Web. Do a general Web search; you can also perform a search for forms or images, and search through the IncyWincy directory (based on the Open Directory, or DMOZ, one of the oldest subject directories on the Web today).

Top Twenty Must-Have Databases on the Invisible Web

We've looked at invisible Web gateways and search engines, which are the two most streamlined ways that you can access the invisible Web quickly and with a minimum of effort. Still, these resources don't even begin to cover all the information you can access—which is why I've put together my list of the must-have invisible Web databases. Basically, these are the ones that you'd want with you on a desert island (along with a good satellite phone and a rubber dinghy . . . but I digress):

The National Portrait Gallery (www.npg.si.edu/): This site is a service of the Smithsonian. Altogether, you're able to search nearly 200,000 historical works of art here, from the Portrait Gallery's collections of paintings, sculpture, prints, drawings, and photographs to the Catalog of American Portraits, a national survey of American portraits in public and private collections across the United States and abroad. You can search by names, dates, or biographical keywords for more than 50,000 portrait sitters or artists before linking to the works of art. An incredibly rich resource.

Project Gutenberg (www.gutenberg.org/wiki/Main_Page): One of my favorite sites on the Web has to be Project Gutenberg, where you can find more than 20,000 free books for downloading (audio books as well).

Hoover's Company Information (www.hoovers.com/free/): You can search for free through most of the Hoover business and company listings. Your search options include the name

▶ One very good resource of invisible Web legal information is FindLaw (www.findlaw.com/), a search engine that offers searchers an extremely comprehensive array of legal information. If you've ever tried to search the surface Web for legal info, you know how frustrating and utterly mind-boggling it can be; FindLaw is an excellent alternative to general search results that offers everything from forms to Supreme Court cases.

or ticker symbol of the company, an A to Z listing, and specific geographical listings.

Kelley Blue Book (www.kbb.com): I bought my last car with the help of the online Kelley Blue Book, a gigantic free database that gives you the market value of new and used cars. It's an invaluable resource to tap into when you're making that auto purchase.

U.S. Bureau of Labor Statistics (www.bls.gov): Want to know how much you should be making in your present position? How about the outlook of that career you're considering, or do you need up-to-the-minute unemployment statistics? The Bureau of Labor Statistics is definitely the place to find all this information and much, much more.

Catalog of U.S. Government Publications (http://catalog.gpo.gov/F): If you're looking for a government form or document, this would be a good place to start. The CGP is the centerpoint for finding federal publications, both current and historical.

The National Archives (www.archives.gov): Find historical documents, genealogical information, and more here at the National Archives, a superb resource that allows you to peek back into history via a variety of historical and archived documents.

ERIC—Education Resources Information Center (www.eric.ed.gov/ERICWebPortal/Home.portal): If you've ever done research in a university library, more likely than not your friendly librarian was tapping into some form of ERIC, one of the most widely used research databases on the Web today with over 1.2 million records available.

The Internet Public Library (www.ipl.org/): This is an enormous subject collection/database that covers a wide range of topics, maintained by a consortium of fourteen different universities.

The CIA Electronic Reading Room (www.foia.cia.gov/): If you've ever wanted to read declassified documents, this would be the place—it's a gold mine of declassified access to all sorts of CIA documents.

The World Factbook ([www.cia.gov/cia/publications/fact book/index.html](www.cia.gov/cia/publications/factbook/index.html)): Get detailed demographic data on every country in the world from the CIA World Factbook: country profiles, geographic information, population statistics, and more.

Thomas (http://thomas.loc.gov): Here is United States legislative information all in one convenient place, courtesy of the Library of Congress. You can find everything from bills and resolutions to information about your representatives right here.

The Library of Congress (www.loc.gov/search/new): An all-in-one search interface for the gigantic Library of Congress is now available; you can search the U.S. historical and cultural collections, prints and photographs, online catalogs, and more from here.

PubMed (www.ncbi.nlm.nih.gov/entrez/query.fcgi?DB=pubmed): PubMed, one of the largest medical databases on the Web, exists as a service of the U.S. National Library of Medicine. Over 16 million pieces of content are available for research here.

USGS Earthquake Hazards Program (http://quake.usgs.gov/): This site offers real-time tracking for earthquakes all over the world, updated research from the field, basic earthquake safety information, and much more.

Federal Aviation Administration (www.fly.faa.gov/flyfaa/usmap.jsp): Get general status reports for every airport in the United States; it's a good place to check before you leave the house for a flight.

Ellis Island Database (www.ellisislandrecords.org/): From the Port of New York, a free database of millions of immigration records. It's an invaluable tool for anyone who is interested in researching their genealogy.

WorldCat (www.worldcat.org/): Search for content both on and off the Web with WorldCat, a unique database that searches the collections of libraries both near you and around the world. WorldCat even offers help from actual librarians—a nice touch.

I could keep going on for a while here—the breadth and variety of information available in invisible Web databases is utterly amazing. However, that should give you enough to chew on for a while.

Using Google to Directly Search the Invisible Web

You can use search engines, such as Google and Yahoo, to search the invisible Web for database information, such as that from a college university or library. Think of these general search engines as the tool you initially use to narrow your search down to invisible Web databases. Basically, almost any database that is available in some form on the Web can be found using Google or your search engine of choice; you just have to use a bit of ingenuity to find it.

For instance, a query for gardening and flowers in Google returns so many results that it's difficult to know what to do with them all, let alone figure out which results are the more credible, especially when you're doing a research project. However, you can use this search string instead to improve your results:

```
flowers database
```

Simple! That's one of the tricks you can use to find invisible Web content—just put the word "database" in your query and more often than not you'll come back lucky. The results for this query had more searchable information regarding flowers than I'll ever need. Plus, many databases are part of an accredited academic (and footnote-able) institution.

Let's try another query: Say you're doing an in-depth report on the past ten years' plane crashes in Argentina. Try a query for "plane crash Argentina" in Google and you'll get mostly news items, which would take a long time to comb through. However, try this query instead:

aviation database

You'll get a lot more information than you can actually use in a report or research project. Basically, typing your subject and "database" in Google or your favorite search engine will net you a big haul of really good, credible, citeworthy results. And the quality of information that you retrieve with this simple query tends to be above and beyond what you would get with your regular Web search results.

Get Linked

Want even more information about the invisible Web? Here are some great resources on my About.com Web Search site that will provide you with more deep Web resources.

WHAT IS THE INVISIBLE WEB?

Is the invisible Web some kind of Area 52-ish, X-Files deal that only those with stamped numbers on their foreheads can access? Well, not exactly. The term "invisible Web" mainly refers to the vast repository of information that search engines and directories don't have direct access to, like databases.

http://about.com/websearch/invisibleweb

THE INTERNET MOVIE DATABASE (IMDB)

The Internet Movie Database is the biggest movie database on the Web. Featuring top movies, movie news, movie reviews, movie trailers, movie showtimes, DVD movie reviews, celebrity profiles, etc., truly a mammoth depository of movie information. This article describes how to find content on IMDb that doesn't often appear in search results.

http://about.com/websearch/imdb

EDUCATIONWORLD— AN EDUCATION DATABASE

EducationWorld is an extremely deep site that not only has a search engine focused solely on educational and teaching-related Web sites, but also has extensive resources for educators and parents. Read this article for a review and how-to of the site.

http://about.com/websearch/educationworld

Chapter 9

Using the Web as Your Personal Librarian

Finding a Topic to Research

To say that the Web is a researcher's dream come true is an understatement. Resources of every kind can be found online, from detailed journals to firsthand accounts to primary sources—not to mention the archival treasures and multimedia references. Whether you're a student looking for information to round out a research report, a businessperson gathering statistics for a comprehensive budget report, or a Web surfer just interested in getting to the root of an issue, you'll find that the Web's assistance is absolutely invaluable.

Search engines are good starting points. The easiest place to start your research is at your friendly neighborhood search engine. However, one search engine does not fit all queries. Even though you'd probably get pretty good results if you did what most

About.com

folks on the Web do these days and just "Googled it," you still
might be missing out on some vital information that is either not in
the Google index or just not on the first, second, third . . . or tenth
page of search results.

Remember, you have many search engine tools in your Web
search toolbox. The problem is not too few tools, but too many!
How do you choose the best tool for the job? Well, it depends on
what you need.

**Sometimes we need help finding a topic to research
first.** Has this ever happened to you? You're assigned an essay or
a science project and you're given free rein to choose the topic . . .
yikes! What do you do? Fortunately, there are Web search tools
that can help with this scenario.

Clusty (http://clusty.com) is one of my favorite search engines
because of one very special feature: clustered results (hence the
name "clusty"). Clusty is a meta search engine; meaning that it
grabs results from a variety of different search engines and search
directories. Type any subject into the Clusty search bar and you'll
be returned not only the standard search engine results, but clustered search results as well—related "suggestions" that build upon
your original query. In addition to being a great way to search for
general information, Clusty is also a superb way to find a topic to
research.

a9.com (www.a9.com) is in part powered by Amazon.com
and Microsoft's Windows Live, and has many interesting features.
However, the feature that I use most often is the layout—a three-
column newspaper template with search "groups" on the far left,
Windows Live results in the middle, and corresponding Amazon.
com book results on the right. Why is this so useful? Because I am
getting another kind of clustered results here, much like Clusty's,
except from different types of sources. Super idea-generator.

Kartoo (www.kartoo.com/) is a visual search engine. In other words, your search results are represented visually rather than in textual list form. Kartoo is ideal for generating research ideas; thanks to the way Kartoo presents search results, you can pretty much plan an entire project outline just from the strength of one query return. For instance, I typed in "bronte" and received back a dozen different subtopics of this venerated author, including biography, books, history, etc.—all with corresponding images, a nice touch.

Infomine (www.infomine.com) is a virtual library of information. Just start browsing through the thousands of topics they cover, and there's no way you won't be able to come up with a good research topic.

Ask (www.ask.com) has a fantastic feature that allows you to narrow or expand any topic you might want to type in. For example, I typed in the word "web," and under the heading "Narrow Your Results" I received these suggestions: live **webcam**, spider web, World Wide Web, etc. For "Expand Your Results," I got Internet Webshots, Webcrawler, etc.—you get the picture. Basically, Ask. com is helping you to start broad and circle in for more details; this is not only helpful when you aren't sure what to research, but also obviously useful when you're looking for more detailed information and need help finding it.

Discovering Quality Results

Okay, so now that we've covered how to find a topic, let's tackle another search engine research challenge: using the Web to find worthwhile results.

When you're using the Web for research, finding quality results becomes extremely important, especially if you're using what you find as an authoritative source. We'll go more into how to actually evaluate Web sources for citeworthiness in Chapter 10; for now,

I'm going to show you a few sites that you can generally rely on to be trustworthy sources of information. (Note: I say "generally" because no one Web source should be relied upon, no matter how reputable. Always be ready to back up your Web sources with print research if needed.)

Some sites are more credible than others. The following sites are ones that are credible sources of information. They have either been compiled by authoritative and scholarly experts in a variety of fields or been endorsed by reputable scholars or librarians. This is by no means an exhaustive list. There are hundreds, if not thousands, of informational sites that are superb for research; these are just the ones that I find myself using the most often.

About.com (http://about.com): I've found answers to some pretty obscure questions at About.com, from the story behind the Da Vinci code to the real story behind many urban legends.

Reference.com (www.reference.com): This is one of my favorite reference sites on the Web for one simple reason: it's extremely simple to use. It's laid out in basic reference categories such as Almanacs, Business, Literature, etc. that you can use to drill down to more specific resources.

The Scholes Library Reference Desk (http://scholes .alfred.edu/ref_desk/ref.html): Think of your friendly neighborhood librarian and you won't be too far off the mark here at Scholes Library. Resources are categorized into types: encyclopedias, dictionaries, etc.

Martindale's Reference Desk (www.martindalecenter .com/): This is one of the best places on the Web to find quality art, business, science, and technology resources. You'll be hard pressed to find one site listed here that is not citeworthy.

Wikipedia (http://en.wikipedia.org/wiki/Main_Page): Wikipedia is a free, multisource encyclopedia—but it's not like any ency-

▶ Many times during the course of various research projects I've undertaken, I've needed to back up various lines of thought with concrete statistics. One of the best places I've found to do that is at the Pew Research Center (http://pewresearch .org/), an organization that gathers facts and figures on a variety of different topics and shares them with the public. It's a good place to find relevant information; they've been an invaluable source to me, especially for technology-related projects.

clopedia you've ever read. Wikipedia is at its heart a **wiki**, which is basically a hub of content that anyone can edit. What this means is that while Wikipedia is a highly useful resource (and one that I use frequently), you must take entries here with a large teaspoon of salt. The information is correct more often than not, but be wary of citing Wikipedia as fact.

Open Directory Reference (www.dmoz.org/Reference/): Your head will spin when you see the number of sites here at the Open Directory's guide to various reference resources on the Web. They're arranged categorically for quick drilldown.

The Internet Public Library (www.ipl.org/): The Internet Public Library is an invaluable resource with thousands of reputable sites, all organized into topical categories that make it easy to find what you're looking for.

Librarians Internet Index (http://lii.org/): One of my very favorite sites on the Web. You could spend hours here lost in the vast variety of information and resources, and since this site was built and maintained by librarians whose goal is to find quality sites, you know that the information you find here is going to be good.

American Memory from the Library of Congress (http://memory.loc.gov/ammem/browse/): Browse the entire American Memory collection from the Library of Congress all in one place, organized by subject ranging from Advertising to Women's History. This is one of the most reputable collections of primary sources (original source documents) you can find anywhere.

The University of Michigan Documents Center (www.lib.umich.edu/govdocs/): Speaking of primary sources, you can't do much better than the Umich Documents Center, a repository for all kinds of government information.

Best Online Documentaries (http://best.online.docus.googlepages.com/): I don't know about you, but I find that I retain information better if it's presented to me in a visual manner. Many

What is a wiki?

▶ A wiki is an open source of content that anyone can edit. Wikis have gained popularity with the rise of Wikipedia, a community encyclopedia; many educators, students, and people in the business world (including myself) have found them to be an invaluable planning tool. For instance, there's PBWiki (http://pbwiki.com/), wikiHow (www.wikihow.com/Main-Page), an open source Web manual, and Wikimapia (www.wikimapia.org/), a Wikipedia/Google mashup that allows users to geotag locations with appropriate articles.

research projects can be well-rounded with relevant, quality documentary treatments—and that's where the site Best Online Documentaries comes in handy. Arranged by categories from Anthropology to Technology, you can find all sorts of full-length documentaries here to augment your research, thereby possibly saving you a trip to the library or university book store.

I could give you another dozen sites off the top of my head, but these mass repositories of information should keep you going for a while.

Finding Information in Specific Categories

Many research projects benefit from specific, discipline-focused information. For example, if you're doing a report on the life cycles of Madagascar bumblebees, you're going to need a source that's targeted.

We covered many source-specific databases in Chapter 8, Digging Deeper with the Invisible Web; however, as I said before, there are hundreds of thousands of databases and other hubs of content that can help you find what you need.

The Web abounds in humanities sites. There are so many great humanities resources on the Web that it's really difficult to limit myself to just a few. For thousands of different art and art-related sites all in one place, I would highly recommend NetSERF's Art section (www.netserf.org/Art/), a collection of at least a dozen different categories of high-quality art resources. Then there's the Arts Database at Yale (www.library.yale.edu/art/databases .html), a superb collection of both arts and humanities databases and resources on the Web (not all of these are available to non-Yale students and researchers, but most are). EDSITEment (www .edsitement.neh.gov/) is a service from the National Endowment for the Humanities, an organization that offers up some of the

TOOLS YOU NEED

▶ Yahoo offers a variety of shortcuts and tools that will help you research your topic. I've put together just a few of these shortcuts in my article titled "Yahoo Search Cheat Sheet" (http://about.com/ websearch/yahoocheatsheet); you'll find that using these Yahoo Search Shortcuts will greatly cut down on your Yahoo search time, and you'll be pleasantly surprised at how much good stuff Yahoo has to offer with just a few simple commands.

world's best humanities resources. Lastly, there's Intute's Arts and Humanities collection (www.intute.ac.uk/artsandhumanities/), over 18,000 quality resources just waiting for you to find them.

Check the credentials of your science sites. When writing up a science or technology report, it's absolutely crucial to get your facts from reputable sources. Coming close just won't cut it in such exact disciplines. Therefore, the sites that you choose for your research must be of the top quality.

I like SciSearch (http://library.dialog.com/bluesheets/html/bl0034 .html); it's somewhat intimidating at first but well worth the effort spent trying to figure it out. Basically, it's an index to articles from scientific journals that are especially useful for a higher-level research paper. Then there's Science.gov (www.science.gov/), the United States' gateway to over 50 million pages of authoritative science and technology information, including up-to-date research, articles, and stats. SciCentral (www.scicentral.com/) is a science news aggregator; this is a super place to get the latest news on a variety of science-related topics. I've mentioned Scirus (www.scirus.com/) before, and it's such a wonderful resource that it's definitely worth mentioning again—it's a science-focused search engine pulling in results from thousands of different high quality sources.

If you're looking for credible sources to back up your research, a great place to start would be EurekAlert (www.eurekalert.org/ pubnews.php?view=titles), another science news aggregator that you can use to drill down deeper into topics that interest you.

Last but not least on my short list would be the Public Library of Science (www.plos.org), a resource put together by a nonprofit consortium of scientists all over the world.

History lives on the Internet. I love finding history sites. Since this is another subject where your facts must be from reliable

▶ Almost every great museum in the world has a Web site, full of information about current exhibits, galleries, and imagery. Many offer in-depth information on their exhibited pieces; it's a good way to get some background when researching art or art history. Learn how to find a museum on the Web here: http://about.com/websearch/findamuseum. Take a leisurely stroll through some of the best art in the world today, right from your computer, including the Met (www.metmuseum.org/), the Getty Museum (www.getty.edu/), and the Smithsonian (www.si.edu/).

sources if you want to use them in a research project, the sites you rely on for information must be trustworthy. To that end, I would highly recommend Best of History Web Sites (www.besthistorysites.net/), a great collection of annotated links to over 1,000 different history Web sites, as well as a huge array of lesson plans and other resources for educators.

The Internet Archive's Wayback Machine (www.archive.org/web/web.php) is a unique site covering events from about 1996 on; their mission is to take Web snapshots of historical events and compile a lasting record. For instance, their coverage of September 11 (http://lcweb2.loc.gov/cocoon/minerva/html/sept11/sept11-about.html) is hands down one of the best collections on the Web of that day.

If you're looking for primary source documents, I would suggest that you visit the University of Oklahoma's chronology of U.S. historical documents (www.law.ou.edu/hist/) or the Avalon Project at Yale Law School (www.yale.edu/lawweb/avalon/avalon.htm); both sources provide thousands of primary source documents and information going back to the seventeenth century.

History buffs will love visiting the National Archives (www.archives.gov/), a wonderful source for American history information, and if you're looking for help with religious history, you can't do much better than the Internet Sacred Text Archive (www.sacred-texts.com/index.htm), a gigantic collection of world religious historical documents, facts, and information of all kinds.

There are so many more resources! Even though I've given you a good listing of specific subject resources to start with here, I've had to leave out way too many great sites because of space limitations. For example, there's the wonderful Virtual Library from the University of Texas School of Law (http://tarlton.law.utexas.edu/vlibrary/index.html), a fantastic collection of legal resources;

Artcyclopedia (www.artcyclopedia.com/), a encyclopedia completely dedicated to works of art with access to over 180,000 entries, and Voice of the Shuttle (http://vos.ucsb.edu/), a large collection of links from all sorts of subject categories.

Again, I can't emphasize enough how important it is to choose quality resources you can trust when selecting sources for a research project. I've given you a few (just a few!) sites here as a jumping-off point, and in Chapter 10, I'll show you how to evaluate sites that you come across as worthy of a citation . . . or not.

Uncovering Timely Information

Depending on the nature of your research project, you might need information that is relatively new—e.g., current news. Let's look at different sources you can tap into to find all kinds of timely information.

You need information that is up to the minute. You can't get much more current than Google News (http://news.google.com); their index is updated at least every fifteen minutes. Then there's Topix (www.topix.net), a news aggregator with in-depth information from over 360,000 sources at the time of this writing. Yahoo News (http://news.yahoo.com/) is also frequently updated, but they don't have as many sources to draw from as Google News and Topix.

You need information that is relatively recent. For more in-depth coverage on information that is relatively new (say, one month), you'll want to check out Yahoo Full Coverage (http://news.yahoo.com/fc;_ylt=ApiR6rJCrrINEEQw6IgVl8es0NUE), a compendium of story hubs categorized by general subject. Google News allows you to filter news coverage by the last hour, the last day, the past week, and the past month, and then you can dive into the

Google News Archives (http://news.google.com/archives) to further refine your search.

You need time-focused historical information. Again I would suggest Google News Archives, but there's also HyperHistory (www.hyperhistory.com/online_n2/History_n2/a.html), a visual timeline of historical events; the Metropolitan Museum of Art's timeline of art history (www.metmuseum.org/toah/splash.htm) with corresponding in-depth articles and galleries; and American History's Today in History (http://memory.loc.gov/ammem/today/today.html), where you can search not only for the current day's information, but also in the archival database.

Locating Quick Facts

We've covered how to find those Web sources that will help us dig deeper for any research project; but what about those times when you just need a quick factual answer? That's when the following resources will come in handy—from answer-finding search engines to sites that follow a basic theme, such as "How does this work," and expand upon it.

You're looking for facts about a specific place. You can't do much better than the CIA World Factbook (www.cia.gov/cia/publications/factbook/index.html); you also might want to try InfoPlease's Countries of the World (www.infoplease.com/countries.html) or the Economist's Country Briefings (www.economist.com/countries/), a more economics-slanted view of countries all over the world; in addition, if you're looking for specific facts about states in America, I would suggest the U.S. Census Bureau's Quick-Facts (http://quickfacts.census.gov/qfd/index.html) interactive map.

ELSEWHERE ON THE WEB

▶ Primary source historical documents are easier to find than ever before with the advent of the Web. Read the U.S. Constitution in its entirety at www.usconstitution.net/, find a whole collection of primary source documents pertaining to early American history at www.constitution.org/primarysources/primarysources.html, look at World War II documents at www.ibiblio.org/pha/, or check out the University of Idaho's collection of over 5,000 primary source documents from all over the world at www.uidaho.edu/special-collections/Other.Repositories.html.

Speaking of maps, the Perry-Castaneda Library Map Collection (www.lib.utexas.edu/maps/) is one of the best current and historical maps sites on the Web today. There is also the excellent National Geographic Map Machine (http://plasma.nationalgeographic.com/mapmachine/).

You're looking for facts on a specific person. If you just need a quick fact, like the date of someone's birth, all you need to do is simply type the person's name into Google or Ask.com (Ask also provides more linked information for most historical figures).

However, if you're looking for more than just cursory information, you'll want to check out Biography.com (www.biography.com/search/), a searchable database of over 15,000 biographies. There's also the American Women's History Research Guide (http://frank.mtsu.edu/~kmiddlet/history/women.html) put together by the Middle Tennessee State University. The Biographical Dictionary at s9.com (www.s9.com/) offers biographies for over 30,000 men and women who have made a difference throughout history.

If you're looking for a more esoteric historical biography site, there's Find A Grave (www.findagrave.com/), a site that keeps track of famous people's graves. HistoryMakers (www.thehistorymakers.com/) is a fascinating site that focuses on achievements in African American history; you'll also want to visit the Congressional Biographical Directory (http://bioguide.congress.gov/biosearch/biosearch.asp) if you need information on various U.S. lawmakers.

You need to know how something works. You're going to have good luck finding out how something works merely by Googling it: for instance, if you want to know how MP3 players work, you could just type in this query: "how do mp3 players work" and you'll get relatively good results. However, for absolutely reliable results that you can use as credible research, there are a few sites that I would suggest as backups to this method.

First, the fantastic eHow (www.ehow.com/), whose motto "How to do just about anything" is pretty dang accurate. Then there's wikiHow (www.wikihow.com/Main-Page_), similar to eHow except that it's an open-source manual that anyone—including you—can edit. That makes it both more reliable and less reliable at the same time—more because errors are quickly corrected, and less because even though I know nothing about electrical wiring, I can still edit that particular project. It's a Catch-22, so be wary. There's also the superb How Stuff Works (www.howstuff works.com/), which is one of my favorite sites simply because of the breadth of their offerings; they cover everything from how the Death Star works to the life cycle of butterflies.

You need general facts quickly. There are some really good search engines out there that serve up search results in an answer format, meaning that instead of getting a whole bunch of links to weed through to find what you're looking for, you just get one instant answer.

Answers.com (www.answers.com/) is probably the best of this niche; there's also the excellent Factbites (www.factbites.com/) and Brainboost (www.brainboost.com/). Ask.com (www.ask.com) has a feature called Smart Answer, which is a bit of a shortcut to finding factual answers you need quickly on a variety of subjects from celebrities to historical events.

Online Tools to Help Research

One of the biggest hurdles in putting together a research project is, well, putting it together. How do I cite sources? Where can I find relevant quotations? What does this word mean exactly? You can get help with all of these tasks and many more using the Web.

For instance, if you need help deciphering pretty much any assigned literary work, you'll want to visit SparkNotes' collection of free study guides (www.sparknotes.com/). This is an invaluable resource that certainly helped me get through all six (yes, six!) of my Shakespeare classes.

There's also Zotero (www.zotero.org), a free Firefox extension that helps you collect, manage, and even cite your research sources. You can also use it to take notes, tag and save searches, or store entire PDF files.

The RefDesk (www.refdesk.com/essentl.html) has an extensive list of what they consider to be the most essential research tools, from almanacs to writing guides. Think of this as the reference section behind the central librarian's desk in any university library.

Need something translated? Try Babel Fish (http://babelfish.alta vista.com/), a free language translator that works with more than fifty world languages. You can also use OneLook (www.onelook .com/) to define not only words but entire phrases, or Thesaurus. com (http://thesaurus.reference.com/) to find different words with similar meanings when the writing well has run dry. To give your project extra pizzazz, try Bartlett's Quotations (www.bartleby .com/), a collection of hundreds of thousands of quotes on any subject you can think of.

Part of every good research project is the citations page. Many resources are popping up all over the Web to help with this least popular of research-oriented tasks; among the best are the Owl at Purdue's APA Formatting and Style Guide (http:// owl.english.purdue.edu/owl/resource/560/01/).

However, there are a number of auto-citation sites on the Web as well. (Note: You'll want to double-check these auto-citations against your assigned style guide; they don't always catch everything.) Among them are the Citation Machine (www.citation

WHAT'S HOT

▶ Get all your diction-ary, thesaurus, and gram-mar needs in one place with YourDictionary.com, a super resource that even offers audio pronunciations of selected words. I know I always need a thesaurus when writing, and this is a good one.

machine.net/); CiteBite (www.citebite.com/), which allows you to directly link to quotes on Web pages; and OttoBib (www.ottobib .com/), where you can simply enter in the book's ISBN and receive an automatic citation—you can even choose the format you need, e.g., MLA, APA, Chicago.

Whew! Lots of information, to be sure, and it's only a sampling. The Web is a fantastic source of information and tools for any kind of research you might be planning, and it just keeps on getting better and better.

Get Linked

Looking for more research and reference sources? Check out these articles on my About.com Web Search site.

FINDARTICLES.COM, AN ARTICLE SEARCH ENGINE

FindArticles, a property of LookSmart, is a search engine dedicated to finding articles "from leading academic, industry and general interest publications." It's an invaluable tool for the casual and advanced Web searcher.

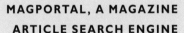
http://about.com/websearch/findarticles

ONELOOK, A SEARCH ENGINE FOR WORDS AND PHRASES

OneLook is a dictionary and translation meta search engine. One-Look searches more than 900 online dictionaries (at the time of this writing) to find whatever definition you're looking for; in addition, you can use OneLook to find translations of a particular word in other languages.

http://about.com/websearch/onelook

MAGPORTAL, A MAGAZINE ARTICLE SEARCH ENGINE

MagPortal is a great research tool that enables the user to find magazine articles on the Web from a variety of different publications.

http://about.com/websearch/magportal

Chapter 10

Evaluating Web Sites for Credibility

Truth and Error on the Web

There are millions of sites on the Web, and all of them are completely accurate, factual, and definitely worth their weight in citations. Right?

Wrong. Actually, this statement couldn't be further from the truth. While there are a great many wonderful sites (many of which I've profiled in this book) that are completely trustworthy and reliable, there are just as many sites out there that are not as consistent with their treatment of the truth as we would like them to be.

Most of the time, this isn't such a big deal—for instance, if you're just idly searching the Web for the latest news on your favorite celebrity, you know that most of the stuff you come across is probably going to be fluff and nonsense. You realize this, and you're prepared for it.

About.com

However, what if you're doing a serious research project or an important school assignment, or finding something that you need for a big development in your workplace? Suddenly, the need for credibility gets much more urgent.

Many people assume that if it's on the Web, it must be true. After all, someone wouldn't go through the trouble of publishing it online if it wasn't accurate. Unfortunately, this is a very misguided assumption. Just because you find it on the Web absolutely does not guarantee that it is worthwhile information. Why? Because anyone can publish whatever they like on the Web with very little effort.

For example, if I really believed that my three cats could do your taxes, I could slap something up within an hour that would be relatively convincing; after all, you don't know exactly how smart my cats are. It's up on the Web, so it must be reliable, right? Obviously, this is an absurd example, but it gives you an idea of how Internet scams are born.

You need to discern truth from fiction on the Web. Whether you're a student, an academic, a businessperson, or just someone who needs truthful information, this is important because an untrustworthy source can at the very least make you look silly; at most, it can get you expelled, fired, or worse. Here are some of the reasons why we need to be on our guard against inaccurate information on the Web:

1. Anyone can publish. My cats doing tax returns was obviously pretty unbelievable, but there are many Web sites out there that don't make it as easy for you to distinguish truth from untruth. You can get ensnared pretty quickly in unreliable facts if you're not careful.

ELSEWHERE ON THE WEB

▶ If you're an educator, you might want to look at Kathy Schrock's Critical Evaluation Surveys, found at http://school.discovery.com/schrockguide/eval.html. These are printable forms for students of all ages, from elementary to college, that can help them critically evaluate Web sites, blogs, and even podcasts. Definitely worth a look if you're teaching your students to have a more critical eye!

2. Most sites do not have outside editorial oversight. If a news reporter puts up something completely nuts on their local news site, eventually someone either on the editorial staff or the public is going to kindly point this out—and this is just one of the reasons why you can rely on most newspaper sites to give you factual information. The more reviewers go through a piece of content before it's allowed up on the Web, the better chance it has of being trustworthy.

3. Not everything is double-checked. I remember (to my embarrassment) writing up what I thought was the best paper of all time for a history class in my freshman year of college; however, I had neglected to do all my homework with one of the Web sites that I used as a source. My professor found glaring errors in my paper and graded me down. Her remarks to me were along the lines of "Your dates were all wrong." If I had bothered to double-check what I had thought was a credible source, I would've discovered that while the main body of information was correct, the dates were completely off-kilter. This is a simple mistake that many people make when they do not double- (and triple-!) check even the most plausible of Web sources.

4. Unlike a library, the Web at large is not maintained by a group of trained experts. If you were to walk into your campus library today and ask a librarian for books on your chosen research subject, he or she would be able to pull up an array of credible sources that have been evaluated, tested, and deemed worthy of citation. Can you do that on the Web? Not exactly. This is not to say that you should not use the Web at all as part of your research; on the contrary, there's seemingly no end to the valuable resources you can unearth online. However, you should utilize common sense when using the Web as part of your reference materials.

WHAT'S HOT

▶ Evaluating sites for trustworthiness is made more fun with Intute's Internet Detective, found at www.vts.intute.ac.uk/detective/index.html. Here, we have the process framed with an intriguing private eye theme, complete with a crime scene, clues, and detective work. I highly recommend this quick little tutorial especially to anyone who's new to college—it does a great job of instructing you how to avoid plagiarism.

5. The Web's weakness is its lack of oversight. Lack of oversight means that the credibility of information on the Web is not necessarily vouched for. I am not suggesting that the Web is not a viable source for any kind of research you might be trying to do. I believe that the Web is a fantastic invention, and it just keeps getting better and better. However, because of the Web's unprecedented and largely unchecked growth, we must all be very cautious when using it as a source, no matter which site we might be looking at.

Tips for Finding Trustworthy Web Sites

In this section, I'll give you some tips to keep in mind when surfing the Web for research, academic or otherwise. These are questions you should ask yourself when you come across a site that looks like a good candidate for a source for your research.

1. What is it that I'm looking for? Many times, a clearly defined focus will help keep me on track and help me find what I'm looking for more efficiently. Rabbit trails are fun, but boy, can they be unproductive!

2. Am I being critical enough? Just because a Web site comes up in the first page of search engine results does not mean that it's an absolutely reliable source. In other words, don't believe everything you read.

3. Am I looking at a big enough range? You've found a great Web site that meets all your research needs—good for you! However, savvy researchers won't ever stop at just one site. Make sure you're gathering enough sources to confirm facts or balance opinions.

4. Would I recommend this Web site to my professor/boss? This might be the best test of all—if you can't confidently suggest that someone in a position of authority over you visit the site you're thinking about using, then it might not be a good choice to include as a source.

Search engines can help you find reliable Web sites. Many searchers believe that once they enter in a query, the most trustworthy site usually will be the one at the very top of the search results. For the most part, this is true. You might remember our discussion way back in Chapter 3 about how search engines rank results; here's a quick refresher course.

The first site listed on your page of search results will probably have a few things going for it that got it to that number one spot: lots of links from other Web sites, a good amount of time spent published online, and relevant content that has been updated on at least a semiregular basis. You might have noticed that I said that the first few sites are reliable "for the most part"; well, that's because while search engines are highly evolved (and getting better all the time), they are not perfect, so bad information can also appear in the first few listings. That's why a critical eye is so important when using the Web for any kind of research.

If you're a student, just use common sense when researching on the Web. Here's a scenario: your professor gives you a research project with an assigned list of sources—for instance, you'll need three encyclopedic sources, two scholarly journal sources, at least three primary source citations, etc. You'll know from reading Chapter 9 on using the Web as your own personal librarian that you can pretty much locate all of this

ASK YOUR GUIDE

What are some consequences of using unreliable sites as sources?

▶ The answer to this is pretty much common sense: if you use a source that is not giving you good information, your project will not only be inaccurate, it will show a lack of critical thinking on your part. Most educators will check the Web sites that you include, and if these sites do not meet the minimum requirements of credibility, you might lose crucial points on an assignment (or have to do it over again).

information on the Web. However, this is where many students get in trouble for a variety of reasons:

WHAT'S HOT

▶ What exactly is plagiarism? Georgetown University has written up a series of in-depth articles on plagiarism at http://gervaseprograms .georgetown.edu/hc/ plagiarism.html. Included here are articles on how to figure out if it's plagiarism or not, what paraphrasing is, common misconceptions, how to avoid plagiarism by citing work, explanations of copyright, and actual examples of plagiarism. It's worth a read if you're at all confused as to what plagiarism might be; I learned a lot from these articles.

- They use random and unchecked Web sites, rather than credible academic sources.
- They use the Web as the primary source for all their research, rather than a supplementary resource. Yes, the Web is a hugely convenient resource, but at some point in your academic career, you'll have to visit the library. The Web is meant to be a complementary tool, not the only tool.
- They use Web sites that only give out one side of the story, rather than present a balanced and accurate view. This can get tricky, but it's very important to track down both viewpoints on potentially divisive issues, especially when you're attempting to win an argument.
- They blatantly cut and paste text from Web sources and fail to cite properly, which is commonly known as plagiarism (and can get you in a heap of trouble). Most professors, if they do discover this, will not only fail you, but are required to report this offense to school authorities. It's just not worth it.

So! To sum up, we've got a few different threads going on here. First, the Web is full of exceptional sources ready to be included in academic research of all kinds. Second, the Web is full of really horrible resources that can not only trip up your research project, but get you in trouble if you are not careful. Sounds like a bit of a paradox, doesn't it? Well, that's where learning to evaluate sites for accuracy on the Web comes into play.

How to Evaluate a Web Site

Judging the truthfulness of information that you find online can be difficult at times. Fiction and reality are not the same thing, but on the Web, it's sometimes hard to tell the difference: for example, there are many sites that claim to have rock-solid evidence that the Holocaust in World War II did not actually happen. If you didn't know any better, you might come across one of these very well-done, scholarly-appearing Web sites and think that they were speaking the truth. That's just one example, and there are many, many more that I could quote you. As P.T. Barnum once famously said, "There's a sucker born every minute."

So how do you divide the wheat from the chaff? How can you tell if something you're reading is true and reliable and worthy of a footnote? You can put Web information through a number of litmus tests to ensure its trustworthiness. Here is a basic Web source evaluation checklist to use to determine if an Internet source is credible enough for an academic or research paper citation:

Who's in charge? Determining the authority of any particular site is especially vital if you're planning to use it as a source for an academic paper or research project. What do I mean by "authority?" It's pretty much common sense here. If you are doing a report on dinosaurs, which site would you choose as a good resource: an official paleontology journal or a hobbyist who just started learning about dinosaurs last week and slapped up a site to explore his new hobby? Sounds simple, until you realize that the hobbyist's site, while actually not a good authority, might look more like an authority on dinosaurs then the paleontology journal. That's why when you're looking at a site for possible inclusion, you must ask yourself the following questions:

Is it absolutely clear which company or organization is responsible for the information on the site? Are you able to find the home page for the linked article that you're looking at? If you can't find the name of the person or organization that is original for the content, you probably don't want to use this source; plus, most academic citation criteria require that you are able to quote the originating source of content.

Is there a link to a page describing what the company or organization does and the people who are involved (an "About Us" page)? This goes right along with finding the source of the content; it's not an absolute requirement, but it does lend more authority to the Web site in question if you can learn more about the person or organization's general background and expertise in the subject.

Is there a valid way of making sure the company or organization is legit—is this a real place that has real contact information? E-mail alone is not enough. Remember, anyone can publish. An actual address, especially for an academically oriented source, will do much to boost the authority of the content.

If you answered "no" to any of these questions, most likely this is not a source you're going to want to include in your bibliography—there's just not enough authority. Let's move on to the next level of Web site evaluation criteria: judging the truthfulness of the information presented.

Is the site telling me the truth? As I've been saying, on the Web you will run into information that is not entirely true, but the falsity might be hard to spot. In addition to determining the authority of a site, you also need to figure out if it's presenting accurate, truthful information to you. Here are a few questions to ask yourself:

Can I easily figure out who wrote the information? If you have to spend more than sixty seconds tracking down the author of the information that you're looking at, you might want to reconsider that particular source. Academic and research-oriented content will almost always have the name of the author right there where you can find it; if you really have to poke around, it's probably not worth a citation.

Are all factual claims clearly substantiated—that is, are there cited (linked) sources? Any Web site that you're thinking about using as part of your research should have clearly linked sources; after all, they've got to cite their sources just like you do. If you read an entire article with lots of facts, figures, and scholarly opinions, yet there are no linked sources, you've got three options: either the author is so incredibly smart that he wrote the entire article off the top of his head without feeling the need to consult any kind of reference; he's made the whole thing up; or he just forgot to link, which is highly unlikely. In all seriousness, if you read a legitimate research source without properly sourced links, you probably will want to find another source.

Are there any glaring grammatical and spelling errors? If there are a lot of really bad spelling and grammatical errors in a potential source, you're probably going to want to rethink it. Good reference articles are usually filtered through a number of editorial controls, and while the odd typo might sometimes get through, a whole host of syntax problems should make you think twice.

How long ago was the page updated? Is there a date stamp on the article somewhere? This particular criterion changes depending

▶ Learn more about how to spot-check domain names for credibility with the University of Illinois's Educators Guide to Credibility and Web Evaluation (http://lrs.ed.uiuc.edu/wp/credibility-2002/homepage.htm), especially the section marked Credibility Indicators, found at http://lrs.ed.uiuc.edu/wp/credibility-2002/methods.htm. At the bottom of this page is more information about examining the actual URL and domain type of a Web site in order to determine credibility; it's a good aid in the process of evaluating a site for trustworthiness.

on the nature of your research. For example, if you're doing a project on Alexander the Great, a recently updated article probably (and I say that with a grain of salt) won't affect the truthfulness of your resource. However, say you're doing a report on the implications of the Enron scandal in the United States. You'll need to find the most up-to-date research out there, so dates suddenly become very important. In addition, most MLA-style citations do require that you cite a date for sources found on the Web; so either way, you'll need to track it down.

Can you verify the expertise of the author? Are the writer's qualifications clearly stated somewhere on the site? This goes to verifying both authority and truthfulness. For example, I could make up a story all about how I'm an expert in glass blowing, complete with everything that might really make me sound as if I know what I'm talking about. However, if you can't find some kind of proof that I know what I'm talking about—whether that be a bio, pictures, linked articles, etc.—then I might not be such a good glass blower after all. Same goes with academic articles; usually you can do a quick Google search of the author's name and the results will help you determine whether the person is an expert in her field.

Once again, if you're not satisfied with the answers to these questions, then you're going to want to find another Web source. That's not to say that your potential source has to meet every single one of these qualifications, but in order for a site to be citeworthy you should feel that it meets at least most of these criteria.

What is your source really trying to tell you? The next step in evaluating a site's credibility is impartiality, or figuring out what's behind the message.

You've got to figure out what's behind the message. Say, for instance, you're researching power motor accidents. The power motor industry would not necessarily be the most neutral of information sources. So in order to find a nonbiased information source, you'll need to determine neutrality.

Ask yourself these questions:

Is there an overwhelming bias in the information? Does the writing seem fair and balanced? Or is the writing overly slanted toward a particular point of view? Academic sources should be fairly objective. For example, if you look up the Battle of Waterloo in an encyclopedia, you probably are not expecting to see a rant on the sartorial habits of Napoleon Bonaparte (if you do, find another encyclopedia, quick!). Find the facts, not opinions, when you're looking for good reference material. Of course, if your topic of research requires opinions, that's a whole 'nother story—but as I mentioned earlier, balanced sources should be found and cited in order to give your project objectivity.

Is the URL appropriate to the content? You should be able to figure out from the site address who the site belongs to, since most organizations and businesses put their name in the URL. This is a good way to quickly determine if the site is legit for your purposes; for example, if you're researching mad cow disease, you probably don't want to get information from the Beef Farmers of America.

Are the ads clearly separated from the content? If you can't easily differentiate which is an ad and which is the content, you might want to move on. There are many Web sites out there designed as legitimate resources that are in reality one giant spammy ad-filled mess; most of the time, these are pretty easy to spot, so this shouldn't be too big a deal.

▸ One of the tools that people can use to find out if something of theirs has been plagiarized on the Web is Copyscape (www.copyscape .com/), a site that finds instances of content taken from the Web without proper attribution. Copyscape works like this: you enter in a snippet of your original content, and Copyscape goes out and tries to find duplicates. It's an easy way to see who's taking unauthorized information.

If the answers to these questions raise doubts in your mind about the site's integrity, then you'll need to reconsider the site as a credible source. Any site that has an inappropriate bias or a hazy line between the advertisements and the content is *not* a good site to use in a research paper or academic project.

The University of Albany has put together a great tutorial on evaluating Web sites, found at http://library.albany.edu/usered/ webeval/. Here they teach you to evaluate Internet resources using a series of six different criteria (author, audience, scholarship, bias, currency, links), figure out whether the Web site you're looking at meets both your needs and established standards of quality, and, best of all, how to apply this critical-thinking process to sources from all mediums, not only the Web.

Avoiding Web Plagiarism

You've found some great sites, they meet your evaluation criteria, and you want to include them as sources. Many people hold the common misconception that because content is on the Web, it is freely available to include in any kind of project you might undertake. In a way, that is a true statement—you can use most any content that you find on the Web, with one important caveat: you must cite the source, otherwise, it's considered plagiarism. Here's a sobering statistic: According to Duke University, the number of students who admit to plagiarizing rose from 10 percent to almost 40 percent between 1999 and 2005. Of those students, 77 percent said that they didn't think cheating was a serious issue.

First, we need a basic definition of plagiarism. Basically, it's taking someone else's content and disguising it, through a number of ways, as your original thoughts. Unfortunately, the Web provides easy opportunities to plagiarize because of its sheer vastness, but I have to tell you: it's relatively simple to figure out when someone is trying to pull this off, and professors have become pretty savvy through a variety of sites and software created especially for this purpose. Plagiarism might be tempting, but it's so not worth it—if you are caught stealing content, you can face a whole horde of unpleasant circumstances.

So you can use content that you find on the Web; it just needs to be properly sourced and cited. (Citation styles vary wildly from teacher to teacher, so make sure you double-check with your professor as to which style is acceptable for your project.)

Plagiarism can take many forms. Here are a few of the most common ways that people plagiarize, either purposefully or unintentionally:

- Failure to cite sources for material included in your project, whether that material is quoted verbatim or put in your own words (paraphrased).
- Taking another student's or employee's work and passing it off as your own.
- Using someone else's ideas without giving proper credit.

And the list goes on and on. Again, I must emphasize that plagiarism is relatively easy to avoid—you just need to give credit where credit is due. Since most academic and research-oriented papers require you to include outside sources in your project, it becomes a simple matter of keeping track of these sources and properly citing them.

A note on citations: In every one of my college classes, I was given different citation methods to follow; therefore, I'm not going to even attempt to tell you how you should cite Web sources.

Check with your professor or employer as to how they would like you to credit your references. At the very least, you should have the author, title, URL, originating organization, and date of publication.

Get Linked

Need more information about evaluating Web sites and using the Web as part of your research project? Here are a few articles from my About.com Web Search site that should help you out.

HOW TO EVALUATE A WEB SOURCE

It can be a challenge to discern the reliability of information that you find on the Web, and the standard is even higher when you're seeking sources for school or work projects.

http://about.com/websearch/evaluateasource

FREE E-BOOKS ON THE WEB

Many sites offer free e-books on the Web. Here are a few sites where you can find free downloadable e-books to use as sources in your research project (properly sourced, of course!).

http://about.com/websearch/ebooks

Chapter 11

Finding Multimedia on the Web

Movies and Videos

There are literally thousands of sites completely dedicated to bringing you multimedia of all kinds on the Web. From full-length movies to streaming podcasts, you can find it on the Web—and it's easier today than ever before to find what you're looking for.

Perhaps the easiest multimedia content to track down on the Web is movies and videos of all kinds. Yes, you can find full-length movies, the latest music videos, documentaries, etc.—and all for free.

We'll stick to the free and legal options. First, any Web site that I recommend is going to be completely free—you will not have to pay for the privilege of viewing any content. If you visit one

About.com

What if a Web site asks me to pay money to watch a video?

▶ Most Web sites these days offer videos completely free to you; they make their money by pasting ads on the Web page itself. So if you're asked to pay money for watching a video, use caution and check the site out: you may be on a site that is not very reputable or may have clicked an advertisement for another Web site by mistake. Or you might actually be on a legit site. Yes, it can be confusing!

of the sites that I have recommended and you are asked to pay, one of two things has likely happened: either that particular site has completely changed its policies or you've accidentally clicked an advertisement (it happens).

Secondly, it is possible to find plenty of full-length feature films on the Web available for free and legal download. Notice I said "legal"? That's the key. Free, downloadable movies are easily located on the Web; however, you won't find the latest blockbuster currently in the theaters on any of the Web sites that I will recommend in this section because there are legal restrictions on posting that kind of thing on the Web.

Sure, there are many ways to get around that, but I'm going to stick to the strictly law-abiding stuff. You *can* download many movies using **BitTorrent** technology, but since BitTorrents are in a hazy area legally I'm going to steer clear for now. (For a very good explanation of how BitTorrents work, I suggest "BitTorrents 101: How Torrents Work" by my friend Paul Gil, the About.com Net for Beginners Guide, at http://about.com/netforbeginners/bittorrents.)

Okay! So now that we've got the somewhat boring disclaimers out of the way, let's find some movies on the Web, shall we?

Finding free videos on the Web is simple. Did you miss last week's American Idol countdown? Are you looking for your favorite cheesy '90s boy band music video? You can use the Web to find these and more. Free movie downloads are more common than you think on the Web. You won't find the most recent blockbusters here, but you will find a huge number of classics, trailers, independent films, documentaries, and more.

At www.jonhs.net/freemovies you'll find free movies that have fallen out of copyright—you can download them legally to your heart's content. OVGuide (www.ovguide.com/) is a meta search (meaning it searches many sites at one time) guide to online movies. Veoh Cult Classics (www.veoh.com/channel/cultclassics) touts B-movie classics; *The Night of the Living Dead, Metropolis, Eraserhead* are all included here. Free Movies Online (www.emol.org/movies/) is a site full of classic movies, cartoons, comedies, etc., all free movie downloads.

The Internet Movie Database (www.imdb.com/) has movie reviews, information about upcoming movie premieres, movie clips, and more. This is the best place to find background information on actors and actresses, by the way. AltaVista Video Search (www.altavista.com/video/default) lets you search for movies and videos on the Web in virtually any format. You can find free movie downloads easily and fast here. At Yahoo Video Search (http://video.search.yahoo.com/) you can search for videos and movies, and you can also submit your own video to Yahoo to be indexed in their database.

With Google Video Search (http://video.google.com/) you can find videos, movies, and TV programs online. I've found full-length documentaries here as well as feature films. Netbroadcaster (www.netbroadcaster.com/new/index.html) features trailers, shorts, independent films, and more. Most of the films on this site are free, but some do require subscription access. Turner Classic Movies (www.turnerclassicmovies.com) has trailers, movie clips, and background information on all your favorite classic films. Hollywood.com (www.hollywood.com/) is another good site for trailers, movie clips, and up-to-the-minute breaking news about new movies.

All Movie Guide (www.allmovie.com/) has a comprehensive database of film synopses and reviews as well as concise actor biographies. Apple Movie Trailers (www.apple.com/trailers/) has an

ELSEWHERE ON THE WEB

▶ Isohunt, a dedicated Bit-Torrent search engine, makes your torrent search much easier. Isohunt does not host these BitTorrent files, it merely helps you find them, which makes it a free and legal service. Learn more about BitTorrents, BitTorrent clients, BitTorrent downloads, and how to do a torrent search here: http://about.com/websearch/torrentsearch.

extensive collection of brand spankin' new movie trailers. This is the best place to go on the Web if you're looking for the latest movie trailer; it has excellent picture quality as well. JoBlo (www .joblo.com/) has reviews, trailers, scripts, interviews, clips, and a lot more. It's one of the more senior movie Web sites; it's been around for a while.

With YouTube (www.youtube.com/) you can upload, watch, and search free videos; this is the first place I go to find TV shows I've missed, movie clips, music videos, etc. However, it should be noted that not all shows, movies, etc. are in their full format on YouTube – sometimes, you have to watch them in parts. There is a YouTube, GoogleVideo, Ifilm Mashup at http://javimoya.com/blog/ youtube_en.php. It's a nice mashup of all three services, but you'll need to know exactly what video you want in order to use it.

Google Video of the Day (www.gvod.blogspot.com/) varies from funny to interesting to extremely weird. LearnOutLoud (www.learnoutloud.com/Free-Audio-Video) has free streaming lectures, audio, and video on a variety of subjects from computing technology to philosophy. VideoBomb (www.videobomb.com/) is a fun way to see what other people are watching.

Truveo (www.truveo.com) is a video search engine that delivers pretty good results; videos are nicely categorized. MeFeedia (www. mefeedia.com/) has videoblogs (video podcasts). Since videoblogs are somewhat tricky to find if you don't know exactly what you're looking for, this is a super resource.

The Open Video Project (www.open-video.org/) is a shared digital video collection managed at the Interaction Design Laboratory, at the University of North Carolina at Chapel Hill. SearchForVideo (www.searchforvideo.com/home/index.html) is a fantastic video search engine with over 6,000 sources currently available. News, entertainment, and extremely popular videos are all searchable

TOOLS YOU NEED

▶ So what do the "pros" use to make their movies on the Web? Popular video blog Rocketboom has quite nicely made available the tools that they use to make their videos, along with the reasons why they like each of their picks: uses, functions, special features, etc. Find out more at the "Rocketboom Online Video Tool List," found at www.rocketboom.com/ extra/video_tools/.

here. About.com's Independent film guide (http://about.com/world-film/onlinefilms/) has a great list of free indie films on the Web that's frequently updated.

Documentaries Online (http://best.online.docus.googlepages.com/) is a simple blog site that is maintained by a documentary fan; he goes around the Web, finds good documentaries, and posts them in their entirety on his site. Atom Films (www.atomfilms.com/) is a collection of humorous short films, cartoons, and animations. Be sure to check out the Star Wars parodies.

RatherGood.com (www.rathergood.com) features a collection of some pretty wild and wacky stuff, from songs to exploding ducks. National Lampoon (www.nationallampoon.com/) has short films and animations from the comic minds at National Lampoon. Some of this stuff is definitely not kid-friendly. Subservient Chicken (www.subservientchicken.com/) is hard to explain; this is more a site where *you* are making the movie. Trust me. You'll enjoy it.

eBaumsWorld (www.top50.ebaumsworld.com/index.html) is a collection of eclectic videos, from stupid to extreme. Definitely funny, but many are not suitable for viewing at the office or in front of younger viewers. OddTodd (www.oddtodd.com/) has flash animations, games, and Mep the Squirrel. How could you not love OddTodd? Be sure to check out the Unemployment films.

There are so many great sites for video media that there isn't enough room to describe them all! Here is a list of more terrific sites:

- **Milk and Cookies** (www.milkandcookies.com/): A wildly eclectic assortment of mostly animated funny shorts.
- **Vmix** (www.vmix.com): A wide variety of user-submitted videos, anything from funny to strange to crazy.

ELSEWHERE ON THE WEB

▶ Did you know that you can watch free online TV channels? Yep, it's true—many of your favorite networks have live, streaming video on the Web, as well as a whole host of channels all around the world. Find out more here: http://about.com/websearch/freetv. By the way, this could be a great way to save some cash on your cable bill.

▶ You can use Google to find a movie or movie theater with showtimes near you. All you need to do is simply type "movies" into Google's search box. You can also search for the name of the movie, for example, *X-Men*. In addition, if you can't think of the name of the movie but know a detail, ask Google to find the name of the movie for you: movie: golden ticket.

- **The Thirty Second Bunny Theatre** (www.angryalien.com/): The bunnies do classic films in thirty seconds or less (seriously). My favorites are *It's a Wonderful Life* and *Alien*.
- **Flurl** (www.flurl.com/): Good source for a variety of videos; there are quite a few NSFW ones here though (acronym stands for Not Safe For Work).
- **Public Domain Torrents** (www.publicdomaintorrents.com/): Remember earlier in this section I said I wouldn't be directing you to torrent sites since there's too much shady legal stuff involved? Public Domain Torrents is one torrent site I can definitely recommend; they only have public domain (meaning legally downloadable) classic movies and B-movies, all totally free.
- **SearchForVideo** (www.searchforvideo.com/): Nicely done video search engine with thousands of video clips available; you can search individual channels, videos from around the Web, categories, etc.
- **In2TV** (http://video.aol.com/video-category/in2tv/2120): Scads of free TV shows, cartoons, and movies here; you can watch full-length Looney Tunes cartoons, classic TV shows such as *Wonder Woman* and *Gilligan's Island*, or browse the dozen-odd categories from Animation to Espanol.
- **Metacafe** (www.metacafe.com): An eclectic collection of videos here; anything from homemade to cartoons and more.
- **Free Public Domain Movies and Documentaries** (www.jonhs.net/freemovies/): Free movies and more, all available for free download.
- **MySpace Videos** (www.myspace.com/index.cfm?fuseaction=vids): MySpace has one of the largest video collections on the Web. You can find a lot of interesting stuff here, anything from viral videos to current news to wild and wacky.

- **Daily Motion** (www.dailymotion.com/): Watch, publish, and share videos here; you can narrow your search by browsing the channels, tags, or user groups.
- **Stumble Video** (www.video.stumbleupon.com/): Just like StumbleUpon, StumbleVideo allows you to find and share good videos; and since all these videos are given quality ratings, you're almost guaranteed to filter out the junk. I say "almost" because the filtering process is not perfect, so use caution if Stumbling in front of younger viewers. A highly addictive site.
- **MotionBox** (www.motionbox.com/): View and share personal videos; a really interesting site that actually helps you edit and organize your video collection.
- **vSocial** (www.vsocial.com/#s:hot): Upload your videos in any format, share them, and view other folks' videos.
- **Blip.tv** (www.blip.tv/): One of the largest video and video-sharing sites on the Web; extremely well done and very easy to use.
- **iFilm** (www.ifilm.com/): One of my favorite places on the Web for great videos, trailers, etc.; plus, you can find plenty of movie background info here.
- **Revver** (www.one.revver.com/revver): Not only can you watch an endless supply of videos here, you can also upload your own and possibly earn some money with the Revver revenue-sharing program (you can learn more about it at www.one.revver.com/go/about).

What about making your own movies? Amazingly enough, you can even find many Web sites that will help you make your own video masterpiece. Some of the better ones out there include:

- **Eyespot** (www.eyespot.com): Make and mix your very own movies here.
- **vPod.tv** (http://portal.vpod.tv): Share and create your own videos, and watch other people's videos.
- **Jumpcut** (www.jumpcut.com/): Create a movie right in your browser window.

There are also specialized movie-related sites. In addition to all these movie and video Web sites, there are a great many sites dedicated to various aspects of moviemaking. A few of the best ones:

- **The Internet Movie Script Database** (www.imsdb.com/): You can read entire scripts of movies here almost as soon as they come out.
- **TuneFind** (www.tunefind.com/): You know that song you liked in that one movie? This is a good place to find out the name and artist.
- **MovieMistakes** (www.moviemistakes.com/): Ever wonder if you've seen something in a movie that wasn't supposed to be there? Check MovieMistakes to see if you're right.
- **ComingSoon** (www.comingsoon.net/): ComingSoon is a good place to get movie scoops, behind-the-scenes images, and leaked movie news.
- **Drive-In Theater** (www.driveintheater.com/index.htm): When you want to find a drive-in theater in the United States, use this site.
- **Cinema Treasures Theater Guide** (http://cinematreasures.org/theater/): Lists of all theaters worldwide that are currently showing classic films.

- **Double Feature Finder** (www.doublefeaturefinder.com/): Use the Double Feature Finder to find local showtimes scheduled back-to-back and spend the entire day at the movies.
- **'80s Movie Rewind** (www.fast-rewind.com/): Your best bet to find information about some of the best movies ever made . . . in the '80s.

Watch Free TV Online

Did you know that you can watch free online TV channels? Here are a few of the best sites for it.

- **LinkTV** (www.linktv.org/experience): Global news, documentaries, TV shows, and movies.
- **CurrentTV** (www.current.tv/): Not a traditional TV network; this is mostly user-created and submitted free online TV.
- **PBS** (www.pbs.org/): Many PBS programs here in a free streaming format; just use this Google query:

```
site:www.pbs.org pbs watch online
```

- **ABC** (www.abc.go.com/): Free online ABC TV shows to download or watch.
- **ChannelChooser** (www.channelchooser.com/): A good place to find many different free online TV channels, all streaming.
- **BBC** (http://news.bbc.co.uk/1/shared/bsp/hi/live_stats/html/map.stm): The BBC's most popular stories; not all the top stories are linked to video, but quite a few are.
- **wwlTv** (www.wwitv.com/portal.htm): For free online TV channels from all over the world; a great selection.

ELSEWHERE ON THE WEB

▶ I don't know about you, but using TV Guide to find out when programs are on in my local area has become kind of a pain. That's where MeeVee comes in. You can use MeeVee not only to keep track of local television listings, but also to find new shows and even store your favorites all in one place. Find out more here: http://about.com/websearch/meevee.

- **DemocracyTV** (www.getdemocracy.com/): Over 600 free online TV channels available here.
- **Jeff's Guide to TV Shows Only Available on the Internet** (http://pulverblog.pulver.com/archives/005282.html): TV fan's great list of all the shows he could find that are only available on the Web—you'll be surprised at how many there are.
- **Yahoo TV** (http://tv.yahoo.com/): Still in the early stages, but you can find good stuff here, especially trailers and pilots from upcoming TV shows.
- **Vanderbilt Television Archive** (http://tvnews.vanderbilt.edu/): What a treasure—over 90,000 hours of news-related programming and information.
- **NBC** (www.nbc.com): Catch online episodes of select NBC TV shows.
- **CBS** (www.cbs.com): Full episodes online of your favorite CBS shows.
- **NewsFilm Library** (www.sc.edu/library/newsfilm): From the University of South Carolina; this collection hosts a part of the Fox MovieTone collection.
- **Choose and Watch** (www.chooseandwatch.com/): A free online TV site with hundreds of channels to choose from.
- **Live Online TV** (www.live-online-tv.com/): A good site with many free channel offerings to choose from.
- **Streamick** (www.streamick.com/): Many, many free online TV channels to choose from here; I especially appreciate that it's so nicely organized into categories.
- **TVLand** (www.tvland.com): Watch old and new TV shows here; I enjoyed getting sucked into an old episode of *Little House on the Prairie*.

- **PeekVid** (www.peekvid.com): A great free online TV repository with hundreds of free shows archived for instant watching.
- **BeelineTV** (www.beelinetv.com/): Free online TV channels from all around the world.

Free Music on the Web

Free downloadable music on the Web really does exist, as long as you're willing to listen to music other than what's on the radio and top 40 (for the most part). Here are a few places on the Web where you can find free music downloads:

- **Del.icio.us** (http://del.icio.us/tag/system:filetype:mp3): I came across this nifty little search trick a while back; you can find all the MP3 files tagged at del.icio.us this way.
- **Indy.tv** (www.indy.tv): Indy makes it easy for you to find great new independent music. Just download Indy and double-click: as it plays songs, you rate what you hear. Indy quickly learns what you like and gets really smart about sending you more music you'll enjoy.
- **Pandora** (www.pandora.com): I was in on the beta testing of Pandora and I loved it. You can create as many specialized radio stations as you want on Pandora, and it will evolve to your specified changes. Right now I have a George Winston, David Wilcox, and a Mindi Smith station. Sweet!
- **Internet Archive:** Audio Archive (www.archive.org/details/audio): This is an absolutely mammoth collection of all styles of music.
- **NPR in Concert** (www.npr.org/templates/story/story.php?storyId=4627437): Here you'll find full concerts by various top artists, such as James Brown and Sinead O'Connor.

WHAT'S HOT

▶ You can use Google to find MP3 files on the Web. Here's how:

-inurl:htm -inurl:html intitle: "index of" "Last modified" mp3 "beethoven".

You are attempting to find directories, so you don't want a Web page (hence the minus sign in front of both the htm and html extensions). You're looking for the root directory, so that's where the "index of" in the title (intitle) comes in. And that MP3 file designation? You can change that to any file you want to look for—wma, pdf, etc.

- **Amazon.com Free Music Downloads** (www.amazon.com/exec/obidos/tg/browse/-/468646/103-9100563-9912638): All sorts of eclectic music is here, not only from independents but from mainstream artists as well.
- **Soundclick** (www.soundclick.com): This is one of my favorite places to find some good tunes; each artist has his or her own page within the Soundclick network.
- **GarageBand** (www.garageband.com): This is another great place to find emerging artists, and each artist has a Web page, forum, etc.
- **Mutopia** (www.mutopiaproject.org): All music in the Mutopia Project is free to download, print out, perform, and distribute. There are now almost 1,000 pieces of music available!
- **AMClassical** (www.amclassical.com): Visit this site for free classical music MP3 downloads; there's a wide variety of styles available.

Free Books and Printed Materials

Many, many sites offer free books that you can download or read online. Here are a few of the best sites that I've found for freebies:

- **ReadPrint** (www.readprint.com/): There are lots of great titles here, including Jane Eyre, 1984, and Hamlet.
- **ManyBooks** (www.manybooks.net): An excellent source of free books for your PDA or iPod. Includes book reviews.
- **The Literature Network** (www.online-literature.com/author_index.php): You can search by author here; many classic authors are represented.
- **Free Computer Books** (www.maththinking.com/boat/booksIndex.html): Every computer subject and programming language you can think of is represented here.

- **LibriVox** (http://librivox.org/): Let the site speak for itself: "LibriVox volunteers record chapters of books in the public domain and release the audio files back onto the net. Our goal is to make all public domain books available as free audio books. We are a totally volunteer, open source, free content, public domain project."
- **LearnOutLoud** (www.learnoutloud.com/Free-Audio-Video): This site has more than 10,000 selections for audio and video learning.
- **Authorama** (www.authorama.com/): Authorama has "completely free books from a variety of different authors, collected here for you to read online or offline."
- **Project Gutenberg** (www.gutenberg.org/): There are more than 20,000 free books in the Project Gutenberg Online Book Catalog, and an additional 100,000 through the Project's partners and affiliates.
- **World Public Library** (http://worldlibrary.net/): This is a rich collection of more than 400,000 unabridged PDF e-books, many of them classics. They also have books in audio MP3 format. There is a membership fee, currently $8.95 per year for an individual.
- **Free Tech Books** (www.freetechbooks.com/): Just what the name of the site says: you can get free technology-related books here.
- **FullBooks** (www.fullbooks.com): There are thousands of books here, organized alphabetically by title.
- **Bartleby e-books** (www.bartleby.com): Bartleby has a huge array of classic literature, all available for free download.
- **Bibliomania** (www.bibliomania.com/bibliomania-static/index .html): This site has over 2,000 classic texts.

Audio Information

The Web offers the listener a vast repository of audio information, from radio stations to podcasts. There is really no end to what you can find here.

There's great radio all over the Web. Can't find anything good to listen to on your local radio stations? No problem—go to the Web. There's no end to the free online radio stations that you can find. Here are just a few:

- **Public Radio Fan** (www.publicradiofan.com/): PublicRadioFan is the best site on the Web to find a public radio station, anywhere in the world. You can search for a free online radio station in a variety of ways, including by location, format, or language, or you can look for programs by name.
- **Last.FM** (www.last.fm): Listen to an eclectic array of music at Last.FM, which has recently been acquired by CBS.
- **Live365** (www.live365.com/index.live): Thousands of radio stations are available here.
- RadioLovers (www.radiolovers.com): This is a wonderful niche site full of old-time radio shows.
- **Radio-Locator** (www.radio-locator.com): Awesome—a radio station search engine.
- **BBC Radio Stream** (www.dave.org.uk/streams): This one's a guide to various BBC radio streams.
- **Windows Radio** (www.windowsmedia.com/mediaguide/radio/?locale=409): And this one's a guide to Windows Media radio stations.
- **AccuRadio** (www.accuradio.com): Over 200 channels of extremely eclectic radio are available here for free.

ELSEWHERE ON THE WEB

▶ Looking for audio content? Pretty much any kind of audio can be found using Yahoo Audio Search, including music (RAM and MP3s, etc.), podcasts, sound effects, interviews, e-books, speeches, and more. Try it yourself at http://audio.search.yahoo.com.

- **Yahoo Launchcast Radio** (http://music.yahoo.com): Yahoo offers lots of radio stations here, and also gives you the option of modifying your own radio station and sharing it with friends.
- **RadioFreeWorld** (www.radiofreeworld.com): Internet radio stations from all over the world.
- **ShoutCast** (www.shoutcast.com): Thousands of radio stations from all over the world are here—there's some pretty eclectic stuff.
- **RadioTower** (www.radiotower.com): RadioTower was one of the first radio station directories on the Web; they now have an index of thousands of stations.
- **AOL Radio** (http://music.aol.com/radioguide/bb.adp): AOL offers free online radio listening featuring XM radio.
- **Pandia Online Radio Station Search** (www.pandia.com/radio/): Pandia has listings for thousands of online radio stations.
- **Pandora** (http://pandora.com): Perfect for anyone who loves music, this is a site that takes your unique musical preferences and programs an entire radio station for you. Pandora is one of the most useful sites on the Web today. It's your very own radio station—and you control what music shows up. This site is also great for finding similar artists to those you already enjoy.

That's just the tip of the iceberg when it comes to online radio stations; there are thousands and thousands of stations to choose from. In addition, if you want to find out if your local radio station is being streamed on the Web, simply type in the call letters to your favorite search engine – most radio stations these days offer some kind of online listening options. You can also search for worldwide

TOOLS YOU NEED

▶ Podcasts are incredibly popular; they're also extremely useful. Some of my favorites include Open Culture's "20 Podcasts that will teach you Spanish, French, Italian, and German" (www.oculture.com/weblog/2007/04/20_podcasts_tha.html); Podiobooks (www.podiobooks.com/), serialized books in podcast form; and Chicago Public Radio's This American Life, found at www.thislife.org/.

radio stations this way, as well as genres, specific bands, and radio personalities.

Podcasts are everywhere on the Web. Now, you might have heard the term "podcast" tossed about lately. Podcasts are simply a way for you to make your voice heard on the Web, talking about pretty much anything. Podcasts are becoming more and more popular, ranging from knitting tutorials to intense technology discussions.

In general, major search engines aren't indexing podcasts in a format that's easy to find, at least for now. However, there are podcast-specific search engines that have solved this problem:

- **Podscope** (www.podscope.com/): Podscope is a specialized search engine that only looks for podcasts, searching for the spoken words within the podcasts themselves.
- **Yahoo Podcasts** (http://podcasts.yahoo.com/): Of all the podcast search engines I've come across, Yahoo Podcasts is the one that I've been able to consistently and successfully use to find good podcasts. Very user-friendly.
- You can also use **Podzinger** (www.podzinger.com/) and Blog-Digger (www.blogdigger.com/index.html) to find podcasts quickly and easily.

Podcast directories are also virtual gold mines for finding good podcasts. Here are a few of my favorites:

- **PodcastAlley.com** (www.podcastalley.com/): This is a podcast lover's dream. Includes the very useful Top Ten Podcasts of the Month (as voted by listeners).

WHAT'S HOT

▶ There are so many great sites completely dedicated to finding the best music to listen to on the Web. Some of my new favorites? Musicovery (www.musicovery.com/), a site that matches your mood to music; FineTune (www.finetune.com/), where you can pick an artist and music is built around that artist's style, and Soma.FM (http://somafm.com/), eleven channels of alternative music broadcasting live from San Francisco.

- **Podcast.net** (www.podcast.net): Podcasts here are categorized by tags; thousands of podcasts in a plethora of subjects are available for free download.
- **NPR Podcast Directory** (www.npr.org/rss/podcast/podcast_directory.php): Not a whole lot of podcasts here, but it's NPR, come on! Quality podcasts in a subject directory format.
- **PodcastBunker** (www.podcastbunker.com/): Their motto is "quality, not quantity," and boy, they're not kidding. One of the best places to find high-quality podcasts on the Web.

In addition, you can find quality podcast directories at Public RadioFan (www.publicradiofan.com/podcasts.html) and of course, the always excellent Apple iTunes podcast directory (www.apple.com/itunes/store/podcasts.html).

In addition to all these fun podcast sites and services, you can use this little trick to find even more podcasts you're interested in:

```
inurl:podcast "global warming"
```

This works well in Google, Yahoo, and Ask.com; not quite as well in MSN, but you can still find a few goodies.

Images

These image search engines, directories, and collections will help you find whatever kind of image you're looking for on the Web, whether it's a piece of clip art, a photograph, a piece of art, or almost anything else you might be searching for. Here are just a few of the many specialized image search engines on the Web.

- **AltaVista Image Search** (www.altavista.com/image/default): Use AltaVista to find images of all kinds on the Web, including photos and graphics or banners and buttons.
- **Google Image Search** (http://images.google.com): Google's huge database will help you find pretty much any image on any topic that you can think of.
- **Yahoo Image Search** (http://images.search.yahoo.com/): Use Yahoo's Advanced Image Search to really narrow down your searches. You can filter by size, coloration, site/domain, and more.
- **ImageAfter** (www.imageafter.com): From the site: "You can download and use any image or texture from our site and use it in your own work, either personal or commercial." Wide variety of images here.
- **Stock.xchng** (www.sxc.hu): This is the first place I go for images on the Web. There are varying licenses with each image, but most are completely fair-use.
- **Flickr** (www.flickr.com): This site has a huge array of different photos. Make sure to check if the photo you want to use is available; not all Flickr users give this kind of permission.
- **YotoPhoto** (http://yotophoto.com): These are all free, fair-use photographs and images.
- **Corbis** (http://pro.corbis.com/splash.aspx): Search through stock photography and pictures.
- **FabFotos** (www.fabfotos.com): This is a high-quality photography collection; it includes only sites with the best quality submissions.
- **Getty Images** (http://creative.gettyimages.com/source/home/homeCreative.aspx): Visit this huge database of searchable images from various leading brands. You can narrow your search to include only royalty-free images.

- **SI Art Image Browser** (www.si.umich.edu/Art_History/): The University of Michigan offers these art, architectural, and museum object images from four different museums and collections, including the their own Museum of Art.
- **University of Colorado Garst Photographic Collection** (http://lib.colostate.edu/wildlife/): This is an amazing collection of over 20,000 images put together by the Garsts as they were filming for Mutual of Omaha's Wild Kingdom television series.
- **American Memory Collections: Photos and Prints** (go to http://memory.loc.gov and type "Original Format: Photos and Prints" into the search box): From the Library of Congress, these collections include Ansel Adams photography, Civil War, and Presidents and First Ladies.
- **Smithsonian Photographic Collection** (http://photo2.si.edu/): Here you can browse through selected images from the Smithsonian collections.
- **Time & Life Pictures** (www.timelifepictures.com/): A fascinating collection of photos and images included in both Time and Life magazines; powered by Getty Images.
- **National Geographic Photography Collection** (www.nationalgeographic.com/media/photography/): The treats here include photo galleries from this acclaimed magazine, gorgeous wallpapers, photo of the day, and more.
- **JSC Digital Image Collection** (http://images.jsc.nasa.gov/): From the site: "This collection of more than 9000 NASA press release photos spans the American manned space program, from the Mercury program to the STS-79 Shuttle mission."
- **Image Collections and Online Art** (www.umich.edu/~hartspc/histart/mother/images.html): Another collection

TOOLS YOU NEED

▶ There are many tools that allow you to actually edit your images online, without the use of a full-fledged image editor. Amazing! The one that I use the most right now is SnipShot (http://snipshot.com/), a tool that allows you basic image adjustment, basic editing tools, and quick image manipulation. Sure, it's not as powerful as a standalone image editor, but it's good for a quick job.

from the University of Michigan; it includes images and art from all over the world.

- **NYPL Digital Gallery** (http://digitalgallery.nypl.org/nypldigital/index.cfm): The New York Public Library's collection of free digital images includes more than 300,000 digitized images available to the public, including many from primary sources.

Note: Please read the fine print before using images from any of these image search engines or image search sites. Different photos and sites have different usage licenses, which can possibly restrict your use of their image.

Get Linked

I've sure given you a lot to look at in this chapter, but there are even more multimedia resources on my About.com Web Search site.

TOP TEN WAYS TO FIND MULTIMEDIA ON THE WEB

Finding multimedia on the Web is easy with my picks for some of the best free movie downloads, free audio clips, and free image sites on the Web. Use these sites to find some great audio files, Bit-Torrent files, movies, movie trailers, and all kinds of multimedia.
http://about.com/websearch/multimedia

TECHNICAL REQUIREMENTS FOR MULTIMEDIA

The Web is a great place to find multimedia files, including images, audio files, and videos. Here are the basic technical requirements for viewing the larger files (audio and video in particular). For images, you won't need anything but a computer with a browser.
http://about.com/websearch/technicalmultimedia

Chapter 12

Mining the Blogosphere

What Is the Blogosphere?

If you've ever read a blog, then you've visited the blogosphere, a catchall term for all the various blogs—also known as online journals—on the Web. First, let's get a good handle on what a blog is. Basically, a blog is anything you want it to be, from a highly personal journal to a publicly available political free-for-all. It's completely up to you.

Make sense? You've probably visited a blog of some kind if you've spent any time at all on the Web, and thus, you've visited the wild and wonderful world of the blogosphere.

So what's so great about the blogosphere? What can you find in the world of blogs? I think I can sum it up in one word: people. Blogs are all about personal, customized content. For instance, I have a personal blog in which I write about my daily life with my family, my cats, and life in general. Sure, it's probably not interesting to anyone but me, but it's got that all-important element

About.com

of "people" in it (you can read it yourself at http://wendyboswell.tumblr.com).

When you start poking around the blogosphere, you're going to find loads of blogs about cats, but you're also going to get blogs centered around someone's political views, another person's take on the latest fashion flubs, somebody else's opinion on technology news, and so much more. The blogosphere is the personal side of the World Wide Web, and there's definitely a lot to explore.

The first blog, most sources seem to agree, was made by Justin Hall. While a student at Swarthmore College, he started his Web-based diary (www.links.net/), which offered one of the earliest guided tours of the Web. Over time, the site came to focus on Hall's life in intimate detail. In December, 2004, New York Times Magazine referred to him as the one who really put blogging on the map. So thanks to Justin's initiative, we can all get our feet wet exploring the blogosphere.

How do you find blogs? There are many ways to find blogs on the Web, but here are three ways that seem to work the best:

- **Blog search engines and directories:** There are quite a few good blog search engines and directories out there that can help you find what you're looking for; we'll go through a few of those further on in the chapter.
- **General search engines:** You can easily find blogs on any chosen topic by just typing "subject blog" (where the word "subject" is replaced by your topic of choice) in your favorite search engine.
- **Word of mouth:** This is how I've found the majority of the blogs that I follow on the Web; not by "literal" word of mouth in most cases, but by following linked recommenda-

TOOLS YOU NEED

▶ In 2005, Michael Bergman, author of one of the most popular Internet search guides and the original discoverer of the deep Web, released Comprehensive Guide to a Professional Blog Site: A WordPress Example. The free eighty-page PDF guide links to eighty additional sources and covers more than 100 topics and how-to tips, ranging from installing software and plug-ins to design, styles, and templates to organizational and effectiveness techniques. Read more at "Free Comprehensive Guide to Blogging" (http://about.com/websearch/bloggingguide).

tions from other blogs and blogrolls (a blogroll is a list of a writer's favorite blogs).

There are also a few blogging platforms (online free services that enable anyone to write a blog simply and easily) that have a neat feature: at the top of all their blogs, readers can click for the next randomly featured blog. I know that Blogger does this and it's a fun way to find blogs that you might not have otherwise found on your own.

Finding Blogs with Blog Search Engines

I mentioned that you can use blog search engines to find blogs that you're interested in, and listed below are some of the engines that I have found to be the most efficient in delivering what I'm looking for. Blog search engines have become more and more sophisticated, and nowadays you can do a blog search on a variety of topics and hit pay dirt. Here is a list of some of the best blog search engines out there—take 'em for a blog-search test drive and see what you think.

- **Daypop** (www.daypop.com): Daypop is a current events search engine. Daypop crawls sites that are updated frequently in order to bring searchers the latest news; included in Daypop's index are newspapers, blogs, online magazines—any site that is updated on a regular basis will make it into Daypop's index. You can use Daypop to search a small slice of the Web for news and information.
- **Blogdex** (www.blogdex.net/): A blog search engine and a "finger on the pulse" kind of deal, Blogdex is put together by MIT and is a service that keeps track of information as it spreads through the blogosphere.

How is a blog different from just a regular Web site?

▶ Actually, it's not really any different, except that a blog is typically updated more frequently. Blogs are just another way to express yourself on the Web—you can talk about your personal life or share pictures, links, videos, audio submission, and pretty much anything you can think of. Blogs have become for many people a creative outlet; you can use your blog to explore and record your life . . . or someone else's. It's all up to you!

- **Technorati** (www.technorati.com/): Technorati is a blog search engine that is a real-time recorder of what is going on in the blogosphere. Currently, Technorati is tracking a whopping 20.8 million sites and 1.7 billion links.
- **Bloogz** (www.bloogz.com/): Search blogs with the Bloogz blog search engine; you can also take a look at which blogs are the most popular at the moment.
- **Blogwise** (www.blogwise.com): Blogwise is more of a blog directory than a blog search engine, but it does have a site search available and an impressive amount of blogs in its directory (over 100,000 at the time of this writing).
- **Ice Rocket Blog Search** (http://blogs.icerocket.com/?&q=): This is an excellent blog search engine that includes the option to search by link. Ice Rocket also has a pretty good advanced search page; you can find it by clicking the Advanced Search link to the right of the search bar.
- **Google Blog Search** (http://blogsearch.google.com/): Google Blog Search is relatively new to the world of blog search engines and at the time of this writing is still in beta. It currently doesn't retrieve many results and it has a lot of usability issues, but given its beta status, these are known issues that hopefully will soon be resolved.
- **BlogPulse** (www.blogpulse.com): BlogPulse is a dream of a blog search engine. It includes really cool BlogPulse user tools such as Trend Search (www.blogpulse.com/trend) and Conversation Tracker (www.blogpulse.com/conversation).
- **Bloglines** (www.bloglines.com/): Not only can you search the blogosphere with the Bloglines blog search engine, you can also subscribe to site feeds and view all your feeds within Bloglines' feed reader.
- **Blogdigger** (www.blogdigger.com/): Blogdigger is a solid blog search engine that also gives you the option to search for

local blogs—blogs that are physically located in your geographical area—an option I immediately added to my bookmarks. You can, too; check it out at http://local.blogdigger.com/index.html.

- **Waypath** (www.waypath.com/): Waypath bills itself as a "blog discovery engine." This blog search engine features the ability to identify topic streams, which basically means that they pull out the meat of every subject post.
- **Findory** (www.findory.com/): Findory is a supercharged blog search engine. Findory not only finds blogs that you're interested in, but also brings you information from a wide variety of sources all over the world, building a customized newspaper of sorts for you. Very cool service; try building your own Findory page.
- **PubSub** (www.pubsub.com/index.php): Think of PubSub as breaking news alerts on steroids—it's an extremely powerful and convenient search service and once you start one, you'll wonder how you ever got along without it.
- **Feedster** (www.feedster.com/): Feedster is a blog search engine with a twist: it searches and indexes anything with a feed, which covers a wide gamut.
- **Sphere** (www.sphere.com/): One of the first things you'll notice about Sphere is that it is extremely uncluttered. There's not much "stuff" to look at or keep track of or attempt to figure out, and since I'm a big fan of the uncluttered look, this was definitely a point in Sphere's favor. The home page has three different blog search tools for you to use: the main search bar, Top Searches for the hour, and Top Searches for the week. It's basically a very streamlined, functional way to search for blogs.
- **Talkdigger** (www.talkdigger.com/): TalkDigger is a search engine that finds which links are talking about links. Make

TOOLS YOU NEED

▶ You might have heard the term "search engine optimization"; basically, this means making your site more visible to both search engines and search engine users. There are lots of great search engine optimization blogs out there, and these are just a few that I read—or try to read, anyway—on a regular basis: SEORoundtable (www.seoroundtable.com), SEOMoz (www.seomoz.org), and JenSense (www.jensense.com). Read more about my favorites at http://about.com/websearch/websiteopblogs.

▶ Blogging has become such an accepted part of the Web at large that they even have their own award organizations. There are the Bloggie Awards (http://2007.bloggies.com/), the Weblog Awards (http://2006.weblogawards.org/), the Canadian Blog Awards (http://cba.myblahg.com/), the Catholic Blog Awards (www.catholicblogawards.com/), the Asia Blog Awards (http://asiablogawards.com/), the Webby Awards (www.webbyawards.com/)—and the list goes on and on. There are even blogging conferences, blogging festivals, blogging workshops—it's an industry in itself.

sense? Well, in a nutshell, TalkDigger lets you enter a URL, and then goes out and finds the sites (from a variety of different search engines) that are linking to it. It's a conversation search engine.

- **LjSEEK** (www.ljseek.com/): LjSEEK.com is a search engine dedicated to sifting through the LiveJournal blogging community. Whether you're a dedicated LiveJournal user or just looking for information, you'll find that LjSEEK comes in handy.

The Best Blogs on the Web

Now that's a controversial title if I ever read one—the "best" blogs? How do you find the best ones? Well, it certainly depends on what you're looking for, what your specific tastes run to. In this section, I'm going to give you my top twenty blogs, the ones I read regularly—these are my own personal favorites for one reason or another, and I believe that there's probably something here for everyone, all over the blogosphere spectrum. Plus, for each selection, I'll give you a mini **blogroll** of sorts, a brief rundown of blogs that are similar to the ones I'm featuring here so you can do some more exploring of your own.

- **Dlisted** (www.dlisted.com/): Probably one of the funniest blogs that I read on the Web. Gossip, dish, dirt—plus some absolutely hilarious commentary. Note: Most of the content on this site is probably inappropriate for younger readers. Similar blogs are PerezHilton.com (www.perezhilton.com), TMZ (www.tmz.com), and The Superficial (www.thesuperficial.com/).
- **BoingBoing** (www.boingboing.net/): It's hard to explain what BoingBoing is all about. It's an extremely eclectic blog full of information from the latest in media to unearthed 1900s

photographs. I love reading what they come up with there; it's like a Best of the Web grab bag. Similar blogs would be Slashdot (http://slashdot.org/) and Fark (www.fark.com/).

- **Lifehacker** (www.lifehacker.com/): Long before I became one of the Lifehacker editors, I was a devoted reader of this extremely useful blog. Every day, timesaving and innovative tips are posted; most are technology-related, but anything that will help readers become more productive in some area of life can be posted. Similar blogs are Lifehack.org (www.lifehack.org), Web Worker Daily (http://webworker daily.com/), and DIY Planner (www.diyplanner.com/).

- **PostSecret** (www.postsecret.blogspot.com/): PostSecret is a blog where people send postcards to an actual, physical address detailing some kind of secret in their lives. Maybe they did actually break the neighbor's window in second grade and are confessing it now to the world—or maybe they are contemplating suicide. It can get that intense. Wonderfully enough, many readers (and the blog owner) chime in with offers of assistance to these hurting people. Updated every Sunday with new secrets. Similar blogs are Group Hug (http://grouphug.us/) and SecretChest (www .secretchest.com/).

- **Dooce** (www.dooce.com/): Dooce is written by Heather Armstrong, a blogger who was initially best known for being fired because of what she wrote on her blog. She's a gifted writer who writes semi-daily about her husband, her daughter, and her dog Chuck, along with her struggles with depression, general observations of life, and did I mention Chuck the Dog? He figures quite prominently as well. It's a hilarious take on the life of a mommy. Similar blogs are Finslippy (www.fin slippy.com), Babylune (www.babylune.com/), and ParentHacks

TOOLS YOU NEED

▶ **Want to learn even more about blogs and blogging? Try About.com's Weblogs site (http://weblogs.about.com/), a veritable cornucopia of blogging information. You can learn the basics of blogging here, as well as how to pick a blogging platform, how to monetize your blog, blog ethics, blogging tools, and much more. There's also the very useful section full of Blogging Tips (http://about.com/weblogs/bloggingtips), where you can read articles on how to make your blog stand out from the rest.**

(www.parenthacks.com/), a blog full of practical how-to tips and tutorials just for parents.

- **Go Fug Yourself** (www.gofugyourself.typepad.com/): Even celebrities have bad hair/fashion days, and the talented Fug Girls are there to document it all. Updated almost every day with new biting but screamingly hilarious commentary. Similar blogs are I Am Fashion (www.iamfashion.blogspot.com/) and The Budget Fashionista (www.thebudgetfashionista.com/).

- **MetaFilter** (www.metafilter.com/): MetaFilter is what is known as a "group blog" or a "community blog," meaning that many people contribute to the content on a regular basis. MetaFilter has a daily updated melting pot of links that have caught the writer's fancy, as well as a fun section titled "Ask MeFi" where anyone can write in with a question for the community to assist them with. A similar blog/Web site would be Digg (www.digg.com/), where everyone is invited to contribute.

- **MicroPersuasion** (www.micropersuasion.com/): Steve Rubel is the author of this blog; he does a tremendous job of keeping track of new technology around the Web and is well-known for being very enthusiastic about stuff he likes. Similar blogs are TechCrunch (www.techcrunch.com/) and Mashable (www.mashable.com/).

- **Overheard in New York** (www.overheardinnewyork.com/): Here's the basic premise behind this blog: strangers who overhear other strangers around the city of New York send their conversations in verbatim, and they are then printed in their entirety for all the world to see. Loads of very strong language and adult situations here, so probably not appropriate for younger readers. Similar blogs are Blogcritics (http://blogcritics.org/) and Kuro5in (www.kuro5hin.org/), but only in the sense that they are also group blogs. By doing a google search for "overheard in" you can find other sites that have taken the Overheard in New York concept elsewhere.

- **Cute Overload** (www.cuteoverload.com/): Be prepared to be utterly overwhelmed by the cuteness here. Smooshy kittens, lovable hedgehogs, soft widdle puppies . . . okay, I've gone too far now. I visit every day for my daily dose of cuteness, and once you visit, I'm pretty sure you'll be a regular as well. Similar blogs are Stuff On My Cat (www.stuffon mycat.com/) and Celebrity Baby Blog (www.celebrity-babies .com/).

- **Scobleizer** (http://scobleizer.com/): Robert Scoble originally gained his fame as the blogging face of Microsoft; he made the huge company more personable with his friendly, insider-look points of view. Scoble has since moved on to greener pastures but continues to be a very vocal voice on the Web at large, blogging about everything from his family to people he interviews in various facets of technology. Similar blogs are Chris Pirillo (http://chris.pirillo.com/) and Om Malik (http://gigaom.com/).

- **Confessions of a Pioneer Woman** (www.thepioneerwoman .com/): Oh, how I look forward to reading this blog every day! It's all about a mother of four who lives on a working ranch with Marlboro Man (yes, really) and a whole cast of interesting characters, and the daily adventures that their life involves. Absolutely hilarious at times, but I appreciate it mostly for the down-to-earth content. Similar blogs are BusyMom (www.busymom.net/), I Heart Farms (www.small farms.typepad.com/), and MommyLife (www.mommylife .net/). Obviously, I'm a big fan of mom blogs!

- **MAKE Blog** (www.makezine.com/blog/): Anyone with any kind of urge toward being crafty will instantly fall in love with the MAKE Blog, a cornucopia of crafts, projects, and generally incredibly useful (for the most part) things to do. Similar blogs are The Knit Sisters (www.knitsisters.com/), Craftzine (www.craftzine.com/blog/), and We Make Money Not Art (www.we-make-money-not-art.com/).
- **101 Cookbooks** (www.101cookbooks.com/): There are quite a few blogs and Web sites completely dedicated to cooking, and I really enjoy this one. The writer has a whole bookshelf full of cookbooks (so do I) and decided to actually start using them, picking a new recipe and featuring it on her blog semi-regularly. I always find some good recipes here. Similar blogs are Megnut (www.megnut.com/), All Cupcakes, All the Time (www.cupcakestakethecake.blogspot.com/), and Dead Man Eating (www.deadmaneating.blogspot.com/), a morbidly fascinating account of condemned inmates' last meal requests.
- **Stereogum** (www.stereogum.com/): Stereogum is all about music, music, music. It's a great place not only to catch up on your favorite artists, but also to find new music that you might not have found otherwise. Similar music blogs are Hype Machine (http://hypem.com/), Idolator (www.idolator.com/), and Culture Bully (www.culturebully.com/).
- **The Huffington Post** (www.huffingtonpost.com/): Need up-to-the-minute political news and commentary? This is a good place to find it. Similar blogs are Little Green Footballs (www.littlegreenfootballs.com/weblog/weblog.php), Daily Kos (www.dailykos.com/), and Michelle Malkin (www.michellemalkin.com/). Note: These are both right-wing and left-wing blogs; I try to get a balanced perspective.

- **Problogger** (www.problogger.net/): Darren Rowse is a professional blogger, meaning that he actually earns a living (and a pretty good one too!) by blogging. He's been at it for a while now and has a lot of wisdom to share; I always come away having learned something new. Similar blogs are Copyblogger (www.copyblogger.com/), Kathy Sierra (www.headrush.typepad.com/), and Amy Gahran (www.rightconversation.com/).
- **Oh No They Didn't!** (http://community.livejournal.com/ohnotheydidnt): This is a community-driven gossip blog, where anyone registered in the LiveJournal community can post (after approval by moderators). Since there are hundreds of people able to post, it's very frequently updated and is one of the best places on the Web to get the fastest celebrity scoops. Similar blogs are Defamer (www.defamer.com/), Pink Is the New Blog (www.trent.blogspot.com/), and Damn ImCute (www.damnimcute.com/).
- **How to Change the World** (http://blog.guykawasaki.com/): Guy Kawasaki is the author of this entrepreneurial-oriented blog, which is full of instructions on how to get along in your workplace more effectively, along with his thoughts on life in general. Similar blogs that give out moneymaking and entrepreneurial tips are Shoemoney (www.shoemoney.com/), the Jason Calacanis Weblog (www.calacanis.com/), and Fred Wilson's A VC in New York (www.avc.blogs.com/a_vc/).
- **Daily Dose of Imagery** (www.wvs.topleftpixel.com/): One of the most beautiful photoblogs (blogs primarily centered around photography) on the Web today. Every day with rare exceptions a new, gorgeously framed image is posted. As an amateur photography fan myself, I really appreciate this particular blog. Similar photoblogs are

Shorpy (www.shorpy.com/) and FlickrBlog (http://blog.flickr.com/).

- **Zach Braff** (www.zachbraff.com): Blogging has even taken off in the celebrity world! If you like Zach Braff, you'll enjoy checking out his blog where he talks about his life and what's going on behind the scenes of his latest projects. There are many other celebrities who have blogs that might be more to your taste; Al Roker (www.alroker.com/journal.cfm), Rosie O'Donnell (www.rosie.com/), and Moby (www.moby.com/journal). I'm hopeful that more celebrities will take up blogging; I for one think it's a great way to connect personally with your fans.

Wow! That's a lot of blogs to check out. I'm sure you'll find at least a few blogs here in my picks that will be right up your alley.

How to Find Blogs You're Interested In

I've mentioned blog search engines, blogrolls, and plain old-fashioned word of mouth as good ways to find blogs that you might be interested in, but there are also a few even more specific ways you can find blogs that are producing the content you want to read.

First, let's investigate the blogroll technique just a bit further. Most blogs have a blogroll somewhere on their pages; this is a list of the blogs that the writer has chosen either because he enjoys reading them or because they are similar to the writer's own blog. For instance, a popular cooking blog might have a blogroll full of other cooking blogs, a sports blog could have a blogroll listing more sports blogs, etc. This is the way that I find most of the blogs that I've ended up adding to my RSS feed reader.

Secondly, Technorati, a blog search engine, is a superb place to find blogs since anyone who has registered their site with

TOOLS YOU NEED

▶ MySpace, the biggest social networking community on the Web, gives each user the space to have his or her own blog. I've got a bunch of great MySpace articles and tutorials for you: how to add music to your MySpace home on the Web (http://about.com/websearch/myspacemusic), and the best music video codes for your MySpace (http://about.com/websearch/myspacevideos).

Technorati is strongly encouraged to "tag," or label, their posts with appropriate subjects. For instance, if I write a post about cats, I would tag my content with the Technorati tag "cats" (most blogging platforms either have built-in tagging support or easy-to-install tagging extensions). So, long story short, you can use Technorati to search for pretty vague subject matter and then drill down to more specific topics—for instance, cats: http://technorati.com/blogs/cats. Once you find a subject that works for you, you can narrow your search even further by using Technorati's advanced search parameters to jiggle various factors in your search, such as authority, popularity, freshness, etc.

Last but not least is Bloglines (www.bloglines.com), which we already talked extensively about in Chapter 5, "Searching the Web with RSS." Bloglines is not only great for keeping track of your RSS feeds; you can use it to find other blogs that you might be interested in.

Here's how: Go to the Bloglines list of Most Popular Feeds (most subscribed-to blogs) at www.bloglines.com/topblogs. These are the blogs that have the highest numbers of people actually subscribed to them via RSS in Bloglines.

You have quite a few options on this page. Under each blog, you'll see three links: Preview, Related Feeds, and Subscribe. If you want to learn more about any of these blogs, you can hit Preview. If you like what you see, you can instantly subscribe to that blog using the Subscribe link; then you can use the Related Feeds link to find blogs that are similar in content to the one that you just previewed.

You can also check out the Feed Directory (www.bloglines.com/dir?mode=0), an alphabetical list of all Bloglines feeds, or the User Directory (www.bloglines.com/dir?mode=1) a directory of Bloglines registered users along with the number of individual subscribers.

WHAT'S HOT

▶ Choosing a blogging platform can be way more complicated than what I outline in this section; however, that's where professional blogger Darren Rowse comes in. He's written a detailed article titled "Choosing a Blog Platform" (www.problogger.net/archives/2006/02/15/choosing-a-blog-platform/). In the article, he teaches us how to figure out our blogging goals, budget, design, and technological aptitude, and then he goes on to give the pros and cons of various blogging platform options. It's a must-read for anyone who wants to get more serious about their blogging!

Last but not least is one of my favorite Bloglines features: Bloglines Quick Picks (**www.bloglines.com/subbundles**). On the left they've given you specific content categories to choose from, ranging from Animal Lover right on down to Wordsmith. Check the plus sign next to the topics that you're interested in and you'll be given at least five blogs that have what you're looking for. It's a fun and fast way to find relevant blogs.

Blogging Platforms

As you can tell by now, blogs are somewhat easy to find using search engines, actual blogrolls, and simple word of mouth—other people sending you a blog that they liked and would like you to check out. However, did you know that you don't only have the option of finding blogs, you can also write one? Yep—and there are all kinds of really great free blogging platforms out there that will host your blog for you on the Web, help you with the technical back-end stuff, and even help you design and choose a template.

Lots of questions come up when choosing a blog platform. It really depends on what you want your blog to do. For instance, if you're just interested in keeping a daily journal of your family, you probably don't need something that is overly fancy, at least not at first. Only you can determine what can meet your needs as far as blogging platforms are concerned; however, that said, I can recommend some good basic blogging services that will help you get going with a minimum of fuss.

The simplest and easiest to use blogging program out there has to be Blogger (**www.blogger.com/**). Sign-up is free, and it took me about two minutes to get a blog actually up and running on the Web. MSN Live Spaces (**http://spaces.live.com/**) is from Microsoft; as with Blogger, you can use this to make a nice-looking blog in a matter of minutes. It's easy to use, and since you are instantly in the MSN community, you're able to browse through blogs that you might not have had the opportunity to find otherwise.

WordPress (**http://wordpress.com/**) is another blogging application that is relatively easy to get up and running; however, it's definitely not as newbie-friendly as Blogger. I use WordPress on some of my personal blogs and I really appreciate how much oomph it has. But if you're not comfortable with a bit of code-tweaking, you probably want to stick with Blogger until you get your feet wet.

Tumblr (**www.tumblr.com/**) is a relatively new service. You can use Tumblr as a sort of "stream of consciousness" blogging platform, posting videos, thoughts, rants, links, pretty much whatever you want. It's extremely simple to set up, and it gives you plenty of options to customize your template.

Twitter (**http://twitter.com/home**) could technically be called a blogging platform; it's a unique service. The best explanation I've heard of Twitter is as a "mini-blogging" application, and I think this is fitting. Basically, you're given your own home page, and you're limited to what you can write in 140 or fewer characters. You can use Twitter to update friends on what you're doing, correspond with people all over the world, or keep a daily online journal of your day (which is what I use it for).

Get Linked

Want to learn more about the blogosphere? Try these resources on my About.com Web search site.

TECHNORATI, A BLOG SEARCH ENGINE

Technorati is a real-time search engine dedicated to the blogosphere. It searches only through blogs to find exactly what you're looking for. At the time of this writing, Technorati was tracking over 22 million sites and over a billion links, a mind-boggling amount.

http://about.com/websearch/technorati

INTERVIEW WITH PROFESSIONAL BLOGGER DARREN ROWSE

I recently had the privilege of interviewing Darren Rowse of Pro Blogger. Read what he had to say about blogging, earning money with blogging, how he got started being a ProBlogger, how to make money from home, and more.

http://about.com/websearch/darrenrowse

Chapter 13

Keeping Your Web Searches Private

What Web Sites Know about You

When you log on to the Web, do you feel anonymous? If you do, then unfortunately you have fallen prey to the same naive thinking that many, many Web searchers do: that what you do on the Web is completely unknown to anyone but you. Au contraire!

You can reveal more than you realize while you Web surf. One of the biggest draws of the Web since its inception is that there are very few laws or regulations governing what goes on, and that's both a good thing and a bad thing. Good, because then we all benefit from free speech; but bad as well, because there are people out there who don't have your best interests in mind, and will exploit your lack of caution.

Why is my search privacy worth guarding?

▸ **We should all have a healthy concern about how private our Web searches are. Not only can our search history be potentially linked to our personally identifying information, but there have been incidents in recent history where individuals' search histories were actually used against them in a court of law. It's a good idea to be knowledgeable about what's going on.**

While you are surfing the Web, there are a few different ways that information is collected about you by every site you visit.

Cookies. No, not the chocolate chip kind, unfortunately. In the context of the Web, cookies are bits of information sent to your browser by Web sites that you visit. Your browser stores and saves these bits of information on your computer (usually in your temporary Internet files folder). The next time you visit that Web site, this information is retrieved so your visit is customized, with less load-time effort for your browser. Cookies are actually very helpful because they help Web sites personalize your visits; however, they can be linked with information that uniquely identifies you.

Your browser: Amazingly enough, your browser can let a Web site know what unique computer address you are coming in from, what kind of operating system you are running, the last link you clicked, and possibly even your e-mail address. This isn't a concern until you realize that there are many security "holes" in Web browsers that allow unscrupulous **hackers** to get in and exploit those holes for their own nefarious purposes. For the most part, these security holes are taken care of as soon as they're spotted, but hackers are constantly on the hunt for new ones.

Search engines: What did you search for last? Was it something . . . a bit embarrassing? Maybe personal? You might not be as anonymous as you think you are. Search engines use cookies to collect information about their users; however, if you decide to register for a free service offered by a search engine (e-mail, picture albums, etc.) then you've given them a name and personal identification to hang that cookie upon. It is not widely known how exactly search engines use this information to track their users, but there's little disagreement that the practice is indeed going on. For more information, I invite you to read Wired's article "What Search Sites Know About You" at **www.wired.com/politics/security/news/2005/04/67062**.

E-commerce Web sites: Have you ever bought something on the Web? I certainly have. If you have navigated to a site without proper security precautions in place on your computer, your financial information is in danger of being stolen.

Existing information: is your information in the Yellow Pages? Do you have your own business? Have you ever been on an electronic mailing list? Most likely there is already a lot of information out there on the Web about you, without your explicit knowledge or consent. Unless you go to great lengths to stop this from happening, it's just one of those facts of Web life that we all have to deal with. (To see how much information might actually be out there, periodically try putting your name into Google—you might be surprised.) There's no law on the books (and there most likely won't be) against publishing this sort of semi-private information on the Web, but there are ways you can protect yourself.

Bad downloads: Back when I was just starting to get into the Web, I thought it would be cool to download a free waterfalls screensaver. Was that ever a bad idea! This free software not only crashed my hard drive, but also installed (without my permission, obviously) spyware on my machine that immediately set to work gathering as much personal and/or sensitive information as possible: such as credit card numbers, bank passwords, e-mail passwords and logins, and a lot more (I was able to stop the spyware before it caused too much damage, thankfully!). I sure learned my lesson the hard way; never download anything that is not from a reliable, reputable source.

E-mail: If your e-mail address appears somewhere on the Web—in a newsgroup, on a Web site, in a seemingly harmless chat room—then you've just provided someone who spams e-mail addresses for a living with all they need to put you on their mailing list (and pretty much never take you off). Spam mail is basically all the "junk" mail you get in your e-mail inbox; it's just like the

TOOLS YOU NEED

▶ If you're as tired as I am of sites forcing you to go through registration just to view their content, than Bug-MeNot (www.bugmenot .com) is for you. It's easy to use and makes life much simpler, not to mention that it's a good guard of your online privacy and enables you to surf anonymously. Read more about BugMeNot in my article titled "Avoid Annoying Registration with Bug-MeNot" (http://about.com/ websearch/bugmenot).

What's the best way to be safe on the Web?

▶ Along with all the suggestions I'm giving you in this chapter, there are also some extra precautions you can take to make sure you're as safe as possible. If you have a blog, use a pseudonym instead of your real name, and don't give out any details that would identify you personally. The Electronic Frontier Foundation (EFF) has an excellent article on how to blog safely on the Web: you can read it at www.eff.org/Privacy/Anonymity/blog-anonymously.php.

unsolicited ads you get in your real mailbox, but it's e-mail. Many people don't realize that their e-mail addresses should be guarded just as carefully as their personal information on the Web, if for nothing else to avoid the annoyance and inconvenience that spam mail can cause you.

A bit daunting, isn't it, to realize all the different ways that your private information can be exploited on the Web! I don't want you to be discouraged and simply throw in the towel, though—there are many ways to safeguard your information and become a more savvy Web searcher.

Ways to Keep Your Search History Private

Phishing is what we call the practice of tricking someone on the Web in order to retrieve their sensitive personal information: passwords, banking information, etc. Find out more about phishing (and how to recognize it) by visitng http://about.com/websearch/phishing faq.

I think the key to being safe on the Web is this: we need to cultivate a healthy fear of how badly both our computers and our personal information can be mangled, but at the same time, we need to understand that there are many precautions we can take that will cover most of our safety bases.

The first precaution that you can take is with your computer, by preventing adware and spyware. This issue is a bit too complex to go into here, so I'll refer you to an article on how to prevent prevent adware and spyware here: http://about.com/antivirus/spywareadware. For free spyware and adware detection software, visit http://about.com/netsecurity/spywaredetection, and to learn more about protecting yourself from spyware, visit http://about.com/netsecurity/protect. For Mac users, find out about virus and spyware prevention here: http://about.com/macs/spywareandvirus. If you are concerned about protecting your identity, this is a good resource: http://about.com/idtheft/protectid.

Now, most of us have no need to hide our search history, but there's no harm in cultivating safer Web searching habits, right? There's nothing particularly cloak-and-dagger in what I'm going to share with you in this section; it mostly consists of plain old-fashioned common sense.

Don't fill out forms on the Web that require personal information. Many Web sites, particularly newspaper sites, tend to make you fill out a whole form with personal information just to access their content.

If you decide to use a "junk" e-mail address (an e-mail address that you use only for online forms, sweepstakes, etc.) you might want to think about using Contactify (www.contactify.com/), a service that allows you to create your own personal contact form on the Web. All it displays is one simple link; people click it and can send you a message, but your real e-mail address is never revealed.

Avoid filling out these needlessly invasive forms if you can. You can usually find the content you're looking for on another site that does not require registration, and spending a little more time searching for duplicate content is preferable to having your personal information sold to other companies so they can fill up your e-mail inbox with personal "offers."

Yep, that's where you get spam! Many of those annoying spam e-mails clogging up your inbox have their origin in some kind of form you might have filled out on the Web, since many of the companies that ask you to fill out these forms actually sell this information to other companies, who then use it in turn to send you advertisements.

ELSEWHERE ON THE WEB

▶ One of the easiest ways for you to lose your Web search privacy is to have your passwords compromised. KeePass, a free password manager, is a safe way around this problem. KeePass is a free download; it's a password manager that helps you manage all your passwords in one secure database that only you have access to. Try it yourself at www.keepass .info.

The best way to avoid many spammy e-mails and safeguard
your online privacy at the same time is to avoid filling out forms on
the Web unless you are completely confident that the company or
Web site asking you to fill out the form has a trustworthy reputation and will not sell your information.

You'll also want to take the time to read the privacy policy of
any Web site that asks you to fill out a form. I know that sounds
like overkill, and if you've ever gotten a peek at the legalese-choked
privacy policies that many Web sites are sporting these days, you
might not agree with this particular piece of advice. However, this
is where you can usually track down what kind of use the company or Web site has planned for your personal information, and
sometimes you're even given the option to opt out of having your
information sold.

I learned a long time ago to use two separate e-mail addresses
on the Web in order to keep my spam level way down. Here's
how it works: I simply went to Hotmail, one of the most popular
free e-mail services on the Web, got myself a free e-mail address,
and then decided that this was going to be the e-mail addy that
ran interference for me whenever I had to fill out a form online.
That way, if I do get spam, it goes to this address instead of my
main e-mail address, where (so far) I've managed to keep my spam
level relatively low. This is also a simple way for you to guard your
anonymity, because the less of your private, personal information
on the Web for everyone to see, the better.

Watch those personal searches. Have you ever done a "vanity search"? We all probably have at one time or another; it simply
consists of you typing your name or other personally identifying
information into your search engine of choice to see what's out
there on the Web.

Now, there's nothing wrong with vanity searches, but if you start making a habit of these personal searches, and start using even more of your personal information, your searches can actually be linked together and it's possible—not very likely, but possible—that if asked in a court of law, your search engine searches can be pieced together in an effort to identify you. For example, when AOL released search data in 2006, even though they replaced personal screen names with random numbers, many people could be identitfied based on their (now public) searches. What kind of personal information are we talking about here?

- your full name, especially if it's a somewhat uncommon name
- your social security number
- your street address and phone number
- your e-mail address
- your driver's license number
- your date of birth
- your credit card numbers

Now, granted, so far in Web history there have been relatively few cases where a search engine has been actually subpoenaed into giving up their search records, but the possibility and the ability to do so should always be kept in mind. Remember this when typing anything private or potentially illegal into a search engine.

In addition, if you are doing this kind of personal search on a public computer—meaning a computer that other people can also access, such as in a library, at work, or in a college computer center—then you have opened yourself up nicely to the wonderful world of identity theft. Any savvy thief would be able to wreak a

WHAT'S HOT

▶ In 2006, AOL released more than 20 million private Web queries from 650,000 AOL users in a shockingly inappropriate breach of privacy. The data included names, addresses, social security numbers, credit card numbers, and a whole host of other personally identifying information. For more information and to find out if your privacy may have been invaded, visit http://about .com/websearch/aolprivacy.

fair amount of havoc with even just two bits of any of the personally identifying information in the list above; it really doesn't take that much.

So how do you prevent your personal information from being compromised? The simplest solution is this: don't put it out there. Don't make it easy for identity thieves to come after you and clean up, so to speak. If I had to choose, I would say that it's quite all right to do a search for your name, but the rest of the list? Ignorance is bliss. There is very little chance that your social security or credit card numbers (for example) are out there languishing away on a Web site somewhere, and searching for them serves little purpose except to give the bad guys some more ammo; however, you can search for portions of this information that can tell you if they've been leaked *without* giving away your full information.

Restrict the search engines you use to do your Web searches. If you log onto the Web through an ISP such as Comcast, Earthlink, etc., don't use their search tools to browse the Web, because they'll easily be able to keep tabs on everything you're doing.

Following that same trail of thought, it's also a wise idea (yet not one that most of us, including me, do on a regular basis) to log out of peripheral search engine services before searching the Web. Many search engines these days have a range of services they offer you, anything from document sharing to instant messaging. Google, for instance, has such useful services that I find myself logged in to at least one at any given time.

Privacy advocates strongly advise against this practice, since once you're logged into your Gmail, for example, your moves are being tracked and logged. It would be relatively simple for that search engine to build up a pretty complete profile of you, if they wanted to. For the sake of privacy, try to remember to log out of

ELSEWHERE ON THE WEB

▶ You can do a lot to boost your search privacy at home since you have control over your machine, but what about at work? You have options, but they are somewhat limited depending on what your corporate Web search privacy policy is. Lifehacker has a good tutorial on how to make the most of your work Web search privacy here: www.lifehacker .com/software/privacy/hack-attack-bolster-your-brows ing-privacy-at-work-228841. php.

peripheral services before using the search engine's primary function: that is, to search the Web.

Now, why should we bother being concerned about search engines tying our searches together? There are a few reasons. First, a lot of people just don't like the idea of search engines knowing what they're searching for and being able to use that information to identify them personally. In addition, while we all feel relatively secure in the knowledge that our searches are not going to be used against us, we have no guarantee that in the future they will not be.

Change your IP address. Okay, first, what in the world is an IP address? Basically, an IP (Internet Protocol) address is the unique numeric signature for each computer connected to the Internet. I have one, you have one, and search engines (and Web sites) are technically able to use your IP address to group all your searches together in one searchable package.

How can you get around this? Simple—you just change your IP address. It's pretty easy to do; just unplug your modem for a few seconds and then plug it back in. Ta da! New IP address. Now, this doesn't work in every situation; for instance, most workplaces will give their workstations a static IP (the IP address does not change no matter what you do), but there are ways around even that (we'll go into that in this chapter when we cover anonymous browsing tools).

Clear your search history. Every single thing you search for is stored somewhere on your computer, and it's a good idea for privacy's sake (not to mention the health of your machine) to clear it out once in a while. It's easy to do this in Windows, but it does take some time and navigating around your computer. Rather than giving you a quite lengthy explanation here, I'm going to refer you

TOOLS YOU NEED

▶ One of the most frequent reader e-mails I receive is about ZabaSearch, a free service that provides publicly accessible information about you all in one place (address, phone number, etc). Many people are concerned, and rightly so, about removing their personal information from ZabaSearch's index. The people at ZabaSearch don't make it easy. Basically, you have to write them a letter that includes particular information. I've written up all the pertinent addresses, instructions, etc. here: http://about.com/websearch/zabasearch.

to wikiHow's excellent and simple tutorial titled "How to Delete Your Usage History in Windows" (www.wikihow.com/Delete-your -Usage-History-Tracks-in-Windows).

Most Web sites have cookies, tiny software programs that track your visits (remember, we talked about cookies at the beginning of this chapter). You don't want to completely disable cookies because your Web search experience will definitely suffer, but you should clean them out every once in a while. For Internet Explorer users, try this simple tutorial from PC World titled "Clear Your Cookies and History" (http://tinyurl.com/2w6klb); for Firefox users, try "Using the Cookie Manager" (www.mozilla.org/projects/ security/pki/psm/help_21/using_priv_help.html).

Most Internet browsers keep track of every Web site you type into the address bar. In Internet Explorer, you can delete your search history by clicking Tools, then Internet Options, then the Clear History button near the bottom of the General tab. In Firefox, all you need to do is go to Tools, then Options, then Privacy and click the Clear button in the History section. Now, this is not a catchall fix—it does not remove your entire search history from your computer, but just your browser—but it's a good start.

Last, but not least, it's a good idea to clean out your cache. In order to promote a faster browsing experience, all browsers keep copies of Web sites you've visited in a temporary "cache" file. The same process I described above to clean out your search history can be used to clean out your cache—you just click different buttons.

Consider using different browsers for different Web activities. Designate one browser window for search, the other for e-mail, and you'll have two different sessions going on with a bit more privacy. For instance, I tend to use Internet Explorer to get into my Hotmail, but then I use Firefox to search Google.

Delete your search engine history. Now, didn't we already talk about deleting search history? Sort of. There's a lot to it. What I'm talking about here is actually deleting the history of your drop-down searches, particularly in Google.

When you do a search in Google, that information is not actually saved at Google; instead, it's logged in your browser, on your hard drive in your temporary Internet files, etc. You clear your Google search history from your browser when you do the procedure just mentioned in the preceding "Clear your search history" section. You can clear it from the actual Google search box in a few easy steps. First, for Internet Explorer:

1. Go to the Tools menu.
2. Select Internet Options and the Content tab.
3. Within the Personal information area, select AutoComplete.
4. Click Clear Forms. You can also uncheck the Forms box in this window to keep this information from being stored in the future.
5. Click OK to exit.

And then for Firefox:

1. Go to the Tools menu.
2. Select Options, then Privacy, then Saved Form Information.
3. Click Clear and uncheck the box.
4. Click OK to exit.

Whew! So, why is it important to do this every once in a while? The less information you have hanging around on your computer for people or systems to track you personally, the better.

ELSEWHERE ON THE WEB

▶ Many people are becoming more and more concerned with how much influence Google wields over the search landscape in general. One of the best sites to find out more about this is Google Watch (www.google-watch.org/), a site that acts as an unofficial "watcher" of Google and keeps tabs on policies that might negatively impact searchers at large. It's a bit on the conspiracy side, however, so do read it with the proverbial grain of salt.

Clear your search toolbar history. If you have a search toolbar installed (as I do), or you use desktop search tools, you're going to want to clean out those caches fairly frequently as well. Yep—those toolbars and desktop search services store information separately from your browser, something not a lot of people realize. If you have the Google Toolbar installed here's how you would clear the search history:

1. Click the Google logo on the Toolbar to access the drop-down menu.
2. Select the Clear Search History option.

There are many other search toolbars out there that you might be using; I strongly suggest that you learn how to clear the search history in whatever search toolbar you choose.

Use a good virus protection and firewall service. Sometimes I forget, being someone who is on the Web all the time and very comfortable with technology, how important a good virus protection and firewall program are in giving me privacy peace of mind. I guesstimate that a good 90 percent of potential privacy hacks are foiled in their tracks by the use of these vital software tools (unless otherwise specified, the following tools are for Windows machines only).

The best place to find good antivirus and firewall software suggestions is About.com's Antivirus Software site (http://antivirus .about.com/); however, if you are looking for something quick, easy, and—most of all—free that you can get up and running today, here are my suggestions:

- Ad-Aware   (www.lavasoftusa.com/products/ad-aware_se_ personal.php): This is one of the most popular anti-spyware programs out there on the market today, and with good reason: it's free and it works. I run Ad-Aware about once a week with the Quick Scan function, once a month for a complete system scan. It's a good way to keep nasty privacy-infringing programs off my computer.

- **Spybot** (www.spybot.info): An excellent spyware "search and destroy" program, also free. I tend to run Spybot at the same time I run my weekly Ad-Aware scan.
- **ClamWin** (www.clamwin.com): A free, open-source antivirus Windows program. ClamWin comes with some pretty powerful features for a free program: you can schedule your virus scans, plus it integrates nicely with Outlook.
- **AVG Free Anti-Virus** (www.free.grisoft.com/freeweb.php/doc/2/): Another Windows-based virus-scanning program. AVG tends to run a bit on the slow side, so you might want to schedule your scans for an overnight run. A free program.
- **Avast** (www.avast.com/eng/down_home.html): Again for Windows users, Avast is a good virus protection program. Avast also scans e-mail and software downloads for possible problems; again, it's a free program.

Many privacy problems can be solved pretty quickly simply by using these and other antivirus and anti-spyware programs; it's just another layer of protection. And while I did list quite a few virus protection programs here for Windows, you Mac users have some pretty powerful tools that can help you protect yourself as well—you can find them at http://about.com/antivirus/macs.

Use common sense. Unfortunately, there are not a lot of Web sites that advertise they are going to steal your information, use your credit card numbers, and rob you blind. That's where common sense comes in. For instance, if you have navigated to a Web site that has products for sale, yet seems to be poorly constructed and unprofessional-looking, then you probably will want to go elsewhere to buy that particular product. Sure, you might be completely safe, but why take a chance? Your privacy is much more important.

Even though I've given you a variety of ways to guard your search privacy in this section, there's one more major tool you have in your search privacy arsenal: anonymous surfing.

Introduction to Anonymous Surfing

People have many reasons for wanting to surf the Web anonymously without being tracked, but they all boil down to the need to protect something or someone. For instance, if you are in a country that has restrictive Web policies, you probably want to hide your browsing habits from the government if you are looking at sites that are contrary to their policies.

If you are at work, you might not want your employer to see that you've been looking for another job. If you are at home searching for prescription drug information, you probably don't want spam e-mails sent to you offering the latest in drug advancements. It's all about privacy.

Anonymous surfing preserves privacy. As I pointed out, people usually get interested in anonymous surfing for various reasons that really just come down to maintaining privacy.

Privacy from other people: You'd be surprised at how much information is available from your Web surfing habits. For instance, by using simple "sniffers" (hacker tools), somebody who really wanted to could find out your IP address, cookies, what's in your browser cache, what kind of computer you're using . . . they could even connect to your hard drive and access your private files, including passwords and banking information.

Privacy from the Web: Say you're searching the Web for information on a drug to help with your arthritis. Your search keywords, IP address, time, etc. will probably be logged and tracked by the Web site that you land on. Best-case scenario is that you just start getting a lot of spammy e-mails in your inbox trying to sell you the new arthritis wonder drug.

Worst-case scenario looks like this: your browsing information is sold to other drug Web site companies, you start getting telemarketing phone calls at dinner time (your phone number is easily accessible unless it is unlisted), you start getting junk mail at home, and lots more. Suffice to say that there are a lot of ways that unscrupulous companies can manipulate the information that you give them on the Web.

How does anonymous surfing work? In a nutshell, anonymous surfing works by putting a buffer between you and the Web site you want to look at, allowing you to view information without being tracked. There are two main ways in which this can be accomplished.

Anonymous or **proxy servers** work by retrieving Web pages for you. They hide your IP address and other important browsing information, so the remote server does not see your information but sees the proxy server's information instead.

However, there is a slight chance that the anonymous server is recording your data, and it is entirely feasible that a malicious proxy server can scoop up everything on your machine. Using an anonymous server with a good user rating and clear privacy policy should avoid this. A list of proxy servers is available at a variety of different sites, including:

● **Public Proxy Servers** (www.publicproxyservers.com/page1 .html)

- **Proxy 4 Free** (www.proxy4free.com/page1.html)
- **Elite Proxy** (www.eliteproxy.us/proxy.php)

For much, much more detailed information about how proxy servers work and how to set up your browser to surf with an anonymous server, I invite you to check out Bradley Mitchell's excellent six-part tutorial titled "Introduction to Proxy Servers" here: http://about.com/compnetworking/proxyservers.

Free Anonymous Proxy Sites and Services

Surfing with an anonymous proxy site or service is simple: all you do is navigate to the anonymous proxy site and enter the URL you'd like to visit anonymously, and you'll be able to surf leaving virtually no trace that you were ever there. The anonymous proxy retrieves the pages before they are delivered to you. This way, the IP address and other browsing information that the remote server sees does not belong to you, it belongs to the anonymous proxy.

That's the good news. The bad news is that these anonymous proxy services tend to slow down your lightning-fast browsing a bit, and there usually will be ads at the top of your browser window (they've got to pay the bills somehow!). But it's worth it if you really need to be invisible on the Web.

There are literally hundreds of free anonymous proxies out there; here are just a few:

- **Anonymouse** (http://anonymouse.org/): Helps you to surf the Web and keep your information private.
- **HideAndGoSurf.com** (www.hideandgosurf.com/): You can choose which information you'd like stripped from the record here.

- **Tor** (http://tor.eff.org/): A great tool to help you anonymize yourself.
- **250 Working Proxies** (www.econsultant.com/proxylist/index.html): The biggest list I've ever seen of anonymous proxies.

Search Privacy Common Sense Checklist

Seems like a lot of steps to take in order to protect your privacy. Trust me, though, it's worth it. If you're at all worried about your privacy or the privacy of your kids when using the Internet, it is important to follow the steps outlined in this chapter. In case you got lost during that detailed explanation, here is a handy checklist that you can use when you find yourself worrying about your privacy on the Net.

- ✔ Don't share your personal information.
- ✔ Familiarize yourself with anonymous browsing.
- ✔ Protect your e-mail address—use a "junk" e-mail address for online offers.
- ✔ Clear your computer's search history on a regular basis.
- ✔ Don't fill out online forms unless they are absolutely secure.
- ✔ Check privacy policies.
- ✔ Invest in a good antivirus and anti-spyware program, and schedule scans on a regular basis.

Voilà! Your privacy has just been protected. If you take all of these steps, your information will be that much safer and you can have a more relaxing surfing experience.

Get Linked

Search privacy is definitely an important issue. Here are some more search privacy resources on my About.com Web search site:

SEARCH ENGINES AND INTERNET PRIVACY

Ever wondered what a search engine's privacy policy looks like? Here are a few for you the next time you'd like some light reading.

⤢ http://about.com/websearch/internetprivacy

THE ANATOMY OF A PHISHING SCAM

Phishing is becoming more and more prevalent on the Web. View the Anatomy of a Phishing Scam image gallery to find out how to identify a phishing scam.

⤢ http://about.com/websearch/phishinganatomy

Chapter 14

Most-Requested Reader Searches

I get a lot of e-mails from readers asking for help on how to find things on the Web more easily, from finding a lost pet to tracking down complicated genealogy records. I tend to get e-mails on a few specific Web search questions in particular: how to find people, how to find public records, how to find various freebies, how to find directions, and how to find . . . well, you can pretty much use your imagination here!

Sites to Help Find People

Finding people on the Web is either really easy or really hard. Very scientific opinion there, wouldn't you say? What I mean is that if someone's information is on the Web already—through publicly accessible information such as the Yellow Pages, business listings, etc.—then it will be relatively simple to track them down. If someone's information is not on the Web—if, for instance, they have an unlisted phone number, a P.O. Box, don't have an e-mail

About.com

address, and are not active on the Web—then it will be harder to find information on them.

That being said, there are a lot of different ways you can use the Web to find information about someone—you just have to be a little creative. Note: Every one of the Web sites that I give you in this section is one that I've tested myself, and as of the time of this writing, they are all free. If you are asked for money, you've either inadvertently clicked an advertisement or that particular Web site has changed its policies.

First, let's look at a few phone directories. These are great places to start your search for someone's phone number or address.

- **Switchboard** (www.switchboard.com): Awarded PC Magazine's Best of the Internet 2004 award; allows you to search for businesses, people, phone numbers, e-mail addresses, and lots more.
- **Lycos People Search** (www.whowhere.com): Searches not only the white and yellow pages, but for professional profiles and alumni e-mail addresses as well.
- **WhitePages.com** (www.whitepages.com): Search by both first and last names to find a phone number.
- **DexOnline** (www.dexknows.com/displayhome.ds): Search for residential, business, and government phone listings.
- **Anywho.com** (www.anywho.com/rl.html): Find a business or person via phone number.

Google can find phone numbers easily. There are three basic Google search operators with which this can be accomplished:

- **bphonebook:** search business listings
- **rphonebook:** search residential listings
- **phonebook:** search all phone listings

To search for residential phone numbers, you would frame your search in Google like this:

```
rphonebook: johnson seattle
```

This search would bring up all the residential listings for Johnson in the city of Seattle. In order to search for a full name, you can do this:

```
rphonebook: sam johnson seattle
```

You can include a middle initial in there if you really want to, but unless the person is listed with that initial, it's probably not worth your while.

To find business phone numbers with Google, you would use this search syntax:

```
bphonebook: refinishing new york
```

This search brings up all the listings for refinishing professionals in New York.

If you're not sure whether what you're looking for is business or residential, you can simply use the Google phonebook operator:

```
phonebook: smith CPA portland
```

This search would bring back all the CPAs in Portland with the last name Smith.

ELSEWHERE ON THE WEB

▶ JournalismNet (www .journalismnet.com/people/) has a well-written article about the variety of ways you can use the Web to find someone. You also might want to look at LibrarySpot's list of people-finding resources at www. libraryspot.com/people.htm; there are general search resources here as well as specific professional organizations, biographies, general statistics, and demographical information.

Google also allows searchers to do a "reverse lookup"—that is, find a name and address attached to a phone number. Here's how you would frame your search:

```
503 555 1212 or phonebook: 503 555 1212
```

The search syntax requires that you have the area code and spaces between the blocks of numbers; it does matter if you put the hyphens in there, so don't do it. The "phonebook" operator searches both the business and residential listings for whatever phone number you put in. As a side note, if you don't want your phone number listed in the Google Phonebook directory, you can visit the Google Phonebook Name Removal page at www.google.com/intl/en/help/pbremoval.html to have it removed.

Many Web sites and search engines offer free people searches. Here are a few of the best ones, both general and specific, that I've been able to find and had good luck with:

- **Yahoo Free People Search** (http://people.yahoo.com): One of the easiest to use interfaces out there. Comprehensive results are delivered quickly. Also allows e-mail search.
- **411 Locate** (www.411locate.com): Instant access to driving directions, reverse lookups, yellow pages, white pages, and more.
- **YourFamily** (www.yourfamily.com): Online since 1996; enables you to find missing family members and start genealogy research.
- **Census Finder** (www.censusfinder.com): Almost 30,000 free census records available online. Searches both locally and internationally.

Can you find unlisted or cell phone numbers on the Web?

▶ In a word, no. Unlisted numbers are not in a phone book, which means that they will not be inputted into a phone directory's Web database. Cell phone numbers are practically unlisted unless you specifically ask for your cell phone number to be included in your local phone book. Every time that I've tried to search for a phone number on the Web and come up empty, it's because the number fits into one of these two categories.

- **FamilySearch** (www.familysearch.org): An extremely comprehensive site put out by the Church of Jesus Christ of Latter-day Saints. Their family records database is one of the largest on the Web.
- **ZoomInfo** (www.zoominfo.com): ZoomInfo is a quick way to find compiled information on both individuals and companies.
- **Pretrieve** (www.pretrieve.com/): Find free public records with Pretrieve, a free public records search engine. Find people online, search for business information, look for address and phone numbers.
- **ZabaSearch** (www.zabasearch.com/): Find people with ZabaSearch.com, a free people search engine. Searches for publicly available records are free but there is a search fee for searches of other documents, such as credit reports.
- **MySpace** (www.myspace.com/): MySpace is one of the most popular sites on the Web for one very good reason: it's a great place to find people for free. You can locate old friends, high school buddies, and more.

In addition, you can use Google for many people searches simply by typing in someone's name; you'd be surprised at how much you can turn up.

There are many obituary sources online. I've also received many e-mails asking for help on how to find obituaries. Usually people are researching their genealogy or family history in general, and just want some help on finding records. Here are a few of the Web sites that I've recommended:

- **Ancestry Social Security Master Death Index** ([www.ancestry .com/search/db.aspx?dbid=3693](www.ancestry.com/search/db.aspx?dbid=3693)): Start your basic research

ELSEWHERE ON THE WEB

▶ How many times have you called up a company only to be lost in voice-recorded hell? Many times, I'm sure. DialA-Human ([www.dialahuman .com/](www.dialahuman.com/)) aims to get you past all that with their alphabetical list of businesses and the secret tricks to get to a real, live human. The next time I call up my insurance company I'm going to consult this Web site first—should save me both some waiting time and unnecessary frustration.

▶ About.com has a ton of great resources for business information. The ones that I use most often for my own business are Mobile Office Technology (http://mobileof fice.about.com/), U.S. Government Info and Resources (http://usgovinfo.about.com/), Tax Planning (http://taxes .about.com/), Freelance and Consulting (http://consulting .about.com/), and Home Business (http://homebusi ness.about.com/).

here, but this site does require paid access for more detailed information. An excellent place to begin since this site has one of the largest family history databases on the Web.

- **The Obituary Daily Times** (www.rootsweb.com/~obituary/): This is a searchable database of obituaries; also available in a free e-mailed newsletter format (over 2,500 entries a day is typical).
- **National Obituary Archive** (www.arrangeonline.com/): The National Obituary Archive is the world's largest repository of obituaries and death records, with more than 55 million individual entries on file. Visitors may search the archive freely to learn about the deaths of friends or family or to explore relationships when building family trees or doing genealogical research.
- **ObitCentral** (www.obitcentral.com/): Obituary Central is an obituary database for finding obituaries and performing cemetery searches.
- **Obituary Listings Index** (www.slipcue.com/obits/obitsmain .html): This site has obituaries of interesting and famous people.
- **Obits.com** (www.obits.com): Obituaries of public figures are here.
- **Boston Public Library Obituary Database** (www.bpl.org/ catalogs/interpro/bpl_search/obits.htm): This is especially useful for serious genealogical searchers; goes back as far as 1971.

Ways to Find Individual and Corporate Business Information

Many sites will let you get some basic business info completely for free, including:

- **Ziggs.com** (www.ziggs.com/): Ziggs is a great place for professionals to find other people in their line of work.
- **LinkedIn** (www.linkedin.com/): LinkedIn is an online network of more than 6 million experienced professionals from around the world, representing 130 industries.
- **Yahoo Local** (http://yp.yahoo.com/): Use Yahoo Local to find businesses near you.
- **BigBook.com** (www.bigbook.com/): Search for U.S. businesses in the online yellow pages.
- **Chamber of Commerce Locator** (www.chamberofcommerce.com/public/index.cfm?): Find a chamber of commerce in the states.
- **U.S. Securities and Exchange** (http://sec.gov/): Find lots of good information about individual businesses here, including salaries and stockholding information.

In addition to these initial informational sites, the Web has plenty of resources for anyone doing a quick business search, looking for business search engines, wanting business research information, or having similar needs. Here are a few resources I've rounded up for you:

- **Business.com** (www.business.com/): An exemplary source for finding any kind of business-related information, from corporate insurance to tax resources.
- **Better Business Bureau** (www.search.bbb.org/): Find out more information about a specific company.
- **AllBusiness** (www.allbusiness.com/): Business search, directories, forms, advice, and much more.
- **TrendWatching** (www.trendwatching.com/): Scours the Web and reports trends in a variety of businesses.

ELSEWHERE ON THE WEB

▶ Small business owners can take advantage of some great tools on the Web to help their businesses run more smoothly. A few that have come across my radar lately: Backpack (www.backpackit.com), an organizational tool; Campfire (www.campfirenow.com), a real-time chat utility for businesses and groups; Dimewise (www.dimewise.com), a financial planning tool; and Google Calendar (www.google.com/calendar), an online calendar that gives users a lot of powerful options when scheduling events.

- **PC World Business Directory** ([http://pcworld.directorym .com/?source=56](http://pcworld.directorym.com/?source=56)): A list of business services; just click and find what you're looking for in your area.
- **SMEAL Search** (http://smealsearch2.psu.edu/index.html/): A specialized search engine that searches for and indexes academic business documents that are in either PDF or PostScript (PS) formats.
- **Where2Go** (www.where2go.com): Find a business on the Web using a variety of search parameters.

Where to Find Public Records

Finding public records on the Web is another topic that I get frequent reader e-mails about. I do need to give you a short disclaimer here: depending on the state or country that you live in, you might not be able to access the more personal public records, such as birth certificates, drivers' licenses, marriage certificates, etc., without (a) showing physical proof of identification and/or (b) paying a fee. Please be sure to check your specific state or country's regulations on these kinds of documents.

A few of the best sites for either finding public records or getting directions on how to obtain them in person are:

- **Google** (www.google.com/): Yes, Google definitely belongs on this list of free public records search sites. Not only is it free, it's also one of the world's largest databases of information. You might be surprised on how much you can turn up on Google with just a simple request for public information; it's a good general place from which to start your search for public records.
- **United States Vital Record Information** (www.vitalrec.com): This is an invaluable site that basically provides vital links

to every state office you might need for any kind of public record. VitalRec explains how to obtain vital records (such as birth certificates, death records, marriage licenses, and divorce decrees) from each state, territory, and county of the United States.

- **Online Searchable Death Indexes and Information** ([www](http://www.deathindexes.com).deathindexes.com): This one is a (mostly) free genealogy search site; excellent for those researching genealogies. From the site: "This website is a directory of online death indexes listed by state and county. Included are death records, death certificate indexes, death notices & registers, obituaries, probate indexes, and cemetery & burial records. Also included is information about searching the Social Security Death Index online."
- **USA.gov** (www.usa.gov/): USA.gov, formerly known as First-Gov.gov, is an absolutely mammoth search engine/portal that gives the searcher direct access to searchable information from the United States government, state governments, and local governments. Every agency that handles public records in the United States can be found somewhere in this huge database.
- **CensusFinder** (www.censusfinder.com/): For the United States, Canada, and the United Kingdom, a free public records search site that helps you find census records from thousands of sources.
- **DirectGov** (UK) (www.direct.gov.uk): DirectGov is a searchable public records database of a wide range of government information and services in the United Kingdom. An excellent place to start for a free public records search.

There are also ways to search for people in the military. If you've ever served in a branch of the United States military and would like to look up someone that you served with, this list of free military people search databases is for you. Unless otherwise noted, all these military people search resources are free.

- **Military Buddy Finder** (www.military.com/Military/Locator/New/Splash): Search over 20 million records for military buddies. Military.com searches for military personnel from four different sources: the Military.com member and Missing Buddy databases, the Department of Defense personnel records obtained under the Freedom of Information Act, and the white pages.
- **USMC Military Reunions** (www.usmc.mil/reunions/reunions.nsf/approved): Search not only for Marine reunions here, but for all services' upcoming and past reunions.
- **The American War Library** (www.members.aol.com/veterans): This is an enormous site and can be overwhelming. Start with the Index contents and work out slowly from there; it's well worth the time you'll need to get acclimated to this wealth of information.
- **The Unofficial Air Force E-mail Locator** (www.usaf-locator.com/): You can post your name to the database for free; at the time of this writing they had over 29,000 listings of past, present, and retired military personnel.
- **Navy WorldWide Locator** (www.npc.navy.mil/CommandSupport/NavyWorldWideLocator/): This site is a great way to track down Navy service members; only family, active duty personnel, and Navy retirees can access this system, however.

- **Shipmate Search** (www.usmm.org/shipmate_search.html): Find personnel from the Navy, Merchant Marine, U.S. Maritime Service, Naval Armed Guard, etc.
- **The Citadel People Search** (www.citadel.edu/r3/tool/people_search/index.shtml): Find Citadel faculty, currently enrolled students, and staff.
- **Department of Defense Locator Services** (www.defenselink.mil/faq/pis/PC04MLTR.html): Make sure you have as much information as possible before using this service; it's extremely useful, but won't work with just partial information.
- **The Vietnam Era POW/MIA Database–Library of Congress** (http://lcweb2.loc.gov/pow/powhome.html): This database was established to assist researchers investigating government documents pertaining to U.S. military personnel listed as unaccounted for as of December 1991.

Digging for Free Downloads

Growing up with a mom whose greatest thrill was Saturday morning garage sales, I have a real love for finding a bargain. And free stuff? Sign me up! Apparently, many of my About Web Search readers feel the same way, since I've gotten many, many e-mails over the years asking where to find good free downloads on the Web.

You can download pretty much anything on the Web, from movies to software to complete full-length books—the list is endless. We went over multimedia in Chapter 11, so let's just move straight on to downloads that are specifically to help or enhance your computer in some way.

How about some specific PC and Mac resources? Whether you're looking for drivers, freeware, shareware, patches, game downloads, or the latest updates to various software packages,

ELSEWHERE ON THE WEB

▶ I just finished reading an excellent article on public records and privacy from the Privacy Rights Clearinghouse titled "From Cradle to Grave: Government Records and Your Privacy," found at www.privacyrights.org/fs/fs11-pub.htm. It's a compelling read that helps make sense of the problem of accountability between the public and the government.

you're sure to find it at one of these free download Web sites. Unless otherwise noted, all the downloads offered at these sites are free; as always, I suggest that you use common sense when downloading software—in other words, don't just start downloading willy-nilly. These sites, while reputable and well-known, will not be able to prevent unscrupulous software from finding its way into your computer if you choose to download it. Make sure you have security and virus protection before downloading anything, and double-check the file download instructions to make sure that the file you are downloading will be compatible with your system.

TOOLS YOU NEED

▶ Is there any end to what you can find on the Web? If there is, I haven't found it yet, and that includes scholarship info. If you're looking for a school scholarship, be sure to check out my favorite site for finding scholarship information: FastWeb (www .fastweb.com), one of the most comprehensive scholarship search resources online. Also see my list of scholarship search and other college information sites on the Web in my article titled "Scholarship Search" (http://about. com/websearch/scholarship search).

- **MajorGeeks** (www.majorgeeks.com): Warning: Use of this site may cause you to excessively download cool programs and feel "geeky."
- **PC World** (www.pcworld.com): Includes downloads, news, reviews, and how-to's (I really like their digital camera tutorials).
- **CNET** (www.cnet.com): Extensive site with not only downloads, but latest technology news and reviews.
- **Windows Updates** (http://windowsupdate.microsoft.com/): The Official Microsoft site for Windows updates; you can also sign up for e-mailed notifications that updates are available.
- **Free Drivers** (http://drivers.softpedia.com/): Lots of different drivers, not only for PCs but for printers, cameras, keyboards, and other equipment.
- **Tucows** (www.tucows.com): One of the most popular shareware and freeware sites on the Net. Includes downloads for Windows, Mac, Linux, and more.
- **Lifehacker Pack** (www.lifehacker.com/software/feature/geek -to-live-lifehacker-pack-149665.php): A must-have packet

of freeware downloads put together by the productivity experts over at Lifehacker.

- **The Forty-Six Best Ever Freeware Utilities** (www.techsupportalert.com/best_46_free_utilities.htm): Forty-six different freeware utilities sorted by function and category.
- **PortableApps** (http://portableapps.com): A portable app is a computer program that you can carry around with you on a portable device and use on any Windows computer. There are lots of really useful downloads here.
- **I want a freeware utility to . . .** (www.econsultant.com/i-want-freeware-utilities/index.html): Extremely useful free utilities that do specific jobs really well and save time and money.

There are many, many more free downloads on the Web available to you; this is just the tip of the iceberg! Let's keep going with even more free downloads.

- **Instant Messenger Clients** (http://about.com/websearch/imclients): Using the Web to talk instantly in real time is possible with instant messenger clients. Here are a few of the best instant messenger programs on the Web.
- **Free Premade MySpace Layouts** (http://about.com/websearch/myspacelayouts): If you're looking for free premade MySpace layouts, you've come to the right place. I've put together a list of my favorite MySpace premade layouts here, and there's something for everyone.
- **Skype** (www.skype.com): Skype is quickly becoming one of the most popular (and cost-effective) ways to make phone calls to anyone in the world. Learn more about Skype and how you can make it work for you.

- **Google Talk** (www.google.com/talk): Communicate with your classmates or profs with Google Talk, a slick, streamlined instant messenger application.
- **Yahoo Widgets** (http://widgets.yahoo.com/): Yahoo Widgets (small software utilities) are a great way to find all the best widgets in one place. In order to get those widgets on your desktop, you'll need to download the Yahoo Widget Engine for Mac or Windows, and then you'll be ready to find and download all the Yahoo Widgets your heart desires.
- **Google Desktop** (http://desktop.google.com): I absolutely could not live without Google Desktop; I use it constantly to find old files, e-mails, chats, etc.

Locating Maps and Directions

I'll admit it: I have a really horrible sense of direction. In fact, I've been known to get lost in the town I've lived in (small town, I might add) for the last ten years! So finding out I could print out maps and directions for pretty much any place I needed to get to was a huge bonus on the Web for me—and, judging from the amount of e-mails I've received, for many readers as well. Here are my favorite sites for figuring out where I need to go.

- **MapQuest** (www.mapquest.com): I use MapQuest at least once a week, more often when I've got three kids to shuttle to various sports events. It's easy to use and gets me where I need to go with a minimum of fuss.
- **Google Maps** (http://maps.google.com): Provides not only driving directions and maps, but also satellite and aerial imagery. In addition, Google Maps allows users to search by keyword for local businesses—a nice feature.
- **AskCity** (http://city.ask.com/city): Ask.com's maps service gives you the standard directions and maps features, but

then goes one step further with their AskCity service. AskCity is a local search, but it's different from other local search map offerings in that it offers widgets, layers, and just plain usability. Think of it as the Happy Meal with not just one good toy, but two (and maybe a couple of extra apple pies inside as well).

A How-to-Find Grab Bag

Almost every time I get a reader e-mail, I'm able to turn it into an article that all my readers can benefit from. In this section, I'm going to give you just a sampling of what my wonderful About Web Search readers have written to ask me to help them find; it's a pretty eclectic selection!

- **Free Language Translation** (http://about.com/websearch/languagetranslation): Free language translation sites on the Web have made it possible for Web searchers to read documents and sites from all over the world, in any language. Have you found something online that you'd like to read, but don't know how to read the language it's presented in? Whether you need to translate something from English to French, Spanish to German, or Swahili to Latin, you'll be able to do it with my list of free language translation sites.
- **Online Radio Stations** (http://about.com/websearch/radiostations): Can't find anything good to listen to on your local radio stations? No problem—go to the Web and you'll be able to find an endless supply of great free online radio stations (my personal favorites are the classical music stations).
- **Free E-cards** (http://about.com/websearch/ecards): Looking for a free e-card? There are a lot of Web sites out there that offer them.

WHAT'S HOT

▶ With gas prices getting as high as they are, it's a good idea to do a bit of Web research first in order to find lower gas prices in your area. I've written up a couple of sites that can help with this here: http://about.com/websearch/findcheapgas. Since prices are going past the $3 mark in my neck of the woods, I plan on using these sites myself, especially Gas Buddy (www.gasbuddy.com/), a site that takes reader submissions for the lowest-price gas.

- **Webcams** (http://about.com/websearch/webcams): You can view free live webcams from all over the world; here are just a few webcams that I found.
- **Free Online Invitations** (http://about.com/websearch/onlineinvitations): Planning a party? There are a few sites on the Web that make it easy for you to pick and send free online invitations.
- **Free E-mail Accounts** (http://about.com/websearch/email accounts): There are plenty of places you can grab a free e-mail account from on the Web; here are a few of my favorites.
- **Free IVR Cheat Sheet** (www.paulenglish.com/ivr/): This one went straight to the printer. Check out Paul English's IVR Cheat Sheet—a detailed list of shortcuts for various companies that will help you skip past the automated voice-system hell. This cheat sheet lists all the secret numbers and tips to bypass the computer and get straight to a real, live human.
- **Free Clip Art** (http://about.com/websearch/clipart): Find clip art and other graphic images for your Web sites using these resources.
- **Free Online Study Guides** (http://about.com/websearch/studyguides): Good online study guides—the kind that don't try to sell you prepackaged essays every five minutes—are few and far between. Here are a few of my favorites.
- **Free Web Games** (http://about.com/websearch/webgames): Looking for free Web games? Here's an image gallery of the best free Web games so you can see what they look like before you get going.
- **Online Jigsaw Puzzles** (http://about.com/websearch/jigsaw puzzles): If you're a fan of jigsaw puzzles, then you'll love my list of free online jigsaw puzzles. All the fun without the lost pieces.

Get Linked

The following list of resources at my About.com Web Search site will provide you with even more information on how to find what you're looking for on the Web.

HOW TO FIND A DOCTOR USING THE WEB

You have many options available to you these days when you hunt for a doctor, and I've found a few Web sites that can help you find a good doctor in your area.

http://about.com/websearch/findadr

THE BEST OPTICAL ILLUSIONS ON THE WEB

One of the most fun activities to do on the Web is find good optical illusions. I don't understand how these work, but they are cool nonetheless. Here are just a few optical illusions I was able to dig up.

http://about.com/websearch/opticalillusions

USE THE WEB TO FIND A FARMER'S MARKET NEAR YOU

Fresh fruit in season, gorgeous flowers, and original handmade crafts all can be found at your local farmer's market—and you can find exactly where using the Web.

http://about.com/websearch/farmersmarket

Chapter 15

Web 2.0

What Is Web 2.0?

In the last fourteen chapters, we've gone over literally hundreds of sites that I've found to be some of the best and most useful (and some not so useful) on the Web. However, there's a new movement quietly beginning to emerge from the Web at large, and this movement has been labeled Web 2.0.

What exactly is Web 2.0? One would assume from the "2.0" label that it's a new manifestation of what we're already familiar with, kind of a new and improved version. That's only partly correct. Web 2.0 is more than anything else a new way for searchers to actually use the Web in a collaborative, interactive way. The term 2.0 doesn't mean that we are "out with the old and in with the new"; quite the contrary! It's just a new perspective on how we use the Web, and how the Web is used for much, much more than just searching.

▶ Most people would generally agree that Tim O'Reilly, founder of the O'Reilly technology publishing house, originally came up with the concept of Web 2.0 after witnessing the crash of so many dot com businesses in the late 1990s and early 2000s.

Now, some of the stuff that's coming out as "new" in Web 2.0 applications and services has definitely been around for longer than this phrase has been in vogue. However, these new kids on the block are taking old concepts and melding them with new ideas, creating and collaborating and sharing previously standalone services with theories that when put together just make sense (kind of like the old peanut butter and chocolate commercials!).

And Web 2.0 isn't just limited to what programmers and techie geeks can do with it, either. Web 2.0 is all about you and me and how *we* can create content, merge ideas, and in essence milk every last drop of usefulness out of the Web that we can get. The Web is no longer a spectator sport—it's all about people, ideas, and collaboration.

So where is this Web 2.0? Is it hidden somewhere special? Do you need a pass or something? No, not at all. Web 2.0 is part of the Web that we all know and love, and it's getting bigger and better all the time. In this chapter, I'm going to share with you just a few of the most popular Web 2.0 sites, concepts, and tools that I use on a daily basis. By the time we're through, you'll see what I mean when I say that Web 2.0 is an idea that's not going to go away anytime soon.

Task Management Tools for Web 2.0

One of the best trends to come out of Web 2.0 is using the Web as a tool to help move toward becoming more organized in every facet of your life. How many of us could use a little more organization? That's what I thought! Well, here are just a few of the best Web 2.0 task manager help sites out there.

- **Stikkit** (www.stikkit.com): Stikkit offers you Web-based sticky notes that you can customize to your own personal to-do list. You can manage your Web bookmarks, your calendar, your task list, your contacts, and anything else you might have going on with Stikkit's system; plus, you can share your notes with others. Stikkit has a lot of really interesting features (desktop widgets!) that make it a powerful standout in the rapidly overcrowding field of Web-based personal organizers.

- **Zirrus** (www.zirr.us): If you're looking for a full-featured Web-based task management tool, then you'll definitely want to give Zirrus a look. Zirrus features include a tag cloud of your designated tasks; you can sort them by priority, color, and/or date. I found Zirrus a bit addicting and quite powerful for a task list manager.

- **GTD TiddlyWiki** (http://shared.snapgrid.com/index.html): This is definitely something worth looking into. GTD (short for Getting to Done) TiddlyWiki is an application that you can freely download to your own machine and use to create your own task lists, organization, etc. The best features about this service? You don't have to be connected to the Internet in order to use it since it's hosted on your own machine; plus, all your to-do tasks can be printed out on paper for you to keep handy. TiddlyWiki does take some time to get used to, but it's very, very worth it.

- **Ta-Da List** (www.tadalist.com): All you need to do to use Ta-Da is sign up (free) and start creating your lists. Not only can you make your own lists, but you can invite others to share your lists, create multiple lists that can be accessed all in one place, or subscribe to your list via RSS, which would then allow you to publish your list in other places (your personal blog or Web site, for example).

- **Todoist** (www.todoist.com): Todoist is a wonderfully simple service that offers you the ability to manage task lists with a variety of features: colors, groupings, even sublists and

TOOLS YOU NEED

▶ Want to browse the Web on the sly when you're actually supposed to be doing something else? Try Work-Friendly (www.workfriendly .net), a simple browser proxy. All you do is navigate to the WorkFriendly Web site, enter in the URL, specify whether you want blue Windows 2003 or gray Windows 2003, and voilà! The Web site comes up as Word text in a Microsoft Word window. Perfect for when you need a little bit of Web time but don't want to get in trouble.

What's the best concept that's come out of Web 2.0 so far?

▶ I would have to say that the best Web 2.0 concept is the idea of the Web as an interactive platform, rather than just a static place to locate relevant content. You can use the Web now for anything you used to use your home computer for: spreadsheets, image editing, collaboration with people all over the world—you name it, there's probably a service out there that's aiming to solve that particular problem.

keyboard shortcuts. You can use the keyboard to execute commands on Todoist instead of clicking your mouse— many people really appreciate that kind of feature, myself included!

- **Workhack** (http://workhack.com): Are you a whiteboard fan? Then you'll love Workhack, a simple site that allows you to start making lists as soon as you type in some identifying text (no sign-up is required). You can visualize and sort your tasks by maximizing or minimizing text (tasks with high priority can be written in large letters, tasks with lower priority can be written in small letters) or organize your list by color. It's an exceedingly simple yet highly functional tool.

- **Jott** (www.jott.com): Want to update your task list, but you're not near a computer? No problem—just call it in with Jott, a service that forwards recorded voice messages to your e-mail, transcribing them into readable text (pretty cool!). Once you get back to the computer, you can use Jott to organize and manage your tasks much like any of the other list management services I've profiled in this section. Definitely a good idea for anyone who finds herself remembering something on the go with nowhere to write it down.

- **FreeMind** (http://freemind.sourceforge.net/wiki/index.php/Main_Page): FreeMind is a free downloadable productivity tool that helps you organize your thoughts and tasks via a mind-mapping methodology: it's kind of like an organized stream of consciousness. That sounds pretty esoteric, but it's well explained on their Web site. I know a lot of folks who have found FreeMind to work very well for them when organizing their task list.

- **Ning** (www.ning.com): Don't like the task manager offerings currently on the market? No problem. Even if you're not a programmer, you can create your very own task list manager (and pretty much anything else Web 2.0) at Ning, a free platform that provides you with the tools you need to create your very own personalized application.

The Web 2.0 Community

One of the primary concepts underpinning the Web 2.0 movement is that of community: sharing content and ideas with others on the greater Web. We first looked at this idea in Chapter 7 on social bookmarking; and we're going to take it a bit further with a few of my favorite Web 2.0 community sites.

- **TripUp** (www.tripup.com): If you're a frequent traveler, you'll definitely want to check out TripUp, a social network that connects travelers all over the world with information and practical advice from people who've already been to the places you want to go to. You can use TripUp to meet people as close as your own neighborhood, or clear across the globe; plus, you can interact with like-minded travelers worldwide to get on-the-ground advice, best places to go, what to avoid, etc. Travel stories, travel videos, and loads of photos are also available (you can upload your own to share with the TripUp community).

- **Wesabe** (www.wesabe.com): Wesabe is a financial community Web site; the premise is that you share your financial struggles and successes with others and learn from each other's mistakes and triumphs. There are loads of great user tips (you can also submit your own best financial suggestions). Plus, Wesabe is a fantastic Web-based money manager— you can actually use it for financial planning and personal finance management. Oh, and one of my favorite features: Wesabe takes your financial info—not specific account numbers, just dollar amounts and general information—

ELSEWHERE ON THE WEB

▶ Google is no longer used just for search; they have a variety of peripheral services that are ideal for getting things done. The technology blogger at Tech No Babble has written up an excellent article on how he uses Gmail, Google Calendar, Google Notebook, and Google Docs and Spreadsheets to make his task list more streamlined—it's very much worth a read. Check it out at "Getting Things Done With Google" (http://starkos .industriousone.com/gettings -things-done-google).

and compares it others' (completely anonymously), and shows you where you could trim the fat or stand to spend a little bit more; it's like a free, personalized budgetary consultation. Finances are one of those things that we either tend to be really good at or really horrible at, and I've personally found Wesabe invaluable for teaching me how to be really good.

- **Stylehive** (www.stylehive.com/home/index.htm): Oh, I love me some Stylehive! Basically, this is where all those really cool style setters and trend mavens hang out and share their shopping wisdom with you. Stylehive is built on the concept of discovering and sharing the hippest stuff out there, from jewelry to apparel to shoes. Once you join the Stylehive community, you can build your own personalized hive that reflects your own personal style, chat with other Stylehive members, subscribe to other Stylehivers' specific picks, and more. I always find something beautiful here.

- **Plazes** (http://beta.plazes.com): Plazes adds a unique physical dimension to the Web—you download the free Plazes software and then the service is able to automatically detect you and tell the world where you might be at any given time. You can use Plazes to connect with other people in your area more easily, follow where your fellow Plazers are, or make new friends all over the world. One of my favorite Plazes features is just people-watching: I love to see what people are up to all over the world.

- **Traineo** (www.traineo.com): Studies have shown that if you want to lose weight and get fit, you'll do better with a buddy. Traineo is a community built on that concept. You get motivation and support from others who share your same fitness and/or weight-loss goals, as well as accountability (you choose four people who will help keep you on track). You can also use Traineo to count calories, track your work-

▸ Make personal goals and find others to work toward these goals with you at Life Tango (www.lifetango.com/), a collaborative goal-setting community. Want to lose some weight? How about travel to Europe, learn Spanish, or spend more time with your family? Once you write down your goals at Life Tango, you can explore the community to find other folks who share the same interests, and then invite these people to help you along your journey.

outs, and visualize your fitness progress, as well as swap tips that have worked for you or share your struggles with the greater Traineo community.

- **BlueDot** (http://bluedot.us/front): BlueDot is a social bookmarking community much like del.icio.us or Netscape, but with a few twists. You can share anything with friends and the greater Web community simply and easily by "dotting" what you find on the Web. Add a BlueDot widget to your blog or Web site, making it easy for your visitors to get to know you and take part in what kind of content you've already discovered. You can create a holiday wishlist of dotted items (handy for sending to people who don't know what to get you!).

- **Frappr** (www.frappr.com): Frappr maps are a fun way for people to communicate and collaborate via an interactive map that displays your whereabouts (similar to already mentioned Plazes). Frappr is specifically aimed at anyone who has a Web site, blog, or even MySpace: you can add a Frappr map to your spot on the Web and you'll see real-time stats on who is visiting the site and where in the world they are. Frappr also is a great way for groups that might be far-flung to come together: for instance, at About.com we have guides who hail from all parts of the globe, so one of our enterprising staff members created a Frappr map for us. Now, we can log on and see where everyone is and connect the name with a geographical location—very handy, and a fun way to get to know one another.

- **Minti** (www.minti.com): Parents need other parents, right? Well, Minti aims to serve this demographic with our very own social community. You can use Minti to get advice from other parents, get your very own family page (upload your own pics!), and make friends with other Minti community

ELSEWHERE ON THE WEB

▶ The Web has a lot of really interesting map "mashups" (two or more applications merged together to make a whole new useful service). One of my favorites is Google Night (http://www-static.cc.gatech.edu/~pesti/night/), a beautiful tweak with Google Maps that shows the world at night. Overlays also include Day, Dusk, Day Map, Dusk Map, and Night Map.

members. The best thing about Minti is that the advice comes from other parents who are "in the trenches," so to speak, instead of glossily produced parenting magazines that make you feel somewhat inadequate for wanting to duct tape your toddler's feet to the floor . . . not that I've ever wanted to do that, of course.

- **Gimme20** (www.gimme20.com): Gimme20 is another fitness-based community site similar to Traineo that connects fitness-oriented folks all over the Web. However, Gimme20 is a bit more workout-focused. You can use Gimme20 to build your own personalized workout based on what you want to do (e.g., build muscle, lose weight, tone your legs) and share workout tips with other Gimme20 community members. It's a good way to get inspired and encouraged.

Sharing Your Content Using Web 2.0

Part of the community aspect of Web 2.0 is the concept of sharing: sharing ideas, sharing content, sharing images, sharing videos—you name it, there's probably a Web 2.0 application that allows you to share it with the greater Web community. It's all about interaction.

- **Critical Metrics** (http://criticalmetrics.com): I'm a huge music buff, so I love when I find something on the Web that introduces me to new music. Here's how Critical Metrics works: they track various music recommendations around the Web and then provide them for you to listen to via a pop-up. Music lovers will really enjoy the eclectic variety of music offered; be sure to check out the "100 Songs We Love" suggestions as well when choosing your playlist.
- **Footnote** (www.footnote.com): This is an intriguing idea that I don't believe has been done before: Footnote puts millions of original source documents up on the Web and then lets

▶ Flickr has inspired plenty of useful tools. One of my personal favorites is Flickrleech (www.flickrleech.net/), a simple site that pulls up as many as 200 Flickr thumbnails at one time. Anyone who plays with Flickr on a regular basis will really appreciate how much easier it is to view mass quantities of photos, instead of tapping the "more" key every two seconds.

you share your thoughts about them by means of online notes. You can also use Footnote to organize your historical document research and share what you find with others—an invaluable tool for researchers and history buffs.

- **Quotiki** (www.quotiki.com/default.aspx): Love quotations? Then you'll want to check out Quotiki, a site that encourages you to share and edit your favorite quotations. Here's how it works: as part of the Quotiki community, you tag, share, submit, and collect quotations, driving the most popular up to the top (much like Digg). Search quotations by tag, author, or key phrases; you can also subscribe to the Most Popular, Top Rated, or Recently Added quote feeds to get your daily quotation fix.

- **MyRecipe** (www.myrecipe.org): Not to be read if you're on a diet, that's for sure. MyRecipe is a place where you can upload and share your best recipes with the community at large, and then e-mail stuff you like to yourself or to others. It's a simple way to explore new ways of preparing food. (I think I might try the chocolate layer cake that's currently on the front page calling my name!)

- **Finetune** (www.finetune.com): Share your musical taste with the world via Finetune, a service that invites you to create a personalized musical playlist and then let others have a go at playing what you like to listen to. One of my favorite Finetune features is the ability to explore and listen to other Finetune community members' playlists—I love discovering what other people are listening to.

- **Senduit** (www.senduit.com): A few weeks ago I had a huge audio file that I needed to send to someone. E-mail just wasn't cutting it because she couldn't accept attachments that big. Enter Senduit, a simple file-sharing application that allows users to share and send anything up to 100 MB.

Here's how it works: navigate to Senduit and upload the file you want to share with someone (took me about twenty seconds to upload a 518 KB file); Senduit then gives you a URL where your file can be accessed. When you click the URL (which becomes inactive after thirty minutes), your file starts downloading immediately. It's an easy, uncomplicated way to share larger files.

- **Standpoint** (www.standpoint.com): This is an incredibly addictive site that allows you to share your beliefs with the Web at large. All you have to do is register, and then start posting your opinions. You can share beliefs on literally anything, from politics to celebrities, to which is the best car to drive. Standpoint calls itself "a social encyclopedia of belief."
- **MediaMaster** (www.mediamaster.com): MediaMaster has to be one of the more innovative services I've come across lately. You can use it to upload your entire musical collection and share it with the world (or just a few selected friends). MediaMaster also has a nifty little widget you can pop easily onto your blog or Web site in order to share your musical tastes; plus, you can even create your very own radio station (great for anyone who's had secret aspirations to be a DJ). Since your music is uploaded onto the MediaMaster servers, you can access it from anywhere that you have an Internet connection. Another plus: since music files typically take up a lot of real estate on your computer, MediaMaster potentially frees up space on your machine.
- **Slidez** (www.slidez.net): Create very impressive looking slideshows from your own photographs and share them with others with Slidez, a site that makes it ridiculously easy to create really professional looking presentations. Easy to use, and easy to install on your site as well.

- **Google My Maps** (http://maps.google.com): Google Maps has been around for a while now (well, at least in Web years) and it's added a new interactive feature called Google My Maps. Basically, this allows you to create your own personalized map and annotate it any way you want. For instance, say you took a tour of Lewis and Clark's journey—you could create an annotated map of your travels complete with notes, videos, and pictures. Each Google My Map you create gets its own URL so you can share it with family and friends; I would think this would be especially fun for family reunions.

- **Myxer** (www.myxertones.com/default): Make, mix, and share your own customized ringtones and wallpapers with Myxer, an easy-to-use site that offers you the chance to not only spin your own ringtone from your own music, but invites you to browse their sizeable catalog for material as well. Myxer takes it a step further and allows you to pillage others' snappy ringtones, make them your own, and even sell them to make a bit of spare change. Note: You'll want to check with your specific carrier as to what charges you might incur for receiving text messages, but other than that, it's completely free.

Web 2.0 Tools and Web Applications

Web 2.0 is all about community and collaboration, but it's also very much about usability—the Web as purposeful platform. Many useful tools have been created out of the Web 2.0 movement, and many more are on the way—tools specifically designed to supplement or supplant traditional desktop software applications. Here are just a few of the best Web 2.0 tools that I've found so far.

ELSEWHERE ON THE WEB

▸ With the advent of Web 2.0 applications, many tasks that previously were only doable with desktop software are being completed more efficiently by Web-based apps. ThinkVitamin decided to see just how far this could go, vowing to make the move from desktop-based computing to complete Web-based information processing. Read it yourself at "Our Office 2.0 Experiment" (www.think vitamin.com/features/web apps/our-office-2-0-experi ment).

- **Campfire** (www.campfirenow.com): What do you do if you have work colleagues scattered all over the globe? You use Campfire, a real-time group chat tool that makes it easy to communicate. I've used Campfire for about a year now and it's so easy—since you're all using the same platform to communicate on the Web, there's none of the awkward and time-wasting maneuvering that would happen if you were all using different chat clients. You don't need to download anything; all you need is an Internet connection, and up to sixty people can be on Campfire all at one time. Amazing!
- **Gmail** (http://gmail.google.com/): Google unveiled Gmail, their e-mail client, a while ago, but they've made so many improvements to it that it definitely deserves a place in our list of stellar Web 2.0 tools. Since Gmail is a Web-based e-mail program, you can access it from anywhere; plus, it's got the biggest storage capability on the Web—you're just not going to run out of room unless you really, really work at it. You can search within Gmail for archived e-mails, and use tagging to categorize and organize your work. And since Gmail is hooked to all the other services in the Google stable, you can interact with them pretty easily.
- **Google Calendar** (http://calendar.google.com/): Google Calendar is probably one of the easiest yet most powerful applications on this list of Web 2.0 tools. Not only can you use it to schedule and prioritize events, you can use it to keep track of work-related tasks, schedule vacations, or send yourself e-mails to remember what you need to do.

There are some great Web-based image editing tools. You don't need anything but your browser and an Internet connection to edit images quickly and easily. Sure, most of these are not as powerful as a full-fledged desktop image editor, but when you just need some simple editing on the fly, they work really well. Here are a few that have come across my radar lately:

- **Wiredness** (www.wiredness.com): Using nothing but your browser, you can perform simple photo editing tasks.
- **Picnik** (www.picnik.com): Edit your digital photos online with a wide assortment of free tools.
- **SnipShot** (http://snipshot.com): Use your browser to crop, snip, resize, enhance, etc. your digital photos—all online.
- **LookWow** (www.lookwow.com): Enhance and brighten your digital photos to bring out the best picture possible; again, right within your browser.

YouTube has inspired lots of tools. The popular video-sharing site YouTube has had quite a crop of useful (and some not-so-useful) tools pop up around it. A few of the ones that I've found interesting are:

- **fTube** (http://mannu.livejournal.com/326881.html): A You-Tube player that downloads the list of the twenty-five most recent videos on the YouTube front page.
- **YouTube Badge** (http://flashandburn.net/youtubeBadge): A simple badge maker that you can use to show screenshots of your six most recently uploaded YouTube videos on your Web site or blog.
- **Video Downloader** (http://javimoya.com/blog/youtube_en.php): Lets you easily download videos directly to your computer from not just YouTube, but also from Google, iFilm, Metacafe, and other sites.

- **YouTubeX** (www.youtubex.com): Quick and easy way to download and save YouTube videos to your computer's hard drive.
- **The Internet TV Charts** (www.worldtv.com/charts): Tracks the most popular videos from YouTube and other video sites; an easy way to see what's getting the most buzz.
- **YouTube Today's Picks** (www.coverpop.com/pop/youtube): A collage of the 101 top rated videos at YouTube.

Here are some great online calendars. I've already mentioned the wonderful Google Calendar, which is the one that I use on a regular basis. However, there are a lot of other Web-based calendar tools out there:

- **30Boxes** (www.30boxes.com): 30Boxes has all kinds of cool features, such as the ability to super-customize your calendar's look and feel and place it on your Web site or blog.
- **Upcoming** (http://upcoming.yahoo.com): This is a social event calendar where users can manage and share calendars.
- **Yahoo Calendar** (http://calendar.yahoo.com): Before I started using Google Calendar, I was using Yahoo's simple yet functional calendar. Easy to use with practical features.
- **Planzo** (www.planzo.com): From the site: "Planzo is a community of online planners and calendars. Create a personal calendar of events for yourself and share it with your friends." Planzo is still in beta at the time of this writing but looks very promising.
- **MyHomePoint** (www.myhomepoint.com): MyHomePoint is a family-oriented planning calendar; I was in the beta program for this one and I totally loved it. Very easy to use, and simple.

- **Eventful** (http://eventful.com): Basically, Eventful is a way to share fun events with other people, using a variety of tools to accomplish this (e.g., alerts, RSS feeds, calendars). For example, I just found out about a concert in my area that I'd really like to go to.
- **HipCal** (www.hipcal.com): I'm not one to resist a cute hippo logo, so HipCal got my vote. Calendar, alerts, address book—all free.
- **Trumba** (www.trumba.com): From the same good people who brought us Visio and PageMaker comes Trumba, a highly functional Web calendar with such interactive features as customizable templates, the ability to share calendars with others and update those who need to be updated, and sync options with Microsoft Outlook. Very nice—simple, uncluttered, and it works (always a good thing).

If you're curious, you can keep track of what's going on with Web 2.0 with these targeted Web 2.0 news tracking Web sites: TechCrunch (www.techcrunch.com), Mashable (www.mashable.com), ReadWriteWeb (www.readwriteweb.com), Solution Watch (www.solutionwatch.com), and Programmable Web (www.programmableweb.com). I subscribe to all of these sites' RSS feeds so I can always know what's happening in Web 2.0 land.

Honestly, I could keep going on and on about the wonderful variety of Web 2.0 services that are out there; in fact, I could write a whole other book on it! I love to see what new innovations people are continually coming up with for Web 2.0 applications and services; it's just another way to make the World Wide Web more interactive, more powerful, and more a part of our everyday lives.

Get Linked

Want to learn more about the emerging technologies that are coming out of Web 2.0? Try these resources at my About.com Web Search site.

**LISTIBLE
INFORMATION**

Here's how Listible works: it's a brilliant combination of tagging, voting and listing—tagging for organization, voting for relevancy, and listing for ranking purposes. Anyone can make a list, and anyone can add to that list (free registration required).
http://about.com/websearch/listible

**ESNIPS
HOW-TO**

Once you sign up for eSnips (it's free and fast), you get a whopping 1GB of storage space to upload and share anything that your little heart desires. You can also download the eSnips Uploader to streamline the process; it's a toolbar, so you can instantly access your eSnips from anywhere on the Web.
http://about.com/websearch/esnips

Appendix A

Glossary

add-ons
small but functional software that can be used to perform additional services.

Amazon.com
one of the largest e-commerce sites on the Web.

API
short for Application Programming Interface; an underlying programming foundation to many Web-based services.

ARPA
short for Advanced Research Projects Agency Networks; they were one of the founding contributors of the Internet as we know it today.

backlinks
refers to links pointing to a certain Web site.

Berners-Lee, Tim
credited with creating the concept of linked content—hyperlinks.

BitTorrent
a peer-to-peer distribution network that allows users to swap files of all kinds.

blog
an online journal.

blogosphere
the term that loosely categorizes all the blogs on the Web.

blogroll
a list of other blogs that a blog owner reads and places on his or her blog.

bookmarks
a saved list of favorite places on the Web.

bookmark managers
tools to manage bookmarks more efficiently.

bookmarklets
small piece of software that adds extra function to a browser.

Boolean search
a specialized form of Web search that uses operators such as AND, OR, and NOT.

browser
software that enables you to view content on the Web.

cache
a storage area for archived copies of Web pages.

cookies
small pieces of software that store visitor data.

Craigslist
a site that offers classified ads to cities all over the world.

deep Web
another term for the invisible Web.

domain name
the actual text name that is associated with and identifies a Web site.

eBay
the Web's largest online auction site.

e-books
books made available on the Web for download.

e-commerce
refers to shopping, buying, and retailing on the Web.

feed
a coded file that contains information from a Web site; usually subscribed to using RSS.

feed reader
a tool used to organize and aggregate subscribed RSS feeds.

feed scrapers
a tool that creates RSS feeds for sites that do not offer them.

Firefox
a browser from Mozilla.

firewall
a hardware or software "wall" that limits unapproved access.

freeware
software that is offered at no cost to download.

Google
one of the world's largest search engines; originally known as BackRub.

hackers

a term that usually refers to people who are experts in computer technology. Depending on the context, hackers are either benign or very dangerous.

home page

the main page of a Web site or the page that you designate as your starting point on the Web.

HTML

short for Hypertext Markup Language.

hyperlinks

coding in text that allows you to link, or connect, to other content on the Web.

hypertext

text that has links to other text somewhere on the Web.

Internet

a network of computer networks that communicates using special protocols to transfer information.

Internet Explorer

Microsoft's browser; also known as IE.

Internet protocols

the variety of methods of communication by which information is transported over the Internet.

invisible Web

term used to refer to the part of the Web that is not easily accessible by search engines.

IP address

the numeric address of a specific computer on the Internet.

ISP

short for Internet Service Provider.

mashups

refers to a site, service, or tool that is the composite result of two or more original sites, services, or tools combined into one.

media player

software that helps you enjoy audio and video content on the Web.

MP3

a file format for music.

multimedia

the general term for media of all kinds, from audio to video.

MySpace

an online social community made up of millions of users, each with his or her own profile.

newsgroups
discussion groups, originally created on Usenet.

Opera
a browser that offers tabbed browsing and security features.

packet switching
the process of breaking down large pieces of information into smaller chunks to be more easily transported over networks.

PageRank
a system started by Google to help organize Web pages for relevancy.

phishing
the act of tricking someone into giving personal information over the Web through a variety of methods.

podcasts
a way that anyone can publish audio content on any subject to the Internet.

pop-up
intrusive ads that "pop up" in front of your browser.

portal sites
large Web sites that offer an all-in-one experience to the user: e-mail, weather, news, etc.

proxy servers
an intermediate server that allows users to search the Web behind an anonymous wall.

RSS
short for Really Simple Syndication or Rich Site Summary; a simple way to distribute content on the Web.

search engine
a tool that helps searchers find what they are looking for on the Web using keywords.

search engine optimization
the process of making a Web site more search- and user-friendly.

social bookmarking
the process of finding bookmarks and sharing them with others, usually in a community.

social Web
refers to a linked, collaborative network of people who share content.

spam
electronic junk mail.

spiders
software that helps index Web sites for search engines.

streaming

refers to the playing of audio and video content in real time without needing to download an entire file.

subnetwork

a network that is part of another larger network.

tabbed browsing

a browser that offers the option to open new Web pages in a tab rather than a whole new browser window.

tag cloud

keywords used to categorize content arranged in one big block for easy access.

tags

keywords used to categorize content.

toolbar

a small piece of functional software that can be added on to a Web browser for faster searching.

top-level domain

the last identifier in a domain name (comes after the dot).

URL

short for Uniform Resource Locator; the unique address of a resource on the Internet.

Web 2.0

the term used to categorize the new wave of Web services currently on the market.

webcam

a digital camera, hooked to a computer, that broadcasts over the Web.

widget

a small piece of software that usually sits on your desktop; used to perform some sort of useful function.

wiki

an open Web site that allows users to add content collaboratively.

wildcard search

a special search syntax that allows you to substitute certain characters (such as an asterisk) to represent words.

World Wide Web

a vast worldwide network of Web sites linked together by hypertextual links.

WYSIWYG

acronym for "what you see is what you get"; commonly applied to HTML editors.

XML

short for Extensible Markup Language.

Appendix B

Other Sites and Further Reading

Web Sites

Web Search

Google Blogoscoped

http://blog.outer-court.com/

Phillip Lenssen does a fantastic job of bringing the most up-to-date news and information on Google here.

Research Buzz

www.researchbuzz.org/wp/

Tara Calishan's site where she journals her findings on the Web; a fascinating read.

ResourceShelf

www.resourceshelf.com

Librarian Gary Price and staff put together a daily updated treasure trove of Web findings.

SearchEngineLand

http://searchengineland.com

Site written by Danny Sullivan, known as the "guru of search."

Librarians' Internet Index

http://lii.org

One of the best places on the Web to find interesting sites.

SearchViews

http://searchviews.com

News and views on the search industry in general.

Phil Bradley's Weblog

http://philbradley.typepad.com/phil_bradleys_weblog/

Written by an experienced Web-searching librarian.

Search Engines

MSN Search

http://blogs.msdn.com/livesearch/default.aspx

The official blog of MSN Search.

Official Google Blog

http://googleblog.blogspot.com

The official blog written by Google staff.

Ask.com Blog

http://blog.ask.com

The official blog of Ask.com.

Google Tutor

www.googletutor.com

An excellent site that gives practical Google user tips.

Inside Google

http://google.blognewschannel.com

Google news, tutorials, and more.

Google Librarian Central

http://librariancentral.blogspot.com

The official blog for Google's outreach to librarians.

RSS

Ten Things You Can Do with Mixed Media RSS

http://marshallk.com/391

A good article on how to create and subscribe to multimedia feeds.

Dapper

www.dapper.net

A new service that allows users to extract and use any information on the Web.

Add This!

www.addthis.com

A social bookmarking and RSS feed button.

Feed Digest

www.feeddigest.com

A service that helps you put automatically updated content on your Web site.

FeedBurner

www.feedburner.com

A promotion and syndication service for RSS feeds.

The Social Web

MySpace

www.myspace.com

One of the Web's largest social networks.

Facebook

www.facebook.com

A social network built around schools and geographical regions.

The Expansion of Social Networks

www.readwriteweb.com/archives/the
_expansion_of_social_networks.php

An excellent article on how social networks are affecting Web search.

LibraryThing

www.librarything.com

Catalog your books online and network with other book lovers.

Goodreads

www.goodreads.com

A social network built around the love of good books.

The Invisible Web

Research Beyond Google

http://oedb.org/library/college-basics/research-beyond-google

Resources beyond just general search engines.

The Invisible Web

www.lib.berkeley.edu/TeachingLib/Guides/Internet/InvisibleWeb.html

From the library at UC Berkeley; an introduction to the invisible Web.

Direct Search

www.freepint.com/gary/direct.htm

A mammoth list of invisible Web resources.

Exposing the Invisible Web to Search Engines

www.searchenginejournal.com/exposing-the-invisible-web-to-search-engines/4771/

A good article on how to expose more sites to search engines' indexing.

Multimedia

iLife Tutorials

www.apple.com/ilife/tutorials/

Apple's multimedia tutorials on iLife and other Apple media platforms.

TV Links

www.tv-links.co.uk

Hundreds of TV shows available for viewing here.

TypeNow

www.typenow.net/themed.htm

Movie-themed fonts, all for free download.

LiveLeak

www.liveleak.com

A video site that is primarily news-oriented.

Blogs

WordPress

http://wordpress.org

An easy-to-use yet powerful blogging platform.

Hype Machine

http://hypem.com/

A great way to discover what the best music blogs are talking about—by listening.

The Top Fifty Productivity Blogs

http://zenhabits.net/2007/04/the-top-50
-productivity-blogs-most-of-which-you-
havent-heard-about/

A write-up of the best productivity blogs on the Web.

The Twenty-Five Basic Styles of Blogging

http://blog.ogilvypr.com/?p=157

Great for those who are new to blogging.

Tumblr

www.tumblr.com

An easy-to-use basic blogging service.

Web 2.0

What Is Web 2.0?

www.oreillynet.com/pub/a/oreilly/tim/
news/2005/09/30/what-is-web-20.html

A five-page paper by Tim O'Reilly on the definition of Web 2.0.

The Complete Web 2.0 Directory

www.go2web20.net/

A comprehensive directory of Web 2.0 tools, services, and sites.

eHub

www.emilychang.com/go/ehub/

A continuously updated site that focuses on Web 2.0 services and innovations.

Web 2.0 Directory

http://web2.econsultant.com/

A list of over 1,200 Web 2.0 sites.

Books

Web Search

Web Search Garage by Tara Calishain

An excellent book by Web search expert Tara Calishain that teaches the basics and beyond of Web searching.

Yahoo to the Max by Randolph Hock

For anyone who wants to get the most out of Yahoo, I highly recommend this book.

Google: The Missing Manual by Sarah Milstein and Rael Dornfest

Google offers much more than searching, and this is the book that explains exactly what you might be missing out on.

Google Hacks by Tara Calishain and Rael Dornfest
A highly researched book that goes under the hood of Google for advanced tips and search tools.

Internet Browsers

Firefox and Thunderbird Garage by Chris Hofmann, Marcia Knous, and John Hedtke
A good book full of Firefox and Thunderbird tweaks and tutorials.

Firefox Hacks by Nigel McFarlane
I would recommend this book for anyone who really wants to get the most out of Firefox.

Internet Annoyances by Preston Gralla
A how-to manual on how to fix common Internet obstacles, from pop-ups to spyware.

Appendix C

Online Tutorials

Chapter 1:
> How to Get Started Searching
> http://about.com/websearch/getstarted

Chapter 2:
> How to Set Your Home Page to Your Favorite
> Web Site
> http://about.com/websearch/sethomepage

Chapter 3:
> How to Make Your Own Search Engine
> http://about.com/websearch/makeasearchen-gine

Chapter 4:
> How to Use Google Base
> http://about.com/websearch/googlebase

Chapter 5:
> How to Get Started with Bloglines
> http://about.com/websearch/bloglines

Chapter 6:
> How to Find a Local Search Engine
> http://about.com/websearch/localsearch

Chapter 7:
> Hot to Get Started with Technorati
> http://about.com/websearch/getstartedtech-norati

Chapter 8:
> Hot to Get School Info with Rate My Teacher
> http://about.com/websearch/getschoolinfo

Chapter 9:
> How to Find PDF Files on the Web
> http://about.com/websearch/findpdfs

Chapter 10:
> How to Use Answers.com to Find Credible
> Information
> http://about.com/websearch/answers

Chapter 11:
How to Find Free MP3's with Google
http://about.com/websearch/findmp3s

Chapter 12:
How to Search Technorati
http://about.com/websearch/searchtechnorati

Chapter 13:
How to Hide Your Online Identity
http://about.com/websearch/hideidentity

Chapter 14:
How to Use the Web to Track Packages
http://about.com/websearch/trackpackages

Chapter 15:
How to Use Flickr Tags
http://about.com/websearch/flickrtags

Appendix D

Yahoo and Google Search Shortcuts

Yahoo Shortcut	Finds Pages That Have...
nokia phone	the words nokia and phone
sailing OR boating	either the word sailing or the word boating
"love me tender"	the exact phrase love me tender
printer -cartridge	the word printer but NOT the word cartridge
Toy Story +2	movie title including the number 2
synonym soda	looks up the word soda and synonyms
define cornucopia	definitions of the word cornucopia
how now * cow	the words how now cow separated by one or more words
+	addition; 978+456
-	subtraction; 978-456
*	multiplication; 978*456
/	division; 978/456
^	raise to a power; 4^18 (4 to the eighteenth power)
convert(conversion)	convert 2 miles to inches
site:(search only one website)	site:websearch.about.com "invisible web"

Yahoo Shortcut	Finds Pages That Have...
link:(find linked pages)	link:www.lifehacker.com
originurlextension:(restrict search to specific filetype)	zoology originurlextension:ppt
title: (search for keywords in page title)	title:Nike
inurl:(restrict search to page URLs)	inurl:chewbacca
site:.edu (specific domain search)	site:.edu, site:.gov, site:.org, etc.
site:country code (restrict search to country)	site:.br "rio de Janeiro"
map	map Portland Oregon
weather	weather 97110
define	define misanthrope
news	news White House
### (find area code)	503
gas (find gas prices)	gas 97132
traffic (find traffic reports)	chicago traffic
search local listings	corvallis oregon plumber
zip codes	zip code watertown new york
movie showtimes	showtimes 45678 (zip)
sports scores	astros scores
stock quotes	quote ncesa
images	cheese images
videos	surf videos
airport info	seatac airport

Yahoo Shortcut	Finds Pages That Have...
flight status	Alaska Airlines 45
aircraft registry	(number of plane) 784r5
book price	type in ISBN number
facts (encyclopedia definitions)	warthogs facts
package tracker	For UPS, type tracking code. FedEx=fedex:tracking code. USPS=usps:tracking code.
patent: (find patent info)	patent:4567894
vehicle history	type in VIN number
time zones	time in paris
yellow page (need zip and topic)	97110 pizza
[!] operator (instantly go to any Yahoo service)	mail! or fantasy football! or reference!
hotels (find hotels)	Yakima hotels

Google Shortcut	Finds Pages That Have...
nokia phone	the words nokia and phone
sailing OR boating	either the word sailing or the word boating
"love me tender"	the exact phrase love me tender
printer -cartridge	the word printer but NOT the word cartridge
Toy Story +2	movie title including the number 2
~auto	looks up the word auto and synonyms
define:serendipity	definitions of the word serendipity

Google Shortcut	Finds Pages That Have...
how now * cow	the words how now cow separated by one or more words
+	addition; 978+456
-	subtraction; 978-456
*	multiplication; 978*456
/	division; 978/456
% of	percentage; 50% of 100
^	raise to a power; 4^18 (4 to the eighteenth power)
old in new (conversion)	45 celsius in Fahrenheit
site:(search only one website)	site:websearch.about.com "invisible web"
link:(find linked pages)	link:www.lifehacker.com
#...#(search within a number range)	nokia phone $200...$300
daterange:(search within specific date range)	bosnia daterange:200508-200510
safesearch: (exclude adult content)	safesearch:breast cancer
info: (find info about a page)	info:www.websearch.about.com
related: (related pages)	related:www.websearch.about.com
cache: (view cached page)	cache:google.com
filetype:(restrict search to specific filetype)	zoology filetype:ppt
allintitle: (search for keywords in page title)	allintitle: "nike" running
inurl:(restrict search to page URLs)	inurl:chewbacca
site:.edu (specific domain search)	site:.edu, site:.gov, site:.org, etc.
site:country code (restrict search to country)	site:.br "rio de Janeiro"

Google Shortcut	Finds Pages That Have...
intext:(search for keyword in body text)	intext:parlor
allintext: (return pages with all words specified in body text)	allintext:north pole
book(search book text)	book The Lord of the Rings
phonebook:(find a phone number)	phonebook:Google CA
bphonebook: (find business phone numbers)	bphonebook:Intel OR
rphonebook:(find residential phone numbers)	rphonebook:Joe Smith Seattle WA
movie:(search for showtimes)	movie:wallace and gromit 97110
stocks:(get a stock quote)	stocks:ncesa
weather:(get local weather)	weather:97132

Index

Note: **Bold** page references indicate ABOUT.com Get Linked information.